JOHN J. KEANE

The Catholic University of America
1887-1896

The Rectorship of John J. Keane

By
PATRICK HENRY AHERN

WASHINGTON, D. C.
THE CATHOLIC UNIVERSITY OF AMERICA PRESS
1948

TO MY PARENTS
PATRICK JOSEPH AHERN (1873-1941)
and
ROSE DEZIEL AHERN

PREFACE

The story of the administration of John Joseph Keane, first rector of the Catholic University of America, should be of interest to all Catholics of the United States since it portrays the early struggles of an institution that is today the pride of the American Catholic people, who have shown an increasingly friendly interest in its welfare and who have contributed so much to its support. The story should likewise be of particular interest to historians, not only because it treats of one of the great institutions of the American Church, but also because it touches a very interesting period in American church history that still remains to be completely investigated and fully told. It was a period of great ecclesiastical figures, of exciting controversies, and of the almost incredibly rapid growth in the American Church. The first rector was one of those striking ecclesiastics, who took a part in the controversies of the time, and who directed the institution that became an important factor in this period of growth and expansion of American Catholicism.

The history of the Catholic University of America for the years that preceded its formal opening on November 13, 1889, has been fully covered by John Tracy Ellis in his recent volume, *The Formative Years of the Catholic University of America*. The first rector played an important role in those years. The present writer confined himself mostly to the functioning university, its growth, its difficulties, and its part in the controversies of the day. Since there had been no prior research done in this field most of the material for the volume was obtained from archieval sources. Unfortunately, many of the personal papers of John J. Keane, John Ireland, and Thomas O'Gorman, which would surely have contained a wealth of material on the subject, have been destroyed or lost. Undoubtedly new light will be shed upon a few uncertain points in this history when the archives of the Congregation of the Propaganda in Rome are opened for the period of the late nineteenth century.

The historian of the Catholic Church in the United States can produce nothing of enduring value without the co-operation of the guardians of the treasures preserved in the archives of American dioceses and institutions. If this work has value it is due in good measure to the courtesy of the Right Reverend Patrick J. McCormick, Rector of the Catholic University of America, who permitted the use of the institution's archives. For similar permissions and courtesies the writer is indebted to the late Most Reverend Michael J. Curley, Archbishop of Baltimore, and his chancellor, the Right Reverend Joseph M. Nelligan; to the Most Reverend Peter L. Ireton, Bishop of Richmond, and his chancellor and vice-chancellor, the Very Reverends Robert O. Hickman and Justin D. McClunn; to the Most Reverend Henry P. Rohlman, Archbishop of Dubuque; to the Right Reverend John M. A. Fearns, rector of St. Joseph's Seminary, Yonkers, New York, and the Reverend Jeremiah J. Brennan, archivist of the Archdiocese of New York; to the Very Reverend James A. Laubacher, S.S., rector of St. Mary's Seminary, Roland Park, and to the Reverend William J. O'Shea, S.S., professor of church history at Roland Park; to the Reverend Joseph I. Malloy, C.S.P., archivist of the Paulist Fathers; and to the staff of the Mullen Library of the Catholic University of America. To each of these the writer wishes to express his sincere thanks.

To the Reverend John Tracy Ellis, the writer owes a special debt of gratitude for suggesting the subject, for loaning him copies of documents, and for his critical reading of the manuscript. The writer is grateful likewise to Professor Richard J. Purcell for his unfailing encouragement. To his associate, the Reverend Peter E. Hogan, S.S.J., he owes a debt of gratitude for invaluable aid during the months of research. Finally to the Most Reverend John Gregory Murray, Archbishop of St. Paul, the writer is grateful for the opportunity to pursue graduate studies, and to his mother, Mrs. Rose Ahern, who made graduate studies financially possible, he will always be grateful.

In its original form this study was submitted to the Catholic University of America as a dissertation for the degree of Master of Arts.

PATRICK HENRY AHERN

The Catholic University of America
June 21, 1948

KEY TO ABBREVIATIONS

ACQR — *American Catholic Quarterly Review.*

ACUA — Archives of the Catholic University of America.

AER — *American Ecclesiastical Review.*

AUND — Archives of the University of Notre Dame.

BCA — Baltimore Cathedral Archives.

CE — *Catholic Encyclopedia.*

CHR — *Catholic Historical Review.*

CUB — *Catholic University Bulletin.*

CW — *Catholic World.*

DAA — Dubuque Archdiocesan Archives.

DAB — *Dictionary of American Biography.*

LThK — *Lexikon für Theologie und Kirche.*

MMBT— Minutes of the Meeting of the Board of Trustees.

NOAA — New Orleans Archdiocesan Archives.

NYAA — New York Archdiocesan Archives.

PFA — Paulist Fathers Archives, New York.

RDA — Richmond Diocesan Archives.

SMSA — Saint Mary's Seminary Archives, Roland Park, Baltimore.

TABLE OF CONTENTS

CHAPTER I

THE OPENING OF THE UNIVERSITY

The Catholic University of America had its remote beginning in the Third Plenary Council of Baltimore that closed its sessions in December, 1884. The fathers of the council heard read a letter from Mary Gwendoline Caldwell offering $300,000 towards the establishment of a university, and from this stimulus there was appointed a committee, composed of the Archbishops of Baltimore, Boston, Philadelphia, Milwaukee, and the Coadjutor Archbishop of New York, the Bishops of St. Paul and Peoria, the Very Reverend John Farley, and Messrs. Reuben Springer, Eugene Kelly, and William Drexel, to receive the promised donation and initiate the movement towards founding the institution. After eight preliminary meetings over a period of nearly two years, this committee informed the Holy Father of the contemplated project in a letter (October 25, 1886) presented by Bishops Ireland and Keane as the board's representatives. The letter asked that the university should forever remain under the government of the bishops of the United States; that the internal discipline of the theological school be placed in the hands of the Society of St. Sulpice; that Washington be chosen as the site of the university; and that the first rector be John J. Keane, Bishop of Richmond, who had agreed to resign his see to take up the difficult task of making the foundation.[1]

By a letter of April 10, 1887, the Sovereign Pontiff canonically instituted the Catholic University of America, and he appointed John J. Keane its first rector, thus giving his approval to the project as it had been proposed. The members of the committee were then incorporated under the General Incorporation Act of

---

[1] John J. Keane was born on September 12, 1839, in Killbarn, Bally-Shannon, County Donegal, Ireland. His family came to this country during the famine year of 1848. After remaining in New Brunswick for two years, they took up permanent residence in Baltimore. He was ordained to the priesthood July 2, 1866, after completing his course in theology at St. Mary's Seminary in Baltimore. He spent his entire period as a priest of the Archdiocese of Baltimore as an assistant at St. Patrick's Church in Washington. In March, 1878, he was appointed fifth Bishop of Richmond. Archbishop James Gibbons consecrated him in St. Peter's Cathedral in Richmond on August 25 of that year. Cf. William J. Kerby, "John J. Keane," *DAB*, X, 267-268.

Congress, enacted for the District of Columbia. After the work had advanced sufficiently, the Board of Trustees sent Keane as their representative with a letter (November 13, 1888) informing the Pope of the progress made in building, and asking his approval of the constitutions of the university. On March 7, 1889, in a letter to Cardinal Gibbons and the archbishops and bishops of the United States, the Holy Father gave his approval to the statutes and laws of the university and endowed it with the rights proper to a lawfully-constituted university. He also conferred on the Archbishop of Baltimore and his successors the office and authority of chancellor. Thus, the Catholic University of America, incorporated by Congress, under the laws of the District of Columbia and governed by a constitution approved by Pope Leo XIII, under the control of the general hierarchy and its separate Board of Trustees, was a unique American university—similar to the great medieval institutions which taught under papal patronage and royal charter.

The recent book of John Tracy Ellis[2] traced the history of the Catholic University of America from the conception of the idea until its birth on November 13, 1889. In this volume a prominent place was given to John J. Keane, Bishop of Richmond, who was chosen the first rector on May 12, 1886, at the seventh meeting of the Board of Trustees.[3] When the choice of the board was announced to the bishop, he protested that he was "utterly unfit, by education and by inclination, to be at the head of a house of study and, still more, to organize a university."[4] Despite these

[2] John Tracy Ellis, *The Formative Years of the Catholic University of America* (Washington, 1946). Cf. [Richard J. Purcell], *The Catholic University of America—A Half Century of Progress* (Washington, 1941); Thomas O'Gorman, "Leo XIII and the Catholic University," *CUB*, I (January, 1895), 19-23. For the act of incorporation and the first trustees, cf. *By-Laws of the Board of Trustees of the Catholic University of America,* (Washington, 1900), Appendix A. For an excellent summary of the evolution of universities, cf. Thomas Bouquillon, "The University of Paris — I," *CUB*, I (July, 1895), 349-369.

[3] ACUA, MMBT, Baltimore, May 12, 1886, p. 15. The choice of John J. Keane as the first rector was honored by the Holy Father in the letter of April 10, 1887, and the formal appointment was made at a meeting of the Board of Trustees in Baltimore on September 7, 1887. Cf. ACUA, MMBT, Baltimore, September 7, 1887, p. 19.

[4] ACUA, "Chronicles of the Catholic University of America from 1885," p. 8. This document will hereafter be referred to as "Chronicles." It is a sixty-two page document written in a record book in Keane's hand. The

2

protests, he was prevailed upon to accept the position and to equip himself for the important task. In order to acquaint himself thoroughly with the organization and direction of a university, he visited the principal Catholic and non-Catholic universities here and abroad and he held conferences with their directors as well as with other men prominent in the field of education.

It was the aim of Bishop Keane, as well as those who wholeheartedly worked for the success of the new university, to make the Catholic University of America one of the best universities in the world. An indispensable factor to the realization of this aim was a corps of professors with proven ability and outstanding reputations for scholarship. Letters that have been brought to light since the publication of Ellis' book give us a clearer picture of Keane's thorough search for the very best talent that was available at the time.

At the very beginning, Keane was aware of the difficult nature of the work which lay before him. There were very few university-trained priests in the United States in the 1880's, and those who had university training did not have a reputation sufficient to warrant an invitation to join the faculty of an institution of higher studies that was founded to present the best in Catholic scholarship. Had Keane been tempted to lose sight of this point there were those who were ready to remind him of it. In a letter to Michael A. Corrigan, Archbishop of New York, Father Robert Fulton, S.J., Provincial of the New York-Maryland Province of the Society of Jesus, who had vigorously opposed the university plan at the Third Plenary Council,[5] had this to say:

With regard to the *personnel,* as far as I can forecast it, there will be no one who has had experience, no traditions, no bond of unity. The professors will probably be drawn from various countries. What guarantee will there be of unity, or even of orthodoxy of doctrine? Which is the reason why the Catholic University course in England and Ireland had failed? [*sic*] Why so many Colleges in the U. S.?[6]

The secular press carried similar stories about the obstacles to be

---

pagination begins with three and ends with sixty-four. Between pages sixty-four and sixty-five there is a supplement consisting of a loose letter written by Keane from San José, California, on October 25, 1896. Ellis referred to this document as the Keane Memorial.

[5] Ellis, *op. cit.,* pp. 103-108.

[6] NYAA, Robert Fulton, S.J., to M. A. Corrigan, New York, September 17, 1886.

met and they stressed particularly the desirability of having the university staffed with American professors. The difficulties were so persistently aired that Keane felt obliged to answer his critics in an article in the *Catholic World* written in the form of a conversation between himself and some men he met on a train:

"I notice," put in Mr. G———, "that your critics doubt whether you will be able, for many a year to come, to bring together a body of distinguished professors in America."

Yes, I answered; we are blessed with a few croaking friends, who will not let us lose sight of the difficulties to be overcome. And this is assuredly not a small one, nor has it been overlooked. For a few years, of course, we will have to look abroad for most of our professors, and we find already that there is no dearth of men of learning and renown willing to unite their lives with such a work in our young republic.[7]

He also informed the public through the pages of the *Catholic American*:

It is the desire of the Board of Directors as well as the wish of the Pope that the corps of professors shall be made up of American talent. That will not be practicable at first, but it will be carried out as soon as possible. . . . As fast as we can find Americans of the necessary calibre to fill the professorships they will be appointed. But for the beginning of the work of instruction the experience of European teachers will have to be depended upon. Owing to the lack of thorough university training in our country, hitherto, competent instructors are scarce in the United States.[8]

In order to emphasize the plan to make the Catholic University of America a thoroughly American institution entirely free from any foreign domination, Keane quoted the Pope as saying:

I wish that it [the Catholic University of America] should be founded by American means, and that it should be conducted by American brains; and if at first you have to call in the help of foreign talent in your faculties, it must be with a view of developing home intellect, of training professors who will gradually form indigenous faculties worthy of the name the university bears.[9]

Keane, therefore, cognizant of the difficulties and of his obliga-

---

[7] John J. Keane, "A Chat about the Catholic University," *CW*, XLVIII (November, 1888), 217.

[8] *Catholic American* (New York), November 24, 1888.

[9] John J. Keane, "Leo XIII and the Catholic University," *CW*, XLVI (November, 1887), 150.

4

tions, took advantage of every opportunity to make personal contact with capable men on European faculties, and he enlisted the aid of others, whose judgment he respected, to evaluate their desirability for the theological faculty. At the same time he scanned the American scene for men of known ability who could be adequately trained by spending some years in Europe and who would eventually replace the European professors who were to be engaged temporarily.

In the fall of 1886, Bishop Keane went to Rome with John Ireland, Bishop of St. Paul, to carry out the commission of the Board of Trustees of the university to obtain Leo XIII's solemn approval of the establishment of the university and the appointment of Keane as first rector. This petition was finally granted on Easter Sunday, April 10, 1887, after many months of anxious waiting. While in Rome, Keane became acquainted with Father Henri Hyvernat, professor of oriental languages and biblical archaeology in the Apollinare, whom he described "as one of the most eminent Egyptologists in the world" and "a disciple of the celebrated Vigoroux [sic] of Paris." Keane had first approached the famous scripture scholar, Abbé Fulcran Vigouroux, S.S., in the hope of obtaining him for the university but Vigouroux suggested that the rector contact his former student, Henri Hyvernat.[10] Keane was so impressed with the young man that he entered a conditional contract with him, which was ratified by the board, and so "he was the first professor chosen for the Catholic University of America."[11]

During this same visit to Rome the Pope recommended Father Edward A. Pace, a young priest of the Diocese of St. Augustine, Florida,[12] who had graduated in Rome with exceptional honors and who had been encouraged by the Holy Father to continue his studies in the hope of one day being "a professor in the great

[10] Ellis, op. cit., p. 350 n. Fulcran Vigouroux (1837-1915) was professor of scripture at the Seminary of St. Sulpice from 1868 until 1890. Cf. L. Dürr, "Fulcran Vigouroux," LThK, X, 611-612.

[11] ACUA, "Chronicles," p. 38. Monsignor James A. Corcoran, of Philadelphia, "was the very first that was asked to join in the faculty. After mature deliberation he declined on account of his age and indifferent health" (Church News (Washington), May 19, 1889). John Gilmary Shea expected to be asked to take a place on the original faculty (Peter Guilday, "John Gilmary Shea," Historical Records and Studies, XVII (July, 1926), 122-123).

[12] Church News (Washington), May 12, 1889.

university to be established at Washington."[13] Thus when Keane and Ireland reported to the Board of Trustees on their trip to Rome they could truthfully say "when the proper time comes, a faculty of Divinity can be brought together that will reflect honor on the University."[14]

Shortly after Keane had returned to America he began his campaign to acquire the services of the young Florida priest who had been so highly recommended to him while in Rome. He wrote to Pace:

I have known you so long and intimately by reputation, & especially since my recent sojourn in Rome, that I feel as if writing to an old friend. . . .

Let me take this opportunity to tell you of the hope in my heart that you will yet be working with me in the Catholic University of America. This is the desire of Prof. Satolli and of the Pope as well as myself. Your good Bishop's need of you is the great obstacle,—for I hope that your desires also would run in that direction. If the Bp. could allow it, my desire w'd be that you should be free for the next two years to perfect your studies in Rome, Louvain, & elsewhere.[15]

Pace's answer was reassuring to the rector's hopes and on October 15, 1887, Keane wrote:

Thanks be to God that your heart is in the University work. May he grant that we may pull together to get it through. Pray hard, and *pull every wire*—and we will do what we can for the same end.[16]

Yet Keane was right in judging that there would be an obstacle in the objection of Bishop John Moore of St. Augustine. Keane told Pace, "Bishop Moore wrote to me . . . that nothing short of a command from the Pope, & then with the loan of a good priest to take your place, would induce him to give you up."[17] It was now

[13] John J. Keane, "Leo XIII and the Catholic University," *CW*, XLVI (November, 1887), 150.

[14] ACUA, "Report of Ireland & Keane to Trustees of the University on Their Mission to Rome," p. 8. This is an eleven page typewritten report signed by Ireland and Keane and dated September 7, 1887.

[15] ACUA, John J. Keane to Edward A. Pace, Winchester, Virginia, September 28, 1887.

[16] ACUA, John J. Keane to Edward A. Pace, Richmond, October 15, 1887.

[17] ACUA, John J. Keane to Edward A. Pace, Richmond, January 9, 1888. Two years before Moore had written to O'Connell: "I am thinking to write a long letter to Mgr. Jacobini about the American College, urging that it be fostered as a seminary of professors for the University" (RDA, O'Connell Papers, John Moore to D. J. O'Connell, St. Augustine, July 21, 1886).

6

time to "pray hard and pull every wire" to bring about Pace's release for further study. However, a command from the Pope did not prove necessary, for John Moore was satisfied with a priest to replace Pace, and he wrote to that effect to Denis J. O'Connell, rector of the North American College in Rome, "Bp. Keane has promised me the loan of a priest to take Pace's place. I am willing to let him go; I have reason to believe that he will do better work at teaching than he is likely to do on the missions."[18] Keane joyfully communicated the news to Pace and asked him to come to Richmond for an interview.[19] This conference culminated in final arrangements for Edward Pace to pursue philosophical and scientific studies in Europe and he set out soon thereafter to accomplish this purpose.[20] After arriving in Europe Pace sent Bishop Keane a letter containing information about university organization for which Keane was very grateful and he asked the young priest to obtain all the information that he could possibly get "especially as to the best method of having the Faculty of Philosophy & Letters grow out of the Fac. of Theology."[21]

Although Keane welcomed all the information on university organization that Father Pace could obtain and, too, depended on him for information concerning the availability and merits of prospective professors during the next few years, he was primarily interested in equipping Pace for his future position in a school of philosophy at the university and with that in view he instructed him:

But I trust that you understand clearly that that [acquiring information on university organization] is not the main object of your time in Europe. It is to become acquainted with the *studies* necessary for

---

[18] RDA, John Moore to D. J. O'Connell, St. Augustine, Florida, February 22, 1888.

[19] ACUA, John J. Keane to Edward A. Pace, Richmond, March 5, 1888.

[20] ACUA, MMBT, Washington, May 24, 1888, p. 20. At this meeting Keane was empowered to defray the expenses of Pace "now in Europe preparing to fill the chair of philosophy." He was also empowered to advance funds to Dr. Hyvernat "now in the East prosecuting studies preparatory to taking the chair of Scripture Exegesis." The Boston *Pilot* reported an interview with Professor Hyvernat by P. L. Connellan, their Roman correspondent, with the Roman date line of May 17: "Prof. Hyvernat . . . has returned to Rome after an absence of eleven months in Oriental lands" (June 15, 1889).

[21] ACUA, John J. Keane to Edward A. Pace, Worcester, July 14, 1888.

a judicious and useful teaching of Philosophy in our day, specially in view of the scientific advances & false theorizing of our days.[22]

At the same time Keane advised young Pace to take every advantage of the freedom given him to pursue his scientific and philosophical studies in the most noted place for each discipline. Although Francesco Satolli, the celebrated professor of dogmatic theology in the College of the Propaganda and in the Roman Seminary who gave invaluable aid to Bishop Keane while he was seeking a corps of professors, was anxious for Pace to spend some time in Rome "so as to be replenished with true Thomism," the rector did not have the same anxiety.[23]

While Keane was carrying on the negotiations for obtaining the release of Pace, he was also corresponding with a number of European professors to ascertain their availabillty for the projected university and to receive their recommendations as to the availability and special qualities of some of their colleagues. After Pace had arrived in Louvain, Keane wrote to him:

As you go about, there are certain persons I wish you could meet and "take the measure of," who have been recommended as Professors. They are: 1. Prof. Pergens, of Louvain, zoologist and paleontologist, recommended by Mgr. Mercier—I do not see what we can have for his specialty for a long time to come. But try to see him and weigh him. 2. M. l'abbé Piat, agrégé de Philosophie of the University of France, strongly recommended by Mgr. d'Hulst, Rector of the Catholic University or Institut of Paris. He speaks of him as a wonder of talent and Philosophical erudition, and says he has lately been studying in Munich, to perfect himself in German. . . . 3. Rev. Dr. Pohle, one of the editors of the philosophical quarterly in Fulda. 4. Rev. Dr. Felten, Professor at Bonn. 5. Rev. Dr. Joseph Schroeder, of Cologne, recommended for theology. 6. I heartily hope that you may happen to get to Innsbruck, so as to see Professor Pastor and Bickel [sic]. With the former, a layman, we have had some preliminary correspondence for Ecclesiastical History. The latter is a very celebrated Orientalist, and I am anxious to know whether he would entertain the thought of coming to America.—Any information that you can find about any of

---

[22] *Ibid.*

[23] *Ibid.* Francesco Satolli (1839-1910) was called to Rome by Leo XIII in 1880. He was appointed professor of dogmatic theology in the Propaganda and (1882) in the Roman Seminary, rector of the Greek College (1884), president of the *Accademia dei Nobili Ecclesiastici* (1886), and Archbishop of Lepanto (1888). Cf. Edward A. Pace, "Francesco Satolli," *CE*, XIII, 486.

8

these persons would be most welcome,—but I don't wish you to go out of your way for it.[24]

This was an impressive array of talent to survey, erudite men all, but future events proved that few of them were destined to share their fate with the new university.

The rector spent the summer of 1888 in the New England states canvassing for the university. Cardinal Gibbons, the chancellor of the university, had advised Keane to seek a good vice-rector while he was making this tour. Priests and bishops in the New England states strongly recommended Philip J. Garrigan, then pastor of St. Bernard's Church at Fitchburg, Massachusetts, in the Diocese of Springfield.[25] Previous to his appointment to this parish, Garrigan had been rector of St. Joseph's Seminary at Troy, New York. This "model priest, polished gentleman, earnest student, excellent administrator,"[26] was proposed to the Board of Trustees by letter and their vote for him was unanimous.[27]

At the meeting of the trustees of the university held on November 13, 1888, Keane requested and received authorization to go to Europe and to "meet personally those who were to be invited to professorial Chairs" and "make contracts with professors." The board limited him to the selection of "not more than six professors including a professor of English Literature."[28] Thus armed with letters to Leo XIII and Giovanni Cardinal Simeoni, Prefect of the Congregation of the Propaganda, signed by the members of the board asking the necessary approval of the statutes of the university, and with the authorization to make contracts with professors, John Keane sailed for Europe on

[24] ACUA, John J. Keane to Edward A. Pace, Worcester, July 14, 1888. Ludwig von Pastor (1854-1928). Cf. I. Ph. Dengel, "Ludwig von Pastor," *LThK*, VII, 1018-1020. Gustav Bickell (1838-1906) taught at Innsbruck from 1874 to 1892. Cf. A. Merk, "Gustav Bickell," *LThK*, II, 342.

[25] ACUA, "Chronicles," p. 27. Garrigan was "just past forty;" after he had completed his studies at Troy seminary he was ordained in 1869; during the years 1873-1876 he had been rector at Troy; 1876-1888, pastor of St. Bernard's Church at Fitchburg, Massachusetts. Cf. Charles G. Herbermann, "The Faculty of the Catholic University," *ACQR*, XIV (October, 1889), 703-704. Also cf. Richard J. Purcell, "Garrigan, Philip Joseph," *DAB*, VII, 167.

[26] NYAA, 1-4, John J. Keane to Jno. M. Farley, Notre Dame, August 18, 1888.

[27] ACUA, MMBT Baltimore, November 13, 1888, p. 22.

[28] *Ibid.*, pp. 22-25.

November 17. He was accompanied by Thomas J. Shahan, who had obtained the permission of his bishop to accept the offer of the board to prepare himself for the chair of canon law by spending some time in Europe in further study.[29] At the time he accepted this invitation Shahan was chancellor of the Diocese of Hartford, a position he had filled for several years after graduating in Rome. After a time in Europe, Shahan decided upon the study of church history rather than canon law and he ultimately returned to the university in 1891 and began his teaching at Washington in that field.[30]

When Bishop Keane arrived in Europe, he stopped at the Sulpician seminary at Issy, in the suburbs of Paris, where he said that he was "going to use his persuasion to engage the Père Lepidi."[31] However, he found later that "Satolli & others say Lepidi *won't do*,"[32] so he searched elsewhere for his dogma professor. It was the rector's intention to visit other institutions of higher learning before going on to Rome, but a letter from Monsignor O'Connell caused him to change his plans and hasten to Rome to meet Archbishop Patrick W. Riordan of San Francisco and Bishop Camillus P. Maes of Covington who were then in the Eternal City.[33] There followed a number of months of anxious waiting before the statutes of the university were finally approved. They were days enlivened by the presence of Bernard J. McQuaid, Bishop of Rochester, who wrote his metropolitan, Archbishop Corrigan of New York, "I have had great fun about the University."[34] In another letter to Corrigan, it was evident that the enlistment of a suitable faculty for the university was one of the sources of amusement:

With Dr. Keane I allude to it [the university] only in a joking way, as for example, when I suggest Lambert as a Prof. of Cont: Theol:

---

[29] RDA, John J. Keane to D. J. O'Connell, Baltimore, November 2 [1888]. The board stipulated that Shahan was not to receive over $700.00 for expenses (ACUA, MMBT, Baltimore, November 13, 1888, p. 24).

[30] ACUA, "Chronicles," p. 39.

[31] James Driscoll to Henri Hyvernat, Issy, November 29, 1888, cited by Ellis, *op. cit.*, p. 350 n. Maria Alberto Lepidi, O.P., was one of the writers who inaugurated the neo-scholastic movement in Belgium.

[32] ACUA, John J. Keane to Edward A. Pace, Rome, January 11, 1889.

[33] BCA, 85-L-9. John J. Keane to J. Card. Gibbons, Rome, December 18, 1888.

[34] NYAA, C-16, Bernard J. McQuaid to M. A. Corrigan, Rome, February 20, 1888.

10

[*sic*] in the university, and Quigley of Toledo, and Smith of New Jersey and Burtsell as adjunct Professors of Canon Law, under Dr. Shahan.[35]

Keane meanwhile mistakingly judged that the interest of Mc-Quaid, even in a "joking way," was a sign of more amicable relations between Rochester and Washington.[36]

When Keane and Ireland were in Rome in the winter of 1886-1887, the Holy Father had advised them to confer with Professor Désiré Mercier,[37] whom the Pope had invited to Rome to expound his views concerning the adaptation of philosophical studies to the special needs of the times.[38] The American bishops heeded this advice and on their return to the United States they reported to the Board of Trustees that "there is reason to believe that, in the frequent conversations held with the eminent professor, his friendly sympathy, advice and co-operation have been permanently secured for our enterprise."[39] When Keane arrived in Rome for the second time in the fall of 1888 he again found Mercier there. This time Mercier was making a strong plea for the establishment of a philosophical institute at the University of Louvain without any apparent success. Keane saw the possibilities in Mercier's plight and he was quick to make overtures to him. In a letter to Pace on December 21, 1888, he said:

I am praying that there may be a Providence in the refusal of the Belgian Bps. to enter into Mgr. Mercier's plan. It was quasi-understood between him and me here in Rome that if he could not carry out his plan in Louvain, he would be willing to come to America. *I want him above all men.* There he could have *carte blanche,* to do all that the

---

[35] NYAA, C-16, Bernard J. McQuaid to M. A. Corrigan, Rome, February 16, 1889. With the exception of Shahan all the men referred to had had difficulties with their bishops.

[36] BCA, 85-P-9, John J. Keane to J. Card. Gibbons, Rome, January 22, 1889.

[37] Désiré Mercier (1851-1926) was appointed professor of thomistic philosophy at Louvain on July 29, 1882. Leo's brief of November, 1889, had founded Mercier's school at Louvain; another in 1894 established it as an integral part of the university under the name of the Institut Supérieur de Philosophie ou l'École Saint-Thomas d'Aquin, and named Mercier as its first president; Archbishop of Malines, 1904; a cardinal priest, 1907. Cf. John A. Gade, *The Life of Cardinal Mercier* (New York, 1935).

[38] ACUA, "Report of Ireland & Keane to Trustees of the University on Their Mission to Rome," p. 7. Cf. John J. Keane, "Leo XIII and the Catholic University," *CW,* XLVI (November, 1887), 152.

[39] ACUA, "Report of Ireland & Keane," p. 8.

11

materials furnished by Providence will make practicable. For some years, he would have only the a b c of his plan—but surely we may hope that God's blessing would make it realizable by degrees. Talk it over with him as you judge prudent. I have written Bp. Maes to do the same when he gets to Louvain—and when I learn that it may be some use to go at it more plainly, I will rejoice to do so.[40]

It was not long before the time came "to go at it more plainly." Three weeks later the rector of the university told Pace:

I yesterday rec'd a letter from Mgr. Mercier, & I have just written a reply showing the impossibility of getting anything from the Holy Father that w'd be a *practical* furtherance of his plan at Louvain. Then I plainly invited & urged him to come to us—explaining that for a couple of years he would be one of the Faculty of Theology, giving a course of Thomistic Philosophy answering the questions of the day, & having only a few ecclesiastical students; but that we would then, please God, organize our Faculty of Philosophy & Letters (as described vaguely in my article on Louvain in Cath. World) which could be organized according to his ideas of a Philosophical Institute, and there would be his field. There would then be lay as well as clerical students, & we would hope for constantly increasing numbers. And starting with the sciences in their connection with philosophy, we would gradually branch out into scientific studies of the highest order.— Here is evidently the field of such a man as Mercier. Talk him into it. Get him willing to begin as a pioneer with little or nothing, & to create.[41]

Mercier was tenacious in his resolve to do everything possible to carry out his plan at Louvain, and Keane, although very desirous of having him for his own university, gave him whatever aid he could:

Mgr. Mercier still clings to Louvain. I can do nothing to help him here. I will write him in that sense in a day or two. I still pray he may have courage and disinterestedness to come to us *& make a beginning* for the sake of Church and truth. Satolli says it is folly to hope to use the Pope as it were to coerce the Bps. The Bps. must be converted first, and he will never do it. He must give up and come with us or be content to grow at a snail's pace where he is. Push him still towards America.[42]

Pushing did not cause Mercier to lose his balance. Although Keane's letters convinced him that there was little hope of obtaining the aid necessary to make his plans for a philosophical

[40] ACUA, John J. Keane to Edward A. Pace, Rome, December 21, 1888.
[41] ACUA, John J. Keane to Edward A. Pace, Rome, January 11, 1889.
[42] ACUA, John J. Keane to Edward A. Pace, Rome, February 8, 1889.

12

institute at Louvain a reality and although Keane's offer was attractive, he still remained cautious:

It seems to become clear that this school [a school of philosophy responding to the aspirations and needs of the age] has little chance of being founded here and your Grace offers me the opportunity to undertake it on a virgin soil with so much generosity and noble largess: I declare it is tempting.

However, Monsignor, the matter is so grave, it has so many different aspects, that *I would not wish to take any engagement at the present*. I desire to work for the purpose of clarifying the situation while reserving my definite judgement.[43]

At the same time Mercier was weakening and beginning to think in terms of coming to America. With this in view he sounded out Keane on the conditions under which he would begin his new work in the United States:

In the first place, I would like to be sure that His Holiness would leave me free in case I should decide to go to America. Perhaps Your Excellency can guess what the Holy Father's dispositions will be. I cannot give up the position His Holiness gave me without his consent. It would be going against my conscience.

In the second place, I would insist that I be not the only one in charge of the heavy task of teaching philosophy. When I had the honor of conferring with the Holy Father about the establishment of a School of Philosophy at Louvain, I said I was acquainted with a man whose help would be of great value for the work and whose collaboration to me seemed *indispensable*. It is the Reverend DeSan, of the Society of Jesus. There is no one equal to him when it comes to keenness of mind, scholarship in philosophy, extensive knowledge of mathematics and of science. He had, after some hesitation, accepted, and the Provincial in Belgium had promised to give his approval for the entrance in the Institute of Louvain. But no one here knows anything about those negotiations. Do you think his nomination would be authorized by the Superior General of the Society and favorably received by the American bishops? These two guarantees having been obtained, there would still remain to be clarified a few less important points, for example, the official title and role which could be assigned to me that I might organize the School of Philosophy without offending anybody and without having to fear an overthrowing on the day when, quod Deus avertat, a rector "qui non cognosceret Joseph" would appear; the certainty of an allowance in case of unfitness, sickness, failure, etc., so as to prevent my having to fall back on my family or become a

---

[43] ACUA, D. Mercier to John J. Keane, Louvain, March 21, 1889 (French).

burden to the ordinary of the diocese I left; the consent of the episcopal council of Belgium or at least the absence of formal opposition from it. These are, Your Excellency, the principal questions which an initial consideration suggests. I submit them to Your Excellency with a view to becoming well informed on the import of the obligation asked of me. When you visit Belgium, we will be able to examine them at leisure.

Be that as it may; whether I follow Your Excellency to Washington or decide not to leave my country, I will be happy to offer my little services. . . .

What tempts me most, deep down in my hearth, about this whole noble project, Monsignor, is to know that I will have to work with a man who scorns the paltry narrowness of our old Europe and who knows how to seek heartily and perseveringly the scientific ascendancy of the Church and the welfare of the leading classes of society.

May the Lord bless your work, Monsignor, and make it fruitful. May he enlighten me as to His Holy Will concerning me and give me strength to accomplish it resolutely or patiently as soon as it is known.[44]

Although Mercier was tending more and more to look to America and the Catholic University of America as a fitting place to carry out his plans for a philosophical institute, he retained his determination to exhaust every possibility for bringing his plan to perfection in Belgium with the aid of the Belgian bishops. The decision was finally made for him. He wrote to Pace on July 8:

You were very kind in telling me that it would have been a great pleasure for you to have me as a companion of labor at Washington; as far as the matter concerned my person, I had really no objection to the plan, but as you may know perhaps, the Holy Father, had better me to stay here [*sic*]. I obeyed, still ready to go everywhere His Sanctity would prefer afterwards.[45]

Thus it was that Keane's hopes were shattered and the university was denied the services of one of the most talented Catholic philosophers of the age.

While Keane was corresponding with Mercier he was "taking the measure" of other professors at Louvain through his able adviser, Edward Pace, and through the ever-helpful Bishop of Covington, Camillus Maes. Keane wrote to Pace on December 21, 1888:

I have also asked Bp. Maes to feel the pulse of Prof. Jungmann as to the chair of dogma with us, and maybe, for a while of Ecclesias-

---

[44] *Ibid.*

[45] ACUA, D. Mercier to "My Dear Friend" [Edward A. Pace], Louvain, July 8, 1889.

14

tical History with it. Keep this quiet, but profit by any possible opportunity to make sounding there.

What do you think of Prof. Colinet? The science of Religion is a branch of importance.[46]

After receiving a letter from Maes in which he was informed that Bernard Jungmann, fifty-six at the time, hesitated about going to America on account of his age,[47] Keane wrote to Pace to put forth every effort to convince the professor that he should come to Washington:

I speak of Jungmann for Dogma, because that is the most important chair to fill, & he is recommended as well fitted for it, both as a Thomist of great talent, & as a historian who could give dogmatic teaching that concrete shape that I would wish all our teaching to have. I have warmed to him, because Satolli & others say Lepidi *won't do*— Satolli says Jungmann could do very well. Bp. Maes writes me that Jungmann hesitates on account of his age, 56. But it seems to me that is a small objection. I have had no correspondence with him, & I would be glad that the ground should, if possible, be prepared before I approach him. Bp. Maes suggested that J. could, *provisionally,* do for ecclesiastical history as well as dogma, as it seems likely that we will fail to get Prof. Pastor for history, as we had hoped, and you know it will take a good while to make students look on ecclesiastical history as more than a secondary study.[48]

Pace's answer to this plea must have given Keane a start, for in a letter to him on February 8, the rector said:

In your last letter you intimated that it might be as well to ask Jungmann only for *Ch. History.* Does this mean that you doubt whether he is fit for the chair of Dogma? It is necessary for me to see very clearly on this point, and you must help me by talking very plainly— I have heard that dogma is his ultimate aim at Louvain, that he is only waiting at his present work till the chair of dogma is vacant. So said Bishop Maes.—And all indications thus far point me towards

---

[46] ACUA, John J. Keane to Edward A. Pace, Rome, December 21, 1888. Philip Colinet was well known because of his writings in philosophical reviews.

[47] Mercier also informed Keane that Jungmann "cannot get used to the idea of changing his environment at fifty-four years of age." He advised Keane that he would have more chance with Jungmann if he "could bring both the expression of a desire and a sign of special esteem from His Holiness" (ACUA, D. Mercier to John J. Keane, Louvain, March 21, 1889 (French)). Jungmann was born in 1833 and died January 12, 1895. Cf. F. Lauchert, "Bernard Jungmann," *LThK*, V, 722.

[48] ACUA, John J. Keane to Edward A. Pace, Rome, January 11, 1889.

him—*there is no one here that I can take, I must* look outside.—The professor must be an eminent man, a Roman student, and thoroughly with the Pope and Satolli in regard to St. Thomas. Satolli again expressed his conviction that Jungmann's knowledge of history & the Fathers ought to fit him for a splendid course of dogma, *the Summa being the text.*

Do me the favor then to look into this matter carefully, by inquiries & even by personal conversation with him. . . . If he will not do, I don't see just whom to ask.[49]

Keane finally offered Jungmann the chair of dogma and on March 18 he received the following reply:

Please accept my thanks for the kind letter and the offer, such an honor to me, of the professorship of dogma at the new Catholic University of America at Washington. The past few days I did not fail to think about that and to refer it to the Lord in my prayers; now I will no longer delay communicating these considerations to you. Much to my regret, they prevent me from complying with your Excellency's desires.

I am in my fifty-seventh year, therefore already quite old and only too well do I feel my physical energy diminish and my strength of mind as well. No doubt, I can still work here, but to undertake such a task, a new and thorough course in dogma, in another country, in an altogether new situation, one needs vigour, assurance, even attraction, all of which I do not have. I cannot acquire those qualities just by an act of the will.

Monsignor Maes thought I was ten years younger, and when he discussed the honorable proposal with me, I insisted on this obstacle of my age, since it sufficed without mentioning many other impediments. Nevertheless, there is another reason which to me is of the greatest importance. I studied philosophy and theology for eight years in Rome at the Germanic-Hungarian College. The special aim of that Institute, for over three hundred years, has been to train priests for work in the provinces of Germany; those parts of Belgium which were formerly part of the old Empire are included. According to arrangements with the Holy See, we take an oath, promising to return and work for salvation of souls in those countries for which the Germanic College was founded. Therefore, I am bound by that oath, and besides I do not want to be freed. Since it is the aim of the Institute and according to an agreement with the Holy See, I am absolutely sure of being in the place where Providence wants me, the more so because I got that position without asking for it, in spite of many difficulties,

---

[49] ACUA, John J. Keane to Edward A. Pace, Rome, February 8, 1889.

16

and I have been able to work sufficiently according to the special aim the Apostolic See has always had in organizing the Germanic College.[50]

One disappointment followed another, for Philip Colinet also refused the offer of a chair at Washington[51] and Keane wrote Pace that "Innsbruck now promises *nothing*. Pastor won't come—& Bickel [*sic*] is considered useless as a professor, can't impart his great learning."[52] When Keane told Gibbons on January 22, "to gather a good corps of Professors,—even the small number of 6,— will be a task of great delicacy & difficulty,"[53] he wrote truly. During his stay in Rome he put forth every endeavor to obtain the Reverend Dr. Checchi, professor of moral theology in the College of the Propaganda, but in vain.[54] Other distinguished professors were recommended to him and, as his negotiations failed with those whom he had first chosen, he passed on to the consideration of them. When it became apparent that Ludwig von Pastor would not come to America, he told Pace to learn what he could about Professor Max Sdralek of Münster for history and Ernst Commer of Breslau for philosophy. Joseph Pohle was under consideration as "having more imagination but less solidity than either of these two."[55]

Keane's major objective in Rome had been accomplished by the first week in March. The final papal approval of the university was given on March 7, 1889.[56] The rector was now free to realize his second objective in going to Europe. On March 20 he left Rome "to visit the principal Universities, & to enlist a corps of Professors." P. L. Connellan, the Roman correspondent for the Boston *Pilot*, reported Keane's itinerary after leaving Rome. "His first visit will be to Pisa, where Professor Gabbs, with whom he is already acquainted, will assist him. . . . Bishop Keane will

[50] ACUA, B. Jungmann to John J. Keane, Louvain, March 18, 1889.

[51] ACUA, Ph. Colinet to John J. Keane, Louvain, April 15, 1889 (French).

[52] ACUA, John J. Keane to Edward A. Pace, Rome, February 8, 1889.

[53] BCA, 85-P-9, John J. Keane to J. Card. Gibbons, Rome, January 22, 1889.

[54] ACUA, "Chronicles," p. 40.

[55] ACUA, John J. Keane to Edward A. Pace, Rome, February 8, 1889. Max Sdralek taught at Breslau (1882-1884) and Münster (1884-1896). Cf. F. X. Seppelt, "Max Sdralek," *LThK*, IX, 389. Ernst Commer (1847-1928) had taught philosophy in Liverpool (1877) and, after receiving his degree of doctor of theology (1880), he taught at Münster (1884-1888) and Breslau (1888-1900). Cf. G. Söhngen, "Ernst Commer," *LThK*, III, 18.

[56] Ellis, *op. cit.*, pp. 344-345.

next proceed to Florence, and pay a visit to the Jesuit house in the very ancient city of Fiesole."[57] In Keane's last audience with the Holy Father, he had told Leo XIII of his intention to go to Fiesole to see the General of the Jesuits in order to ask for the celebrated August Lehmkuhl for the chair of moral theology. In the "Chronicles" Keane wrote: "To my great surprise, the Pope had never heard of him. But when I explained, he promised, proprio motu, to give me a letter to the Father General, urging him to grant my request."[58] The bishop presented this letter to the General of the Jesuits at Fiesole and "the Father General explained that Fr. L. was in such a condition of health that he was unable to teach, & would be probably never able again.—That ended the matter of the professorship."[59]

Austria was the next scene of the quest for professors. Theology was taught in the faculties of Graz, Innsbruck, Cracow, Lemberg, Prague, Olmütz, Salzburg, and Vienna.[60] At Innsbruck was the theologate of the Austrian and Hungarian provinces of the Society of Jesus besides the theological school for a greater part of northern Tyrol.[61] Bishop Keane was very anxious to obtain some men from this famous university but his correspondence with them had given ample proof that it was impossible. Hence he confined his visit to Vienna, the second oldest university of the former Holy Roman Empire, whose Catholic character by this time was limited to the theological faculty.[62] Keane was welcomed by all the professors at Vienna because "Mgr. Merry del Val, a very eminent young prelate, gave me a letter to his father, who is the

[57] Boston *Pilot*, March 30, 1889. This is the only reference to Keane's journey to Pisa. Since all chairs of theology were suppressed throughout Italy in 1873, it is unlikely that he went to the University of Pisa in search of professors. Cf. U. Benigni, "University of Pisa," *CE*, XII, 112.

[58] ACUA, "Chronicles," p. 40. August Lehmkuhl, S.J., (1834-1918) was very desirable because he had studied at Ditton Hall, England and because of his text book on moral theology. Cf. K. Hilgenreiner, "August Lehmkuhl," *LThK*, VI, 454.

[59] ACUA, "Chronicles," p. 40-41. This account continues: "But I entered at considerable length on a discussion with him of the too evident unfriendliness of the Jesuits toward the University, and of the notion, which I proved to him to be groundless, that the University was a measure of hostility or rivalry towards the Jesuits. He gave all possible assurances of friendliness &c., and I went away hoping my visit would do some good."

[60] Edward A. Pace, "Universities," *CE*, XV, 188-198.

[61] M. J. Ahern, "Innsbruck University," *CE*, VIII, 24-25.

[62] Leopold Senfelder, "University of Vienna," *CE*, XV, 421-423.

18

Spanish ambassador at Vienna."[63] During his visit he wrote Monsignor O'Connell at Rome that, "my visit here has been useful, giving me insights that will serve to avert blunders.— The notion here as to sacred studies is, that Rome is stronger as to Dogma, but far weaker than Vienna as to Scriptural and historical studies. I think *these* and philosophy (in its broadest sense) ought to be our aim & our characteristics."[64] The next day Keane wrote to Pace that his visit to Vienna had been instructive, "but I am still at sea as to *men*. I start for Munich tomorrow— will be there only two or three days. . . . Thence I will go to Fulda, to see Pohle."[65]

In Germany at this time, there were theological faculties at Bonn, Breslau, Freiburg, Munich, Münster, Strassburg, Tübingen, and Würzburg. These were state institutions where the professors were appointed and paid by the state, but those appointed to the theological faculties had to be approved by the bishops.[66] Munich did not yield any professors, so Keane hastened to Fulda to see if Joseph Pohle would consent to join the pioneer band in America. Pohle was particularly desirable because of his erudition, his reputation, his knowledge of the English language, and his age. He had received the degrees of doctor of philosophy, doctor of theology, and licentiate in canon law at the Gregorian University in Rome, and at this time he was teaching in the seminary at Fulda and was one of the editors of the *Philosophical Year Book* of the Görres Society. Some years before, the *Kulturkampf* had proscribed his usefulness in Germany and he had taught for a while in Switzerland and in the seminary of the

---

[63] *Church News* (Washington), May 12, 1889.

[64] RDA, John J. Keane to D. J. O'Connell, Vienna, March 30, [1889]. Keane's state of mind was revealed in this letter: "While I feel the need of making all possible noise on these inaugural and preparatory occasions, I am praying in an anxious heart all the time that the outcome may be to the Church's credit & utility & not to the contrary. Do join with me always in that supplication.

"The rescript [from Cardinal Simeoni on May 23, 1889] has turned out admirably. But won't it make some people mad! O *how hard* a position has Providence placed a fellow in who detests strife & diplomacy, & who, on the other hand, has danger from a quick Irish temper besides, which it usually takes far more effort to control than people know of! May God keep his poor servant."

[65] ACUA, John J. Keane to Edward A. Pace, Vienna, March 31, 1889.

[66] Edward A. Pace, "Universities," *CE*, XV, 188-198.

19

Diocese of Leeds in England.[67] Keane was elated when he wrote O'Connell:

Rev. Dr. Pohle, Professor of the Seminary here, has accepted the Chair of Philosophy in our University. He is considered by all who know him as one of the foremost men of the day in philosophical studies—and is a model priest. He was seven years at the German College in Rome, where he must have been ordained about 12 years ago, as he is now 36 years of age. During the Kulturkampf, he taught theology at Leeds, England, & speaks English well.

And let me ask of you a great service. He, like the other students of the German College, took an oath to work in Germany. He must get a dispensation from this. The Holy Father will be sure to grant it, as he desires that we should succeed in getting our corps of Professors.[68]

On the same day Bishop Keane wrote the chancellor of the university relating his satisfaction with the work accomplished in Rome and reiterating that "the task of gathering together a small corps of Professors is a task full of difficulties."[69] He did not tell Cardinal Gibbons, however, that he had obtained the services of "one of the first philosophers of Germany."

The rector next visited the University of Bonn. There he offered a chair to Felten, who was engaged at the time in teaching sacred scripture. Felten considered the offer seriously and he later wrote Keane that, "after having consulted with some friends and with the kind-hearted Archbishop of Cologne," he had come to the conclusion that he could not accept the honorable offer. In the same letter Felten recommended Louis Claude Fillion, a Sulpician, "a biblical scholar and a writer of name," and if the Sulpicians, "who have done so much for America already," refused to release Fillion, he recommended "l'abbé Martin, Professeur a l'école supérieure de Théologie de Paris."[70]

Keane remained in the region of the lower Rhine where, following the advice of Felten, he contacted Joseph Schroeder at the archdiocesan seminary of Cologne. At this time Schroeder was

[67] Charles G. Herbermann, "The Faculty of the Catholic University," *A CQR*, XIV (October, 1889), 708-709.

[68] RDA, John J. Keane to D. J. O'Connell, Fulda, April 5, 1889.

[69] BCA, 85-V-8, John J. Keane to J. Card. Gibbons, Fulda, April 5, 1889.

[70] ACUA, Joseph Felten to "My Lord" [John J. Keane], Bonn, April 14, 1889. Louis Claude Fillion (1843-1927) was professor in the seminary of Rheims and later a professor in the Catholic Institute of Paris. Cf. J. Freundorfer, "Louis Claude Fillion," *LThK*, IV, 1.

only forty years old but he had gained a reputation as a linguist, an orator, a writer, and a serious scholar. While in residence at the German College at Rome, he passed the public examinations in philosophy and theology and "the doctor's hat was awarded to him amid the hearty applause of all present." He could not return to Germany to exercise his ministry because of the May Laws, so he spent the years until the *Kulturkampf* was abandoned teaching in the Seminary of St. Trond, at Liége, Belgium. After his return to Germany in 1887, Schroeder was appointed pastor of the Church of St. John the Baptist at Cologne. Within a year the Cologne seminary lost its professor of dogmatic theology, Dr. Matthias Joseph Scheeben, and Archbishop Krementz of Cologne chose Schroeder to take the chair of dogma and morals.[71] It was while occupying this position that Bishop Keane's offer came to him and he obtained the consent of his archbishop to leave the Archdiocese of Cologne and to accept the chair of dogma offered by the rector of the Catholic University of America. Keane wrote O'Connell that Schroeder "is considered one of the ablest professors in Germany," and he requested that O'Connell obtain a dispensation from the oath to teach in Germany that had been taken when Schroeder was at the German College in Rome. The rector now had three of his professors, Hyvernat for sacred scripture, Pohle for thomistic philosophy, and Schroeder for dogmatic theology. The search was henceforth confined to professors for moral philosophy, church history, canon law, and English literature.

John Keane had entertained hopes of obtaining Max Sdralek for church history when he visited the Royal Academy at Münster. Sdralek was away when the rector arrived and thus it was not until later that he learned that the able professor intended to remain in Germany.[72] While at Münster, Keane offered the chair of moral theology to Joseph Rappenhöner, who had been teaching the subject for a year. The young professor later declined the offer because of "my father's objection." Rappenhöner added, however, that he would appreciate being kept in mind in the

---

[71] Charles G. Herbermann, "The Faculty of the Catholic University," *ACQR*, XIV (October, 1889), 704-705. John B. Hogan described Schroeder after their first meeting as "a big burley German with a good-natured look beaming through his glasses" (SMSA, Baltimore, J. B. Hogan, S.S., to Charles B. Rex, S.S., Baltimore, October 27, 1889).

[72] ACUA, Jos. Rappenhöner to John J. Keane, Münster, April 15, 1889.

future in case a professorial chair should fall vacant at Washington as he desired to work with Dr. Pohle.[73]

Belgium and particularly the University of Louvain, "the best organized Catholic University in the world," was the next field to be thoroughly searched. The successive refusals of Mercier, Jungmann, and Colinet to accept his offer of posts had in no way dampened Keane's high regard for the university that he considered to be the model that the Catholic University of America should keep before its eyes.[74] After spending several days at Louvain without any further success, he went to Liége. He offered the chair of church history to Godefroid Kurth, who had won fame for his many historical writings. Kurth, "after consultation with religious persons and asking God's help," decided not to leave Europe.[75]

The American rector now turned to France. He looked to the five Catholic institutes of France at Angers, Lille, Lyons, Paris, and Toulouse as his final hope. These five centers had been established as independent Catholic institutions after 1875, and Lille was now the most flourishing of them all.[76] Although Keane failed to find the professors he needed in these institutions, he did obtain a former professor at Lille, Thomas Bouquillon, for the chair of moral theology. Bouquillon, a native of Belgium, had spent ten years teaching moral theology in the seminary of Bruges after he had received the degree of doctor of theology upon completion of his studies at the Gregorian University. In 1877 he was appointed to the Catholic Institute at Lille, where his ability as a teacher and a writer became known to European theologians, especially upon publication of his manual of moral theology, *Theologia moralis fundamentalis.* To assure himself leisure for the preparation of a new edition of his work on moral theology, the professor retired to the Benedictine abbey at Maredsous. When Keane was visiting Louvain in search of professors, Bernard

---

[73] *Ibid.* Rappenhöner taught moral theology at the Royal Academy at Münster from 1888-1891. After that he taught at the University of Bonn. Cf. Jos. Rappenhöner, *Allgemeine Moral theologie* (Munich, 1893), p. i.

[74] John J. Keane, "The Catholic University of Louvain," *CW,* XLVI (January, 1888), 525-534.

[75] ACUA, Godefroid Kurth to "Monseigneur" [John J. Keane], Liége, April 15, 1889. Kurth was professor of history at Liége from 1872 until 1906. Cf. E. de Moreau, "Godefroid Kurth," *LThK,* VI, 316.

[76] John J. Keane, "The Catholic Universities of France," *CW,* XLVII (June, 1888), 289-297.

22

Jungmann called the rector's attention to this retired friend and colleague. Edward Pace was dispatched to "take his measure" and he reported that Bouquillon was certainly suitable but it would take some delicate urging to move him to cast his lot with the new university. Since the rector was to return to the United States in a few weeks, he and Pace judiciously and effectively moved him to accept through the mails.[77]

Paris was the next stopping place. His mission was now near completion and his search was almost over. Keane usually stayed with J. H. Icard, S.S., the Superior General of the Sulpicians, when in Paris, and this time he had the added pleasure of the company of Father Pace who had left Louvain in March to pursue further studies at the Catholic Institute of Paris.[78] While in Paris Keane had several conferences with the rector of the Catholic Institute and he "saw all there was at the Sorbonne, and adopted all their useful ideas."[79]

It had been Bishop Keane's intention, when he left for Europe, to secure a Roman for canon law. While in Rome, he was urged to take Sebastian G. Messmer, professor of dogmatic theology at Seton Hall, the seminary of the Diocese of Newark. Keane

[77] H. Rommel, *Thomas Bouquillon* (Bruges, 1903), passim. ACUA, Bouquillon Papers, Edward A. Pace to Th. Bouquillon, Paris, April 22, 1889; John J. Keane to Th. Bouquillon, Liverpool, April 27, 1889. Cf. "Memorial Exercises for Dr. Bouquillon," *C UB*, I X (January, 1903), 157-163. Bouquillon was born at Warneton in Belgium, May 16, 1842, and he died in Belgium on November 2, 1902. Charles G. Herbermann in his article, "The Faculty of the Catholic University," gave his age as "about forty-two" and erroneously stated that "he had prepared himself for the professor's chair by careful, conscientious, and intelligent toil at the University of Louvain, and his scholarship there was so marked and so well appreciated that he was appointed to a professor's chair in Belgium immediately after his ordination" (*A CQR*, XIV (October, 1889), 710-711). Cf. William J. Kerby, "Thomas Bouquillon," *CE*, II, 716. Camillus P. Maes, Bishop of Covington, gave this interesting description of Bouquillon shortly before the professor's death: "Do you know Bouquillon?" If so, you can picture him to yourself, bending forward, opening wide his big black eyes, and with thumb and index fingers of extended hand pressed together, and, with startled voice of deep conviction saying deliberately and with scanded [sic] utterance: 'Mais, Monseigneur . . . c'est difficile.' Then, suddenly propelling himself forward to the edge of his chair and staring at me: 'Monseigneur!' he exclaimed, 'mais . . . c'est . . . dangereux!' " (AUND (Photostat) Camillus P. Maes to "My dear Friend" [Daniel Hudson], Covington, October 9, 1902).

[78] RDA, P. R. Heffron to D. J. O'Connell, Louvain, March 3, 1889.

[79] *Church News* (Washington), May 12, 1889.

obtained the permission of Bishop Winand M. Wigger of Newark, who was then in Rome, and cabled the offer to Messmer.[80] The latter was a native of Switzerland. He had completed his studies at Innsbruck and shortly after his ordination in 1871 he came to the United States and began teaching dogmatic theology at Seton Hall. His outstanding ability as a theologian led to his appointment as one of the secretaries of the Third Plenary Council of Baltimore in 1884.[81] When he received the offer of the chair of canon law, he did not rely on his own judgment as to his fitness. He wrote to Cardinal Gibbons and Archbishop Corrigan to ask them whether they would consider him to be "a fit subject for the position, intellectually, morally & socially, and whether you approve of the nomination made by Bp. Keane. Your answer will decide whether I shall accept or not."[82] He also told Corrigan that "the position would just suit my taste & inclination." The two prelates seconded Keane's nomination and Messmer cabled his acceptance to the rector. Shortly thereafter Messmer wrote Gibbons to thank him "for the kind words spoken to me in your letter."[83]

By the third week in April, 1889, Keane had reason to rejoice, as his European mission was accomplished. He told Pace, "my heart is full of gratitude for the blessings that have prospered my mission beyond my hopes."[84] He also told Pace that he had a "jubilant letter" from Schroeder and one from Bouquillon "full of doubts, which I hope I have removed by a long letter." Before sailing for America, Keane wrote to Denis O'Connell:

Our corps of professors to begin with, will be:

Dr. Schroeder, Dogma	Dr. Hyvernat, Old Testament
Dr. Bouquillon, Moral	Dr. Pohle, Thomistic Philosophy.
Dr. Messmer, Canon Law	

These are all first class men & make a fine start. Pace and Shahan

---

[80] ACUA, "Chronicles," p. 40.

[81] Charles G. Herbermann, "The Faculty of the Catholic University," *ACQR*, XIV (October, 1889), 710.

[82] BCA, 85-W-3, S. G. Messmer to J. Card. Gibbons, South Orange, April 7, 1889; NYAA, C-24, S. G. Messmer to M. A. Corrigan, South Orange, April 3, 1889.

[83] BCA, 85-W-10, S. G. Messmer to J. Card. Gibbons, South Orange, April 15, 1889.

[84] ACUA, John J. Keane to Edward A. Pace, Queenstown, Sunday morning, 1889.

will fall in line ere long. I regret not having found a satisfactory Prof. of Ecclesiastical History—but that will come in time.[85]

He also urged O'Connell again to obtain the dispensation from the German College oath for Schroeder and Pohle.

Bishop Keane was welcomed home on Sunday, May 5, by Philip J. Garrigan, the vice-rector of the university. He gave interviews to the newspapers which informed the country of the success of his mission and made all aware of the fact that the university would be staffed by brilliant minds when it would open in the coming autumn. The press also announced that Charles Warren Stoddard had been engaged for the chair of English literature. Stoddard had a reputation as a lecturer and writer and he had taught English literature in 1885-1886 at the University of Notre Dame.[86] The newspaper accounts of the new faculty also gave rise to some speculation as to who would be called to complete the faculty. Bishop Foley of Detroit wrote Cardinal Gibbons:

> It has appeared in the newspapers and is confirmed in the "Dacotah [sic] Catholic" that Dr. Marty is to lecture on Plain-Chant, as one of the grand professors of the University. Everybody is laughing out in the West and asking if this is the higher education to be given after so much effort and expense.[87]

It was idle speculation on Marty because it had been announced previously that Joseph Graf was to be the musical director of the university. Father Graf, a native of Germany, had been musical director of the Cathedral of the Assumption in Baltimore for eight years before receiving his appointment to the same position at the Catholic University of America.[88]

---

[85] RDA, John J. Keane to D. J. O'Connell, Liverpool, April 27, [1889]. If Cardinal Manning was quoted correctly, he had a different regard for the value of the men Keane obtained. He supposedly said: "Bishop Keane could have found enough mediocrities in his own country without going across the Atlantic for others" (Maurice Francis Egan, *Recollections of a Happy Life* (New York, 1924), p. 185).

[86] New York *Evening Telegram*, May 16, 1869. Cf. Charles G. Herbermann, "The Faculty of the Catholic University," *A CQR*, XIV (October, 1889) 706-707.

[87] BCA, 86-U-12, John Foley to J. Card. Gibbons, Detroit, July 11, 1889.

[88] ACUA, Garrigan Papers, John J. Keane to P. J. Garrigan, Cincinnati, June 6, 1889. Cf. New York *Evening Telegram*, May 16, 1889. After the first year the trustees authorized Fr. Graf's services to be continued at a salary of not more than $500 (ACUA, MMBT, Washington, July 23, 1890, p. 31).

25

Other names were presented to Keane and the Board of Trustees as suitable candidates for positions in the university. In a strong letter to Cardinal Gibbons, William Byrne, vicar general of the Archdiocese of Boston, recommended Charles P. Grannan, professor of dogma and sacred scripture in Mount Saint Mary's Seminary at Emmitsburg:

He made the best course of Sacred Scripture that Rome could give under the late Prof. Ubaldi. He is a pupil of the Propaganda and bears the degree of S.T.D. which he earned in that institution. He has taught Sacred Scripture and Theology for about seven years at Emmitsburg, with general approval and distinguished success. . . . He is willing to study two or three years in Germany or elsewhere, to perfect himself in the subject that may be assigned to him. This he will do at his own expense, if required, having friends who will aid him.[89]

This recommendation was not fully considered until the fall of the year when a slight misunderstanding developed between Archbishop Corrigan, Grannan's superior, and Keane as to the extent of the preliminary advances that had been made. Keane took particular pains to correct any false impression that had been made on Corrigan, whose support of the university was so badly needed, and Keane assured Corrigan that *"no invitation whatsoever had thus far been given him"* and "no thought has been entertained of entering into an agreement with him, until we should first have your assurance that it would be pleasing to you, both

---

Difficulties then developed and Cardinal Gibbons wrote to Keane: "His employment in the first instance, as I intimated to you at the time, was undesirable" (ACUA, J. Card. Gibbons to John J. Keane, Baltimore, September 26, 1890). When Graf decided to leave the university, Keane wrote to Garrigan: "I agree with you, it is well that Fr. Graf has gone. The arrangement as it was could not be satisfactory to either side." The rector advised Garrigan to see Professor Gloetzner and to inquire as to his willingness to teach at the university (ACUA, Garrigan Papers, John J. Keane to Philip J. Garrigan, Detroit, November 7, 1890). When it was found that Professor Gloetzner would not be willing to assume the burden, the rector advised other alternatives (ACUA, Garrigan Papers, John J. Keane to P. J. Garrigan, Kansas City, Kansas, November 21, 1890). It is evident that some of the priest-students were engaged in the directing of music during the years that followed, Kerby being among them (ACUA, W. J. Kerby to P. J. Garrigan, Dubuque, September 17, 1894).

[89] BCA, 86-F-5, William Byrne to J. Card. Gibbons, Boston, July 25, 1889.

as his Ordinary and as a member of the Board of Directors."[90]
Corrigan, after accepting this explanation of the misunderstanding, gave his full consent as Grannan's ordinary and as a member of the board, stating at the same time, "in case the University or Mt. St. Mary's do not need Dr. Grannan, abundance of work awaits him at home, where he would be very useful, and very welcome."[91] After receipt of this satisfactory letter, Keane consulted with Cardinal Gibbons and they decided to invite Grannan "to prepare for future work in the University by some years of study in Europe." He also sent Corrigan a letter to tell him that he appreciated his "valuable service thus given to the work."[92]

Another name that occasioned considerable correspondence between Keane and the Board of Trustees in the period just before the university's opening was that of St. George Mivart. It was recorded in the minutes of the second meeting of the board in 1885 that "Prof. St. George Mivart [was] desirable as prof. of science."[93] It is quite likely that Bishop Ireland made the suggestion, for it was he who now strongly urged Keane to secure the services of Mivart at once.[94] Keane wrote Corrigan:

His name would add greatly to the reputation of the Univ.;—nay it is urged that, without the prestige of some such man, our Faculty, no matter how learned & eloquent in Latin will count for very little in the estimation of the American public, whose expectations ought to count for something with us.[95]

Keane also urged that any suspicions about his orthodoxy ought to be considered entirely removed "especially by the letter of

[90] NYAA, C-16, John J. Keane to M. A. Corrigan, Washington, September 11, 1889.

[91] NYAA, C-16, M. A. Corrigan to John J. Keane, New York, September 16, 1889, copy.

[92] NYAA, C-16, John J. Keane to M. A. Corrigan, Washington, September 20, 1889. The trustees of the university agreed to pay the expenses of Pace, Shahan, and Messmer. Grannan had agreed to pay his own expenses (ACUA, MMBT, Baltimore, November 12, 1889, p. 27).

[93] ACUA, MMBT, New York, January 27, 1885, p. 6.

[94] ACUA, John J. Keane to Edward A. Pace, Washington, August 7, 1889. Again in 1892, Ireland said: "I do not forgive you the loss to Mivart. Don't be afraid of good sound liberalism" (ACUA, John Ireland to John J. Keane, Rome, April 26, 1892).

[95] NYAA, C-16, John J. Keane to M. A. Corrigan, Cape May, New Jersey, August 2, 1889.

27

commendation & benediction sent him by the Holy Father, on account of his recent work on Truth."[96] It was Corrigan's opinion, however, that it would not be wise to invite opposition at the start or to afford unnecessarily any grounds for criticism. Corrigan realized that Mivart's attainments were very valuable but he believed that he would serve the university better later on in the chair of natural science when secular students attended the institution. "If I do not mistake," Corrigan said, "Professor Mybart's [sic] difficulties have occurred chiefly, when he left the field of science for the domain of theology."[97] Archbishop Patrick J. Ryan of Philadelphia wrote to Gibbons at the same time, saying that he had talked of the Mivart case with Archbishop Williams of Boston and the latter had given excellent reasons for "first consulting Card. Manning or someone equally competent to judge as to Mivart's present position as a Christian philosopher."[98] Ryan also felt that to invite a man suspected of unsound philosophy would be injurious to the university. Gibbons informed Ryan that the engagement of Mivart was postponed until further investigation and Ryan passed this information on to the Archbishop of New York.[99] This cautious attitude of some members of the Board of Trustees and the prayers that Keane requested of Pace "that God may guide to a wise solution of so important a problem" saved the university from embarrassment, for Mivart later rejected some points of Catholic teaching which resulted in his being excommunicated.[100]

Besides the regular faculty the Board of Trustees engaged two Paulists, Augustine F. Hewit and George M. Searle, the former to lecture on church history and the latter on astronomy and physics. Both these men were converts and Father Hewit was among the original group that founded the Paulists in 1858. The

[96] *Ibid.*

[97] NYAA, C-39, M. A. Corrigan to John J. Keane, New York, August 5, 1889, copy.

[98] BCA, 83-M-3, P. J. Ryan to J. Card. Gibbons, Philadelphia, September 8, 1889.

[99] NYAA, C-17, P. J. Ryan to M. A. Corrigan, Philadelphia, September 21, 1889.

[100] The correspondence between Herbert Cardinal Vaughan and St. George Mivart relative to his rejection of certain teachings of the Catholic Church was printed in the American newspapers and proved a subject of general interest at the time. Cf. New York *Sun*, February 8, 1900; *Catholic Standard and Times* (Philadelphia), February 17, 1900.

Paulists were the first to establish a house of studies at the university and Keane was quick to make use of the talents of these two capable men. Hewit had exercised his talents for writing since publishing his autobiography in 1846 and he had been one of the editors of the works of Bishop John England. Searle had been an assistant professor at the Naval Academy in Annapolis for four years, and for nearly two years he had served as assistant at the Harvard Observatory. After he joined the Paulists, he published a volume, *Elements of Geometry*, which was highly praised in scientific journals.[101]

Very important in the life of the future university was the director of the divinity college. The first director was the Very Reverend John B. Hogan, S.S. Hogan's name was suggested in the second meeting of the Board of Trustees, held in New York in 1885, "as most suitable for Rector of the New University."[102] This suggestion was somewhat strange since it was the intention of the hierarchy to have the university under the direction of the secular clergy, but it was an evidence of the esteem in which Hogan was held by some members of the board. At the seventh meeting of the board, held in Baltimore on May 12, 1886, Gibbons was directed to communicate with the Superior General of the Sulpicians with a view to placing these fathers in charge of the discipline of the priest-students of the university.[103] Keane later entered into a contract with Father Icard, the Superior General,[104] and Hogan, who was then rector of St. John's Seminary, Brighton, Massachusetts, was appointed to the Washington post by Icard. At the time of this appointment there was a question of the Sulpicians taking charge of All Hallows College near Dublin, and it seemed a foregone conclusion that had they assumed control there Hogan would have been placed at the head of that institution. "It was even in view of this that, when sending him to the University, Fr. Icard informed Bishop Keane, that he might withdraw him after a few years."[105] Besides directing

---

[101] Charles G. Herbermann, "The Faculty of the Catholic University," *A CQR*, XIV (October, 1889), 711-713.

[102] ACUA, MMBT, New York, January 27, 1885, p. 6.

[103] ACUA, MMBT, Baltimore, May 12, 1886, p. 13.

[104] ACUA, Garrigan Papers, John J. Keane to P. J. Garrigan, Paris, November 27, 1888.

[105] NYAA, C-42, A. Magnien, S.S., to M. A. Corrigan, Baltimore, January 14, 1892. This letter was written at the time Corrigan was seeking a rector for

the studies and discipline of Divinity College at the university Hogan lectured three times a week on ascetical theology.[106] For an assistant in the direction of studies and discipline, Father Hogan had Alexis Orban, S.S., who was also librarian and conducted private classes in geology.[107]

Thus at the time of the opening of the Catholic University of America in November, 1889, the aim of the hierarchy and officials of the university to have a distinguished faculty worthy of the institution's place in American Catholic life was realized. True, it was not a complete staff but within a few years the faculty of theology was brought to full strength and as time passed the other schools were added according to the original plan. The Board of Trustees, through the efforts of the first rector, obtained men of outstanding talent for further preparation in European countries and in time the teaching staff of the university became predominantly American.

A suitable faculty having been obtained, the next matter in order of importance was the gathering of a student body that would profit by the advanced courses that were to be offered by the distinguished group of pioneer professors. Shortly after Keane had finished gathering his corps of professors he began a tour of the United States to recruit the first students. He visited "several of the principal seminaries of the country, addressing the students concerning the University, and seeing the Bps. of such students as seemed fit & willing to come."[108] The rector had indicated previously that the university would aim to reach the heights in scholarship and, therefore, any students who did not have the same ideals would find no place in the new institution. In an article in the *Catholic World* in 1888, he had said:

---

the seminary that he intended to open in New York. Abbé Magnien thought that Father Hogan could be spared: "I feel convinced that our Superior will have less difficulty in providing for the University than in finding a president for your seminary."

[106] *Solemnities of the Dedication and Opening of the Catholic University of America, November 13, 1889. Official Report* (Baltimore, 1890), p. 76.

[107] *Ibid.*

[108] ACUA, "Chronicles," p. 42. Before the rector returned to Washington after his trip to Europe to get professors, he addressed the students of Niagara Seminary, Seton Hall, and St. Mary's Seminary, Baltimore (ACUA, Garrigan Papers, John J. Keane to P. J. Garrigan, Troy, New York, May 12, 1889).

I need hardly say that our Catholic University will never consent to enter into the race with the professional schools whose system is short measure and quick speed. It can aim at nothing short of thorough scholarship, and can accept no students who aim at less. It may well be that her students therefore will be, for sometime to come, comparatively few; but those few will be the best, and their example cannot fail to gradually spread abroad an inspiration after deeper learning.[109]

As the bishop had foreseen, the number of students was limited. He told Edward Pace at the end of his tour that "I hope we will start with nearly 50 students,"[110] but actually only thirty-two had reported on the first day of classes.[111] This compared favorably with some of the most celebrated of the European universities. "The number of Divinity students in the Catholic University [Institute] of Paris, is not large, has probably never exceeded fifty."[112] At Louvain the number of divinity students fluctuated between thirty and sixty: "In 1888 it was 63; in 1889, 29; in 1891, 40, and in 1892, 38."[113]

It is surprising to note the attitude of John Foley, Bishop of Detroit, with regard to canon law, an attitude that would have impeded Keane's work of gathering students for advanced studies if it had been shared by the other bishops of the country:

Please teach my boys common sense and a zeal for the salvation of souls and also to be gentlemen. Do not give them too much canon-law. We have a surfeit of it out here and it is, as far as I can see, a great impediment to usefulness.[114]

[109] John J. Keane, "The University of Strassburg," *CW*, XLVI (February, 1888), 646-647.

[110] ACUA, John J. Keane to Edward A. Pace, Washington, August 7, 1889. The rector's search for students carried him over a good portion of the nation. He kept Garrigan informed of the progress he was making (ACUA, Garrigan Papers, John J. Keane to P. J. Garrigan, Cincinnati, June 6, 1889; Notre Dame, June 13, 1889; Chicago, June 14, 1889; Milwaukee, June 15, 1889).

[111] SMSA, J. B. Hogan, S.S., to Charles B. Rex, S.S., Washington, November 19, 1889. More students arrived after the first classes. For a list of the first students, cf. *Solemnities of the Dedication*, p. 83. Also cf. *Year-Book of Catholic University of America, 1894-'95* (Washington, 1894), pp. 37-41 for a list of all the students and their origin between the years 1889 and 1894.

[112] J. J. Keane, "The Catholic Universities of France," *CW*, XLVII (June, 1888), 294.

[113] *Fourth Annual Report of the Rector of the Catholic University of America* (Washington, 1893), p. 30.

[114] SMSA, John Foley to A. Magnien, S.S., Detroit, September 14, 1889.

Some bishops were very skeptical about the university's future. Bishop Wigger of Newark had been informed by Bernard J. McQuaid of Rochester that St. Andrew's Seminary in his diocese had thirty-nine students, and in his answer the Newark prelate pessimistically stated: "I am inclined to think that our Catholic *University* will scarcely have as many to begin with."[115] The next year Keane was notified by the rector of the seminary at Troy that one of the bishops of the Province of New York had protested against his being permitted to address the students.[116] This protest had been lodged by Bishop McQuaid of Rochester who had little sympathy with the university and its work. He told Corrigan:

> The Papers announced that Bp. Keane was to set out on a drumming tour to the chief seminaries of the U. S. to gather students for the next year's work. I wrote to Dr. Gabriels protesting, so far as I had any right, against a second invasion of Troy. The Doctor answered that he would be careful to hinder a repetition of what was done before.[117]

As we shall see later, the rector met with similar opposition during his term of office, but the majority of the bishops of the country co-operated with him to the best of their ability, at least to the extent that they did not raise barriers against him or actively hinder him in fulfilling his commission from the hierarchy of the country whom he represented in their university.

The number of students attending the first classes was swelled by the members of the Society of Missionary Priests of St. Paul the Apostle (the Paulists). This community was the first to accept the invitation tendered by the Board of Trustees to all religious congregations to establish houses of study around the university.[118] Keane had voiced the intentions of the board to extend such an invitation two years before the university opened:

> We look forward with glad expectancy to the day when our divinity college will be surrounded with homes in which students not only of

---

[115] Archives of the Diocese of Rochester, W. Wigger to B. J. McQuaid, New Jersey, September 25, 1889.

[116] ACUA, "Chronicles," p. 42.

[117] NYAA, C-16, B. J. McQuaid to M. A. Corrigan, Rochester, May 6, 1890.

[118] [Philip J. Garrigan], "Present Aspect of the Catholic University," *A ER*, I (August, 1889), 293. "Students belonging to religious communities may reside in separate houses, under the supervision of their respective superiors, and attend the lectures at the University."

32

various dioceses or provinces, but also the various religious congregations will live and study under such discipline as their superiors may determine, and at the same time attend the university courses, thus imbibing at once the spirit of their institute and the noblest streams of sacred learning, and building up a real republic of letters.[119]

The Paulists were allowed the use of the Middleton Mansion, located on the university grounds a short distance southeast of Caldwell Hall, which they called St. Thomas College. In 1891 a contract was entered into between the Catholic University of America and the Paulist Fathers:

Ap'l 8th, 1891.

The Board of Directors of the Catholic University of America agree to grant to the Paulist Fathers a lease of their present holding for 25 years. At the expiration of their lease all buildings are to revert to the University without compensation. If before the expiration of their lease the Board should deem it necessary to resume possession of their property, they may do so after due notice, but in that case the Paulists are to receive indemnity for improvements made by them, such indemnity to be in proportion to the unexpired term of their lease. It is further stipulated that no extension of their buildings or considerable improvements be undertaken without the approval of the Board. . . .[120]

The first year there were ten students in residence at St. Thomas College supervised by Fathers Hewit and Searle.[121]

While Keane was seeking professors and canvassing the country for students, the building that was to house the university was being rushed to completion under the direction of the vice rector, Philip J. Garrigan. The rector had prepared the plans for the building himself after those that had been submitted in competition from thirteen architects, three of whom received prizes, were found to be impractical.[122] The board adopted the rector's plans in their meeting at Baltimore on September 7, 1887, and they appointed a building committee, consisting of Archbishop

[119] J. J. Keane "The Roman Universities," *CW*, XLVI (December, 1887), 320.

[120] ACUA, MMBT, Washington, April 8, 1891, pp. 33-34. The Paulists later signed the agreement entered into by the religious bodies establishing houses of study in connection with the university. Augustine F. Hewit, C.S.P., signed for the Paulists and Keane for the university on April 11, 1893 (ACUA, original).

[121] SMSA, J. B. Hogan, S.S., to Charles B. Rex, S.S., Washington, November 19, 1889.

[122] ACUA, "Chronicles," p. 23.

Williams, Bishop Keane, and Mr. Waggaman, with power to make contracts which were binding when endorsed by the president of the board.[123] Keane's plans were "put in working shape by Mr. E. Francis Baldwin, of Baldwin & Pennington, well-known architects of Baltimore,"[124] who co-operated with Joseph Harrahan, the builder, and Edward Brady, the superintendent,[125] to erect the structure in the short time between the laying of the cornerstone on May 24, 1888, and the opening of the university on November 13, 1889. The building was not quite complete when classes began, due to the fact that the electric wires had been wrongly laid, necessitating digging up floors and tearing down ceilings to get at them and relay them.[126] The work was finally completed in December of the first scholastic year.[127]

Two weeks before the opening of the university a description of Caldwell Hall appeared in the Boston *Pilot*:

The new building is intended to be one of a noble group surmounting a hill upon which it stands overlooking the country for miles around. It is built of Georgetown gneiss rock, with Ohio sandstone trimmings. The main or central part of the building is five stories high, while the two wings are four stories. Only the front elevation of the building is in view as you approach it from the roadway, which gives one a wrong impression of its size on first sight. The architecture is modernized Romanesque, and the finials of the pinnacles will be surmounted with ideal figures of ancient philosophers. The arches of the windows will be adorned with similar smaller statues. The arcade corridor extends from the north to south ends of the ground floor of the building, and the arcade entrance will be surmounted with a marble statue of our Lord and Saviour. The public lecture hall of the University is situated in the south west corner, and will seat about three hundred people. The main corridor will be adorned with a marble statue of the Virgin,

---

[123] ACUA, MMBT, Baltimore, September 7, 1887, p. 18. Mr. Baldwin changed many of the ideas that Keane had submitted so as to keep the cost of the building within the amount specified by the rector. Among the changes the architect suggested that stone be used instead of brick (ACUA, E. F. Baldwin to John J. Keane, September 5, 1887). The plans were submitted with this letter.

[124] ACUA, "Chronicles," p. 23.

[125] *Ibid.*, p. 42.

[126] SMSA, J. B. Hogan, S.S., to Charles B. Rex, S.S., Washington, November 19, 1889.

[127] SMSA, J. B. Hogan, S.S., to Charles B. Rex, S.S., Washington, December 19, 1889.

34

CALDWELL HALL

the gift of Madame LaRoux, of Paris, costing 5,000 francs. The magnificent painting of Pope Leo XIII will soon be put in place in one of the parlors near the main entrance. The corridors will contain statues of St. Paul and St. Thomas Aquinas. The latter, which will represent the patron saint of the institution, will be a fac-simile of the statue which stands on the Pincian Hill at Rome, which was the gift of the English Catholic residents of the city. The organ, presented by Mrs. James F. Barbour, of this city, will be put in the chapel at once. In addition to the lecture halls, chapel, and parlors, the first floor will contain spacious classrooms, dining-rooms, and kitchen. The thirteen altars in the building will all be of marble and designed after the most artistic models. The floors of the entire building are of North Carolina pine, and laid double, so as to prevent sound from traveling from one story to another. The professors and students will have their study-rooms on the second and third floors, each being alloted two rooms. The fifth floor will be used as a gymnasium and recreation hall.[128]

The preparatory work was now completed and all was in readiness for the grand inauguration which took place on November 13, 1889.[129] After the impressive ceremonies attended by a large number of civil and religious dignitaries, the students assembled in the chapel at half past eight o'clock to begin their spiritual retreat which was conducted by the rector and Father Hogan. On Monday morning, November 18, Bishop Keane celebrated the Mass of the Holy Ghost. After the Mass the professors of theology knelt before the altar and recited aloud the profession of faith and kissed the gospels "as a pledge of their faithful adhesion to the same in all their teaching."[130] Then all assembled in one of the lecture halls to hear the opening discourse delivered by the rector. The following day, Tuesday, November 19, each of the professors met his individual classes and the work had begun in earnest.[131]

[128] Boston *Pilot*, October 26, 1889. The statue of the Immaculate Conception mentioned in the news item was ordered by Keane on April 25, 1889. It was to cost $1000 (ACUA, F. Mayer to John J. Keane, Munich, April 27, 1889).

[129] Cf. Ellis, *op. cit.*, pp. 267-299.

[130] *Constitutiones Catholicae Universitatis Americae a Sancta Sede approbatae cum documentis annexis* (Romae, 1889). *Constitutiones Facultatis Theologicae*, cap. III, n. 111.

[131] *Solemnities of the Dedication*, pp. 75-76.

CHAPTER II

UNIVERSITY LIFE

The first year of the university's existence was spent in efforts to perfect its organization according to the norms prescribed in the constitution. The faculty of theology chose Monsignor Joseph Schroeder as its dean, Dr. Thomas Bouquillon as vice dean, and Dr. Henri Hyvernat as secretary.[1] The academic senate, consisting of "the Rector as presiding officer, the Vice-Rector, the General Secretary, the Presidents of the Colleges, the Deans of the different Faculties, and besides of two Professors from each Faculty,"[2] was organized and held meetings not only monthly as required by law, but "almost weekly," because the work had to be studied and regulated in all its details.[3] In reporting on these first days, Keane wrote:

All were eager to put things in the best shape. We had the experience of all other institutions in Europe & America; we were untrammeled by any traditions of mere routine & red tape; we were guided by the experience of the able men composing our Faculty, especially by the wonderful erudition & sagacity of Dr. Bouquillon; we had the advice of Very Rev. Father Hewit, Superior General of the Paulists, who had come to preside over the studies of their scholastics in the St. Thomas College which they had founded in connection with the University, & who, by our invitation, attended the meetings of the Senate during the three years he lived with us.[4]

In the beginning the students were allowed to attend all the courses, as far as they could, so as to test their strength. Keane had been informed by Monsignor J. B. Abbeloos, rector of the University of Louvain, that experience there had demonstrated that no student could attend all the divinity courses and do justice to each. Abbeloos had been agitating the question of forming optional groups of studies for some time, but he had been hindered

[1] ACUA, "Chronicles of the Catholic University of America from 1885," p. 45. Cf. *Year-Book of the Catholic University of America, 1894-'95* (Washington, 1894), p. 12.

[2] *Constitutiones Catholicae Universitatis Americae a Sancta Sede approbatae cum documentis annexis* (Romae, 1889), Cap. VI, n. 1.

[3] ACUA, "Chronicles," p. 45.

[4] *Ibid.*

36

from so doing by the traditional conservatism of the faculties.[5] After about six weeks, the academic senate divided the studies of the School of Theology into four departments, namely: dogmatic, moral, scriptural, and historical studies.[6] The students were permitted to specialize in any one department or select courses in the different departments with the approval of the faculty. If a student selected courses in the different departments, he obtained his degree of licentiate or doctorate in theology by taking an examination in the principal course in each of the four departments. If he specialized in any one of the departments, that speciality was mentioned in the diploma.

The first year the examination for the degree of baccalaureate in theology was given at the close of Lent, thereafter it was held about a month after the opening of classes. This degree was conferred as a reward for excellence in the seminary course of divinity which preceded admission to the university. The examination consisted of "questions in dogmatic theology, moral theology, sacred scripture (with the Hebrew tongue), and ecclesiastical history, so arranged as to sufficiently summarize the entire seminary course in these various branches."[7] Students who had secured the baccalaureate elsewhere could take the examination at the university if they desired the additional honor of the university degree.[8]

Not all of the students entered the university with the idea of acquiring a degree. It was announced before the formal opening that students could "pursue some special course of study for a longer or shorter time without regard to degrees."[9] These special students did not constitute the majority of the "pioneer group," although they were considerable in number. The matriculates, those who had complied with all the conditions established by the university as prerequisites to full admission to graduate courses and had been accepted as candidates for degrees, found that high

[5] *Ibid.*, p. 46.

[6] *Ibid.* Each professor taught five hours a week the first year besides conducting private scholastic exercises. Owing to the increase of professors and the multiplication of courses the number of weekly lessons obligatory on each professor was reduced to four hours a week in the second year. Cf. *Year-Book of the Catholic University of America, 1894-'95* (Washington, 1894), pp. 12-14.

[7] Cincinnati *Evening Post*, August 29, 1890.

[8] Philadelphia *Press*, February 4, 1890; New York *Sun*, February 13, 1890; Chicago *Times*, March 2, 1890.

[9] Boston *Pilot*, September 28, 1889.

37

standards had been set by the university for the degrees of licentiate and doctorate in theology. This was in keeping with Keane's request to the Board of Trustees that they instruct the committee on studies, consisting of Gibbons, Williams, and Ireland, "to require a degree of excellence for graduating higher than the minimum called for by the statutes."[10] To obtain the licentiate in sacred theology the candidate was required to spend successfully two years in university studies. If the student chose a specialty, profound knowledge of that specialty was demanded. If a general study only was chosen, a solid and sufficient acquaintance with the subjects of the four departments was required.[11] The candidate had to pass a six hour written examination and defend fifty theses in an oral examination, first privately, then publicly. To obtain the doctorate in sacred theology, the student had to spend two years in study after obtaining the licentiate. The candidate had to write a thesis of at least one hundred printed octavo pages on some subject of sacred science selected by himself and approved by the faculty. The book had to manifest original power and personal research and it had to be approved by the faculty and published. After the other requirements were satisfied, the candidate was required to sustain publicly seventy-five theses, along with the dissertation, for three hours on each of two consecutive days.[12]

Keane wrote in later years:

From the beginning the students were made to appreciate the difference between the text-book recitations of the Seminary & the personal research which was to be the chief characteristic of University work.

Hence the formation of Academies (the German *"Seminar"*) in each of the Departments, as far as practicable.[13]

A month after the university opened the Abbé Hogan wrote to

[10] ACUA, MMBT, Baltimore, November 12, 1889, p. 28. The minimum set by the statutes was the requirements for degrees in the graduate institutions in Rome.

[11] Cincinnati *Evening Post*, August 29, 1890.

[12] *Year-Book of the Catholic University of America, 1893-'94* (Washington 1893), pp. 26-27.

[13] ACUA, "Chronicles," pp. 47-48. The *Seminarium* or academy of moral studies was inaugurated during 1890-91. The *seminaria* or academies of psychology and church history were added in 1891-1892. The exegetical academy was opened in 1892-1893. Cf. *Year-Book of the Catholic University of America, 1894-'95*, pp. 13-14.

38

his friend, Father Rex, that "studies are coming into shape—I confess rather slowly."[14] Shortly after that in writing to Pace, Keane expressed his entire satisfaction with the conditions of the university and he said, "the ground is feeling solid beneath our feet."[15] After the first year's work, Archbishop Ireland, as chairman of the board's committee on studies, reported to the Board of Trustees that the work was "very good under the circumstances."[16]

The rector and the president of Divinity College found their chief difficulty the first year in the organization of the internal discipline, or the rule of the student's daily life. The rule required that all students live in common under the direction of the priests of St. Sulpice. There were exercises in common consisting of a half-hour meditation each day, an examination of conscience before dinner, a lecture or spiritual conference of a half hour, and evening prayers. Besides the breviary and the celebration of Mass each day, the priest-students recited the rosary and visited the Blessed Sacrament in private. On Sundays and feast days they had public recitation of the office. One day a week they were at liberty to leave the campus. The scholastic work each year was preceded by the exercises of a spiritual retreat.[17] Concerning this aspect of university life Keane wrote at the close of his rectorship:

Our first body of students,—"the pioneers" as we called them,—. . . . were young men of fine qualities. But several of them were imbued with the notion that the University should be totally different from a Seminary in regard to rule & personal restraint or control. Some thought that there sh'd be no spiritual exercises in common,—that each one should be trusted to see to all such things for himself. They resented supervision of their coming & going & all need of permission, &c.

---

[14] SMSA, J. B. Hogan, S.S., to Charles B. Rex, S.S., Washington, December 19, 1889.

[15] ACUA, John J. Keane to Edward A. Pace, Washington, January 9, 1890.

[16] ACUA, MMBT, Boston, July 24, 1890, p. 29.

[17] ACUA, "Seminaire des Étudiants en Théologie de l'Université Catholique de l'Amérique." This is a one page report in French signed by Father John B. Hogan, S.S., president of the Divinity College. The report has no date. It was written between the opening of the university and 1894 when Father Hogan left the university. It was written after the university had been open for some time, for it said: "Already favorable reports have come to us from various parts of the country relative to those who spent some time in our midst."

This gave matter for much serious deliberation, & caused no small solicitude to Father Hogan & myself. Some of the Professors rather shared the conviction of the students.

But after mature reflection, & consultation with the Cardinal Chancellor &c., we resolved to stand inflexibly by the principle that the spiritual & priestly life & training of the student was at least as essential as their intellectual development. Common spiritual exercises were considered essential for the securing of regularity. Limitations of personal liberty had been reduced to the minimum considered essential to the maintenance of good order. So it was resolved to stand by the rule, and the students were very kindly but very firmly told that whoever would not accept the rule must leave the University. [18]

Hogan particularly was dissatisfied with the spirit that prevailed among the students. He told Father Rex at the end of the first scholastic year: "It is pretty well understood on all sides that there must be less of the *go as you like methods next year*—that the discipline if not positively bracing, must not be relaxing—that a rule is a rule for all, and has to be kept."[19] One of the students who left the university during its first years wrote his views on the rules to the superior of St. Mary's Seminary at Baltimore and they were decidedly at variance with those of the rector and Abbé Hogan:

[18] ACUA, "Chronicles," pp. 48-49.

[19] SMSA, J. B. Hogan, S.S., to Charles B. Rex, S.S., Washington, May 10, 1890. In a lengthy report to the rector toward the end of the first year, consisting of eleven well-developed points, Hogan expressed his dissatisfaction with the order of the institution and he complained of the general disregard for the rule on the part of the students and the faculty. He said: "The general discipline of the house has not been satisfactory. Many of the rules have been set aside by a certain number, some privately, others openly and steadily. ... Already it has come to be spoken of as a place where people do pretty much as they like, and a number of them not half what they might" (ACUA, John B. Hogan, S.S., to John J. Keane, Washington, May 22, 1890). Joseph Pohle expressed this view: "As for the domestic discipline, I do not know whether the right medium between personal liberty and law has yet been found. There exists no doubt a great amount of dissatisfaction among the students which might easily break out into a dangerous agitation and bring on disastrous results, as soon as a free expression of their prejudices would gain a widespread diffusion among the clergy of the country. Would it not be better to devise a new plan in which the character of the students as true University's men would be fully recognized and their prejudices as if they were only treated as Seminarians or grammar school boys efficaciously stopped? I would propose to have the students themselves work out a code of rules by which they should be governed, and so give them back that feeling of personal freedom which is so essential and important an element of a free country and of an American citizen. I know

40

I hope for the sake of the University that they will make some changes in the rule. It was a disappointment to me in many ways to find there a system of discipline substantially the same as in the seminary. While I admit the necessity of certain regulations in every community, I do not admit the necessity of all the restrictions and limitations set forth in the rule of the University, and most of all do I object to the watching, that thing so distasteful and so disgusting to any one who has even a spark of manhood in him. I assure you it made my blood boil to see the restless eyes of the President [Hogan] cast from face to face at all the public exercises. Such a thing as that, though the Sulpitians are accused of it, I never saw in Baltimore and when it was laid at their door, I have always stoutly denied it. You would not do so nor would Father Dumont. . . .

Priests who go to the University from the mission mean business. They are not idlers, they are not pleasure-seekers, they are not disgraced, they are not untrustworthy. They are serious men possessing the confidence of their Bishop, fond of study, ready to give up much for the sake of knowledge.[20]

During the second year, the president of Divinity College wrote to his friend, Charles Rex: "Here things are better than last year yet anything but perfect."[21] By the beginning of the third year he seemed a bit more satisfied: "The young men have

---

that I am treading on dangerous ground, but I feel bound in conscience, on account of the manifold signs of dissatisfaction, and bitter feeling, freely expressed by the students, to single out the fact & put it before your Lordship" (ACUA, "Some Remarks on the way the University ought to be made more efficient," Joseph Pohle). Ireland told Keane: "If there are objectors, the ring leaders should be quietly asked to go home. The mass of students will soon settle down to the rule. . . . I sincerely trust that my students are not among the objectors. If they are, I will recall them at once, & replace them by worthier men" (ACUA, John Ireland to John J. Keane, St. Paul, December 7, 1889).

[20] SMSA, A student at the university in 1890-1891.

[21] SMSA, J. B. Hogan, S.S., to Charles B. Rex, S.S., Washington, January 5, 1891. At the end of this school year Hogan told Keane: "All complain that the students (i.e., many of them) are unmannered, disrespectful and self-willed, and that several have taken their work too easy. . . . Most of the young men who come here feel no need of improving spiritually. Some of them almost resent the notion of anyone bothering them about it. They find fault constantly with every one of their superiors. . . . I do wish that in the future you and Dr. Garrigan will be less ready to accept without questioning the complaints students may make of me in this connection. . . ." (ACUA, John B. Hogan, S.S., to John J. Keane, On Board Royal Mail Steamer *Arizona*, June 19, 1891).

41

not undertaken this time to run the house."[22] Each year the Board of Trustees' committee on discipline approved Hogan's recommendations for strict compliance with the rules of the university, particularly those that pertained to the students' a-tendance at all devotional exercises, and the one that forbade smoking in private rooms.[23] In 1892 Hogan's report on discipline stressed the need of sanctions for infractions of the rules, so the board recommended that a system of demerits be adopted and re-ports sent to the several bishops. Expulsion was sanctioned in grave cases.[24] Naturally such a measure could have been used only in extreme cases, especially at the beginning and while there was no assurance that such action would be backed up by hierarchical authority outside the institution. Hence, sanctions were difficult to apply with the result that none was effectively employed.

The students alleged as an excuse for their infraction of the rules, particularly that which forbade smoking in their rooms, the example of the professors, who, like themselves, were ordained priests with the same spiritual obligations, and who smoked in their rooms and in the corridors.[25] The authorities also had dif-ficulty in making the students report on time at the opening of the first term, so as not to miss the retreat, or to be punctual in returning from the Easter recess. Also they found it difficult to persuade the priest-students to retire early and rise in the morning in time to attend meditation.[26] Nevertheless, by the end of the second year the "unrest & quasi-resistance of the students had almost disappeared . . . and henceforth not a trace of it remained."[27] The trustees' committee on discipline was gratified by Hogan's report on the excellent observation of the rules during the university's fifth year[28] and, except for Dumont's complaint that the students did not attend to their daily medi-tation and examination of conscience, the next year's report was equally gratifying to the board.[29]

[22] SMSA, J. B. Hogan, S.S., to Charles B. Rex, S.S., Ellicott City, Maryland, October 4, 1891.
[23] ACUA, MMBT, Boston, July 24, 1890, p. 30; Washington, April 8, 1891, pp. 32-33.
[24] ACUA, MMBT, Washington, April 27, 1892, p. 35; April 11, 1893, p. 41.
[25] NYAA, CUA file "1892 — Dr. Hogan's Report on Discipline."
[26] Ibid.; ACUA, "Report on Discipline by Father Dumont, April 15, 1896."
[27] ACUA, "Chronicles," p. 49.
[28] ACUA, MMBT, Washington, April 4, 1894, p. 46.
[29] ACUA, MMBT, Washington, October 1, 1895, p. 49.

In January, 1890, a number of students organized a literary society that was "originally intended to develop skill in debate and in the use of dialectics."[30] Bishop Keane was moderator of this society in its formative years and during his administration it was very active in the life of the university. The members gave receptions for visiting dignitaries and they established the custom of presenting a well-prepared program on the principal feasts and on the national holidays. As time went on it became an academic center in which the results of actual class work or of private research carried out upon lines indicated by the professors were presented in the shape of essays, reviews, and communications of a more or less formal nature.[31]

In the eyes of the rector one of the most important features of the newly established university was the public lectures. While he and John Ireland were in Rome in 1886-1887 fulfilling the commission entrusted to them by the Board of Trustees, they had met a "distinguished Prelate who was for several years a Professor of the Sorbonne in Paris" who gave them information on lectures before the public that were given at that institution. This he regarded as of paramount importance. The two American prelates had consulted with other experienced educators, who were also convinced of their importance, and who, in turn, convinced the rector and the Bishop of St. Paul that they should be established as a principal feature of the projected university. There were a number of motives for developing this feature of university life. First, it would fill a need for those people who were seeking truth and who would be ready to listen were it fittingly presented. Secondly, it would summarize for the students the matter studied in the classes and "it would train them in the all-important art of presenting learned subjects in a popular form with correctness and elegance." Finally, it would "increase the popular esteem that would thence accrue to the University."[32] The necessity of presenting popular lectures had assumed such a great importance in the minds of Keane and Ireland that they recommended the site of the university be changed so that it would be more accessible to the people living in Washington.[33]

[30] *CUB*, I (January, 1895), 93.

[31] *Ibid.*

[32] ACUA, "Report of Ireland and Keane to Trustees of the University on Their Mission to Rome," pp. 8-9.

[33] *Ibid.*; ACUA, MMBT, Baltimore, September 7, 1887, p. 17.

43

When this proposal was considered by the board, seven members voted to retain the site that had been purchased while six members voted to change the site. The board then adopted the alternate plan of renting or building a hall in the city for the purpose of giving the lectures.[34] Keane later admitted that this was a "fortunate decision, as our influence subsequently brought about the construction of the Eckington rail-road, which brought us into quicker communication with the centre of the city than would be practicable from any other available site."[35]

The popular lectures were begun in January of the first scholastic year. They were given on Wednesday and Friday afternoons by the rector and professors of the university and by learned men who had been proposed to and approved by the Board of Trustees.[36] A lively interest was maintained in them by the announcements that appeared in the press and by the excerpts from the lectures that the newspapers printed in their columns.[37] The popular scientific lectures, illustrated by slides and experiments, given on Friday afternoons by Father George M. Searle, C.S.P., were attended by the largest numbers and seemed to meet with the greatest general interest and approval. All were well attended and enthusiastically received. After the second year the Board of Trustees restricted the number of lectures to one a week and they exempted the students from any obligation to attend them.[38] During Keane's administration they continued to be prominently featured and, among other things, they were responsible for sustaining the public's interest in the university and keeping the institution's name in the pages of the secular papers.

Vespers sung "in rigid adherence to the Gregorian chant" in the university chapel on Sundays and feast days made "a new attraction to Washingtonians, who throng to the university in large numbers."[39] On Sunday, January 3, 1891, the rector began

---

[34] ACUA, MMBT, Baltimore, September 7, 1887, p. 18.

[35] ACUA, "Chronicles," pp. 21-22.

[36] ACUA, MMBT, Baltimore, November 12, 1889, p. 27.

[37] New York *Herald*, January 20, 1890; Washington *Post*, January 30, 1890; Washington *Evening Star*, February 7, 13, 20, 1890; New York *Tribune*, May 12, 1890; New York *Tablet*, June 14, 1890; Washington *Evening Star*, March 2, 19, 1891; Washington *Post*, December 18, 1891; "University Chronicle," *CUB*, I (April, 1895), 264.

[38] ACUA, MMBT, Washington, April 8, 1891, p. 32.

[39] New York *Herald*, January 20, 1890.

44

the practice of giving sermons at vespers, a practice that was continued regularly thereafter.[40]   In fact, many practices that became traditional were introduced during the first years of the university's work. The constitutions declared:

The Blessed Virgin Mary, Immaculately Conceived, the Protectress of the Church in the United States of America, shall also be the Heavenly Patron of the University, and her feast day shall be celebrated solemnly each year on the 8th of December.[41]

Accordingly, each year a pontifical high Mass was celebrated by the rector or by some other member of the hierarchy. The professors of the faculty of theology had as their patron St. Paul the Apostle. Since the feast of St. Paul fell each year within the summer vacation (June 29), the feast of the conversion of St. Paul the Apostle (January 25) was solemnly celebrated.[42]   In accordance with the apostolic letter of His Holiness, Pope Leo XIII, given on August 4, 1880, the university honored with special veneration St. Thomas Aquinas, the patron of Catholic schools throughout the world, by celebrating his feast (March 7) with due solemnity.[43]   Hogan declared that the celebration of St. Thomas' feast in 1890 was a success, "especially the reception given to the Cardinal."[44] Shortly after the celebration of the feast of St. Thomas, the university had the first public disputations. Hogan told Rex: "They were hardly better than those you have in Brighton. . . . showing more how hard it is to do anything good in forma scholastica, at least for people such as we have to deal with."[45]

By the first week in April, 1890, a beautiful altar made by Francis and A[ME] Jacquier, of Caen and Paris, France, was installed in St. Paul's Chapel, "now the most beautiful chapel in

[40] Washington *Post*, January 4, 1891.

[41] *Constitutiones*, Cap. XI, n. 1.

[42] *Ibid., Constitutiones Facultatis Theologicae*, Cap. VI.

[43] *Constitutiones*, Cap. XI, n. 2.

[44] SMSA, J. B. Hogan, S.S., to Charles B. Rex, S.S., Washington, March 12, 1890. The Washington *Post*, March 3, 1890, gave a list of the guests which included all the prominent clerics in the vicinity.

[45] SMSA, J. B. Hogan, S.S., to Charles B. Rex, S.S., Washington, March 12, 1890.

45

the United States and one of the finest in the world."[46] The New
York *Tribune* gave the following description of it:

The front of the altar will be an alto relievo of the "Last Supper"
upon a gold background. Upon it in the centre will stand the exquisitely
carved tabernacle, each side of which will be sculptures, also in alto
relievo, that on the left representing the "Sacrifice of the Paschal
Lamb" and that on the right the "Manna in the Wilderness." [47]

On the second Sunday in April this altar was consecrated by
Bishop Keane and the vice rector sang the high Mass.[48] Within
the same period the Chapel of the Sacred Heart of Jesus, the
private chapel of Bishop Keane, was furnished "at the expense of
the devout women of Washington,"[49] and the Stations of the
Cross were erected in St. Paul's Chapel. These stations were
made by the Royal Bavarian Art Institute at Munich, the same
company that provided the fine group windows for the sanctuary
and the twelve single figure windows for the nave of the chapel.[50]
Here, in June, 1890, Miss Mary Elizabeth Breckenridge Caldwell,
"Lina," who had donated $50,000 for the erection of the divinity
chapel, was married to Baron Moritz Curt Freiherr von Zedwitz,
a native of Saxony, who was then German minister to the Republic of Mexico, and described by *Age* as "thirty-nine and handsome."[51] John Lancaster Spalding, Bishop of Peoria, performed
the marriage ceremony in the presence of Cardinal Gibbons,
Bishop Keane, and about a hundred guests.[52]

The first school year came to a close on June 20, when nineteen,
half of the priest-students, received the degree of bachelor of

[46] New Tork *Tribune*, April 19, 1890. Twelve altars for this chapel were
made by the same company. They arrived early in 1889 (ACUA, Francis
Jacquier to John J. Keane, Caen, February 23, 1889 (French)). The main
altar cost 10,000 francs (ACUA, Itemized bill).

[47] New York *Tribune*, March 31, 1890.

[48] *Ibid.*, April 19, 1890.

[49] *Ibid.*

[50] *Ibid.*, March 31, 1890. Cf. ACUA, Benziger Bros. to John J. Keane, New
York, August 20, 1888.

[51] *Age* (York, Pennsylvania), June 21, 1890.

[52] Baltimore *Sun*, June 18, 1890. Bishop Spalding informed Keane that the
baron was not a Catholic (ACUA, J. L. Spalding to John J. Keane, Peoria,
May 13, 1890). Keane got permission from the cardinal to have the marriage
performed in the chapel, for which Spalding was grateful (ACUA, J. L. Spalding
to John J. Keane, Peoria, May 21, 1890).

46

theology.[53] Keane, in his first annual report, gave thanks "to the signal assistance of Providence, to the admirable energy and harmonious unity of our Faculty, and to the brave and good spirit of our students" that brought a happy solution to the difficulties "naturally to be expected in the starting of so important a work." He could say, with gratitude, that the first year had been a success.[54]

The second scholastic year opened on the feast of St. Michael the Archangel, September 29. Keane urged the thirty-three students from nineteen dioceses and the fifteen Paulists, two of whom were students and the rest merely attending some courses, "to imitate the great prince of the heavenly host, in his enthusiasm for God and the truth, and to descend boldly into the great battleground of thought, having for a war-cry the name of Michael."[55] The theology faculty received two new members: Sebastian G. Messmer, who had been designated for the teaching of canon law before the opening of the university and who had spent the intervening time in preparation for his post by pursuing studies in Rome,[56] and Father Thomas O'Gorman, who, by the unanimous approbation of the faculty,[57] had been invited by the Board of Trustees to assume the chair of ecclesiastical history.[58] O'Gorman had been a professor in the Seminary of St. Thomas in St. Paul, Minnesota, for five years when he accepted the invi-

[53] Baltimore *America*, July 29, 1890.

[54] ACUA, "First Annual Report of the Catholic University of America, July 1890." This is a typewritten report, with no pagination, bound with printed reports that are labeled: "Annual Reports of the Rector 1-7, 1890-1896. Office of the Treasurer."

[55] *Second Annual Report of the Rector of the Catholic University of America, April, 1891* (Washington, 1891), p. 26. The New York *Sun* announced that there would be sixty students. Among them would be "several Benedictine monks who had been professors in [a] California College. . . . Rev. A. Russell Nevins, formerly an episcopal minister, Mr. Frederick Power, who was once an Anglican monk, having belonged to the Cowley Fathers" (September 1, 1890). There were two Benedictines and Father A. Russell Nevins, C.S.P., listed among the students for that year, but Power was not listed.

[56] *Supra*, pp. 23-24. Cf. *Solemnities of the Dedication and Opening of the Catholic University of America, November 13th, 1889. Official Report* (Baltimore, 1890), p. 91. Also cf. New York *Tribune*, July 29, 1890.

[57] *Second Annual Report of the Rector*, p. 3. This is the report of the dean of the faculty made to the rector on March 19, 1891.

[58] ACUA, MMBT, Boston, July 24, 1890.

tation to teach church history at the university.[59] Toward the end of his first year at the university he received the degree of doctor of divinity from the Holy Father by apostolic letter, an honor calculated "to give to our work a new token of his paternal solicitude, and to honor at the same time the merits of our colleague," the rector reported.[60]

Each of the professors gave four lectures a week. The dean of the faculty considered that number of lectures "amply sufficient to habituate to assiduous industry every serious student who realizes the object of his presence in the University." As far as the professors were concerned, they considered four lectures, rather than five, "consistent with the exceptional preparation which genuine University work requires."[61] Besides the lectures given by the faculty of theology, George M. Searle, director of the observatory, lectured on astronomy, Professor Stoddard on English literature, Professor Victor H. Bazerque on French literature, and Professor Webster Egarly on elocution. Hogan was decidedly disgusted with the showing of the students on St. Thomas' day of 1891. He told Rex: "The Jesuits who attended might well compare themselves with us in a sense of legitimate pride."[62]

At the completion of the second year only six students received the degree of baccalaureate in theology.[63] Yet, any disap-

[59] Thomas O'Gorman was born in Boston on May 1, 1843. His boyhood was spent in Chicago and St. Paul. From the latter he was sent to France with John Ireland to be educated for the priesthood. He was ordained in St. Paul in 1865 and he worked there for eleven years as a missionary. In 1877 he united with the Paulist Fathers in their mission work. In 1885 he was appointed a professor in the Seminary of St. Thomas in St. Paul and he taught philosophy and theology there. He remained at the university from 1890 until 1896, when he was consecrated bishop and installed in the Diocese of Sioux Falls. He died on September 18, 1921. Cf. "University Chronicle," *C UB*, II (April, 1896), 215. Also cf. Richard J. Purcell, "O'Gorman, Thomas," *DAB*, XIV, 3.

[60] *Second Annual Report of the Rector*, p. 4. O'Gorman had O'Connell to thank for the honor (ACUA, D. J. O'Connell to John J. Keane, Rome, October 27, 1890). In 1891, Archbishop Ryan of Philadelphia wanted the rector to permit O'Gorman to resign his position at the university so as to attend exclusively to the Indian Bureau in Father Stephan's place (ACUA, P. J. Ryan to John J. Keane, Philadelphia, December 16, 1891).

[61] *Second Annual Report of the Rector*, p. 4.

[62] SMSA, John B. Hogan, S.S., to Charles B. Rex, S.S., Washington, March 12, 1891.

[63] *Second Annual Report of the Rector*, p. 26.

48

pointment that may have been experienced because of the small number who received degrees was offset by the first fruits of the university's work. Five students and a professor in the scholasticate of the Marists won the degree of licentiate in sacred theology.[64] They had spent two years in serious application to higher studies under the careful supervision of the faculty. These were the students whom Ireland told:

When you shall be advanced in years, and the university shall become the wonder of America and of Europe as the first seat of learning in Christendom you will all say to the young generations growing up around you, 'I was a pioneer in that university!'[65]

At the meeting of the Board of Trustees in April, 1891, Keane urged the members to make the bishops of the country aware of the special advantages of the institution by keeping a number of their subjects in attendance.[66] Gibbons, at the request of and in the name of the board, sent a letter to all the bishops of the country informing them that the faculty of theology was so far developed that "it was able to offer to studious ecclesiastics an almost complete system of post-graduate divinity studies, such as was contemplated by the Third Plenary Council." He urged each bishop to have at least one student, and as many more as possible, in residence at the university:

that thus the objects had in view by the Plenary Council may be realized; that the desires and expectation in this regard so strongly and repeatedly urged upon us by our Holy Father, the Pope, may be fulfilled, and that this institution, with which, in the eyes of the world, the honor and welfare of the Church in America are so largely bound up, may reach the degree of reputation and usefulness which is its due.[67]

The Board of Trustees had begun the policy of allowing those who had completed three years of undergraduate theology to enter the university. Gibbons, in his letter to the bishops,

[64] *Third Annual Report of the Rector of the Catholic University of America, April, 1891* (Washington, 1892), pp. 6-7.

[65] New York *Tribune*, May 12, 1890. Ireland had given this talk at a reception in his honor on May 5. Father Peter Yorke of the Archdiocese of San Francisco, one of the recipients of the licentiate, had delivered an address of welcome on the occasion of Ireland's visit.

[66] ACUA, MMBT, Washington, April 8, 1891, pp. 32-33.

[67] ACUA, J. Card. Gibbons to the Archbishops and Bishops of the United, States, Baltimore, May 1, 1891 (printed).

stressed the necessity of allowing the students who entered under this policy to remain at least two years, and he also urged all the bishops to allow their students to stay at least two years to work for the degrees offered by the university. "Let us all," he said, "from end to end of the land, vie with one another in advancing the University to its full development, in multiplying its students, in making it indeed a glory to the Church and a blessing to America."[68]

Despite the appeal of the chancellor of the university, the enrollment did not increase during the third year. Thirty-three students, the majority of whom were not priests,[69] attended the lectures of the faculty of theology that had been augmented by the addition of three priests who had been preparing for their work in Europe. Charles P. Grannan came to fill the chair of scriptural exegesis, thus making up for the deficiencies in the course given by Professor Hyvernat. Thomas J. Shahan began his teaching of early ecclesiastical history, and Edward A. Pace of psychology.[70] During the year the faculty suffered a serious loss when Sebastian G. Messmer, professor of canon law, was appointed by the Holy See as fourth Bishop of Green Bay. Messmer received the official information of his appointment from Propaganda through Frederick X. Katzer, Archbishop of Milwaukee, on December 14, 1891. The professor had prior knowledge of the likelihood of his being thus honored. He had asked Denis O'Connell, then in Rome, to forestall the appointment because he considered it a bad policy to take young men from the university who had just begun their work after special training for it. The outspoken Archbishop of St. Paul also expressed this view to Keane: "You must educate your professors, & then hold on to them—making bishops only of those who are not worth keeping as professors."[71] Messmer also rightly considered that it would be easier to find the right man for Green Bay than to find a suitable man for teaching canon law. Because of these considerations he declined the appointment when it

[68] *Ibid.*

[69] SMSA, J. B. Hogan, S.S., to Charles B. Rex, S.S., Ellicott City, Maryland October 4, 1891. He said: "few brilliant . . . several profs. have scarce any students. Dr. Schroeder has only three."

[70] *Official Announcements for the Scholastic Year 1891-2* (Washington, 1891), p. 5.

[71] ACUA, John Ireland to John J. Keane, Rome, April 26, 1892.

first reached him, and he appealed to Cardinal Gibbons to write to Rome on his behalf. The cardinal, however, refused to work against his appointment to Green Bay, although he lamented his loss to the university. Messmer also asked Archbishop Corrigan to write to Cardinal Parocchi, a member of the Congregation of Propaganda, on his behalf.[72] In his endeavor to "escape the mitre," Keane gave him full co-operation.[73] In spite of all these efforts to remain at the university, the Holy Father commanded him to accept the appointment and Cardinal Simeoni, the Prefect of the Congregation of the Propaganda, sent the papal brief of appointment (December 14, 1891). The professor deferred his consecration until March 27, the fourth Sunday of Lent, so that he could continue his work at the university as long as possible and still be installed in his see before Holy Week.[74] His loss was viewed as serious by the faculty because it was impossible to replace him immediately, but canon law was taught for the remainder of the year by the combined efforts of the rest of the professors.

During that year some dissatisfaction developed among the regular professors because of the inequality of their salaries. The cardinal chancellor, after careful consideration of the circumstances, raised all the salaries to the same figure. The harmony that resulted was deemed an ample return for the financial burden involved.[75] This action of the cardinal was approved by the Board of Trustees when they met in the spring of 1892.[76]

The baccalaureate in theology was attained by only three students during the third year. Thomas Bouquillon, in his report to the trustees as dean of the School of Theology, gave a number of reasons for the scarcity of candidates. Many of the students had received their degree at other institutions where the work and

[72] NYAA, C-35. S. G. Messmer to M. A. Corrigan, Washington, December 15, 1891.

[73] ACUA, "Chronicles," p. 55.

[74] NYAA, C-42, S. G. Messmer to M. A. Corrigan, Washington, February 6, 1892. Bishop McQuaid of Rochester preached on the day of Messmer's consecration (NYAA, C-42, S. G. Messmer to M. A. Corrigan, Washington, February 17, 1892). He also told Corrigan: "I really do not know whether it is a regret or not to let you know that my dear colleagues on the faculty have ordered a *mitra pretiosa* for me" (NYAA, C-44, S. G. Messmer to M. A. Corrigan, Washington, March 13, 1892).

[75] *Third Annual Report of the Rector*, p. 4.

[76] ACUA, MMBT, Washington, April 27, 1892, p. 36.

51

requirements were easier and others did not make any attempt to obtain the degree. He requested that the trustees urge the bishops to impress their students with the necessity of taking degrees and to allow their students to remain at the university long enough to complete their studies for advanced degrees.[77] The chancellor of the university once more appealed to the bishops of the United States to send students to the university,[78] a practice which did not result in an increase in the number of students, as might have been expected, but it may have been instrumental in keeping a sufficient number in attendance to prevent the university from dying.

The fourth year of the university's life opened on September 27 with thirty matriculated students.[79] There were no changes in the faculty and the rector found it impossible to fill the chair vacated by the promotion of Messmer. Hyvernat taught more scriptural archaelogy and Schroeder taught one of the great treatises of dogma proper, rather than merely matter pertaining to the particular treatise *De Locis Theologicis*, according to directions given by the Board of Trustees' committee on studies and discipline.[80] Archbishop Francesco Satolli, ablegate to the United States, resided at the university from the time of his coming in the autumn of 1892 until he moved to more suitable quarters at Second and I Streets, N.W., in November, 1893, following his appointment as the first permanent delegate to the United States (January 24, 1893).[81] Satolli gave a series of conferences on St. Thomas Aquinas on Tuesdays and Fridays beginning November 22, 1892. Keane in his *Fourth Annual Report*, expressed special pleasure and gratitude to the apostolic delegate for the conferences and he said:

They have most strikingly demonstrated the incomparable superiority of the works of St. Thomas to all other text books for advanced

---

[77] *Third Annual Report of the Rector*, p. 7.

[78] *Fourth Annual Report of the Rector of the Catholic University of America, March, 1893* (Washington, 1893), p. 30.

[79] *Ibid.*, p. 4. For the names of the students, cf. *Year-Book of the Catholic University of America, 1893-'94* (Washington, 1893), pp. 35-36.

[80] ACUA, MMBT, Washington, April 27, 1892, p. 35. This request of the board was communicated by the rector to the dean of the faculty of theology, who read it at the faculty meeting on May 1, 1892 (ACUA, John J. Keane to Rev. Th. Bouquillon, D.D., Dean of the Faculty of Divinity, April 28, 1892).

[81] Washington *Post*, November 16, 1893.

theological studies, a lesson which, in compliance with the expressed wish of the Holy Father, we shall bear in practical remembrance in the courses of the University.[82]

The Paulists, and the Marists who had established a house of studies near the university in 1892,[83] did not have any students sufficiently advanced to be regularly matriculated in the university, but at the request of the directors of these two houses of study, the university senate allowed the more advanced of their students to attend such courses as they could follow with profit as a "temporary privilege."[84] At the end of the fourth year's work, four received their baccalaureate in theology and five received their licentiate.[85]

The relatively small number of students continued to be a problem during the rest of Keane's administration. Each year he requested the Board of Trustees to stir the bishops of the country from their indifference and neglect of their own institution. Each year Gibbons wrote to all the bishops, but with only limited success. The dean of the faculty also urged the board to increase the enrollment but, at the same time, he insisted "that quality is the chief consideration."[86] The dean also advanced a number of reasons for keeping students at the university until they had taken higher degrees, among them being the necessity of developing the talents of young men who would be capable of perpetuating the faculty and the great need of Catholic leaders in all fields of knowledge:

We plead not so much for the University as for the Church in this country. Science in every department of knowledge and activity is advancing independent of the Church, often contrary to her. We are constantly reminded in the Press, great and small, that Catholics are behind the race; that the Church has no men to lead in the new paths

---

[82] *Fourth Annual Report of the Rector*, p. 5.

[83] *Infra*, p. 88.

[84] *Fourth Annual Report of the Rector*, p. 6.

[85] *Year-Book of the Catholic University of America 1893-'94*, p. 36. William J. Kerby, later a professor of sociology at the university, received his baccalaureate that year.

[86] *Fourth Annual Report of the Rector*, p. 30. Bouquillon had replaced Schroeder as dean of the faculty in 1891. O'Gorman replaced Bouquillon in 1893 (NYAA, G-4, J. J. Keane to M. A. Corrigan, Washington, October 19, 1893). Charles P. Grannan followed O'Gorman in 1895 (NYAA, G-16, J. J. Keane to M. A. Corrigan, Washington, June 24, 1895). Also cf. *Year-Book of the Catholic University of America 1894-'95* (Washington, 1894), pp. 12-15.

now trod by learning. How shall the reproach be contradicted or avoided unless the one University we have in this land be fostered in its work by every needed contrivance? [87]

In the same report the rector quoted the encyclical letter of Leo XIII to the Spanish bishops (October 25, 1893), in which the Holy Father recalled the glory of the old universities of Spain, and notably the theological schools of Salamanca and Alcalá, and attributed the decadence of sacred studies in that country to the disappearance of the Catholic universities and their colleges. The Pope said: "The disappearance of the old universities brought about a lack of capable professors for the seminaries." The rector applied the words to the American university by saying: "No words could define with more precison and force the office of the Faculty of Theology in a University, to form teachers, who in turn are to direct Catholic thought."[88]

During the fifth scholastic year (1893-1894) the number of matriculated students decreased, there being only twenty-five from seventeen dioceses and one student from Canada.[89] The Paulists and Marists had thirty students who pursued elementary theological studies under professors of their own communities.[90] The chair of canon law was filled this year by Dr. George Peries, a graduate of the Catholic Institute at Paris. Peries had been recommended by Father Pauline F. Dissez, S.S., of St. Mary's Seminary in Baltimore. Shahan knew him and spoke highly of him both as a priest and as a scholar. Bouquillon knew him for his writings and considered him a superior mind. To avoid making any regrettable mistake in the choice of a professor to fill the important chair of canon law, Bouquillon was sent to Europe in the summer of 1893 to make inquiries about Peries in Louvain and in Paris. As a result of these investigations, Bouquillon found that he could recommend Peries without qualification.[91]

[87] *Fifth Annual Report of the Rector of the Catholic University of America, March, 1894* (Washington, 1894), pp. 24-25.

[88] *Ibid.*, pp. 23-24.

[89] *Year-Book of the Catholic University if America 1894-'95* (Washington, 1894), p. 41.

[90] *Fifth Annual Report of the Rector*, p. 23.

[91] BCA, 91-B-3, John J. Keane to J. Card. Gibbons, Washington, August 2, 1893; NYAA, CUA file, John J. Keane to M. A. Corrigan, Washington, August 2, 1893. When Martin Marty sent his vote for Peries he advised the rector: "If the thing has to be done over again I think it is the safest course to

54

The Cardinal Archbishop of Paris, in granting Peries the necessary permission to accept the invitation to go to the United States, paid a high tribute to his learning and priestly qualities.[92]

The faculty received another addition with the return of Father Daniel Quinn, who had taken with honor his degree of doctor of philosophy at the University of Athens. He began the scholastic year with a course of New Testament exegesis and philology.[93] These gains were partially offset at the end of the year by the loss of Joseph Pohle who had accepted the Prussian government's invitation to the chair of dogma in the Royal Academy at Münster.[94] At the meeting of the Board of Trustees on April 4, 1894, the committee on studies and discipline recommended that the chair vacated by Pohle be offered to Father Hogan, president of Divinity College. If he refused to accept it, the faculty's recommendation of Dr. Grannan would be adopted.[95] This turned out to be an unhappy decision because the faculty had not been consulted according to the norms of the constitutions. For a number of reasons, the faculty opposed the nomination of Hogan to the chair of apologetics[96] and they communicated their decision to the chancellor directly when the rector refused to forward it.[97] Gibbons handled the situation with his usual tact, suggesting that the appointment be allowed to stand until the next meeting of the board if Father Hogan would be willing to accept it on those conditions.[98] But, as a matter of fact, Hogan did not accept the appointment and the faculty recommended that an American be selected, preferably one who had studied at the university "as an encouragement for our own young ecclesiastics and especially for our own students."[99] Father Charles Aiken of the

---

get our canonist from Rome" (ACUA, Martin Marty to John J. Keane, Sioux Falls, South Dakota, August 6, 1893).

[92] *Fifth Annual Report of the Rector*, p. 3.

[93] *Ibid.*

[94] *Ibid.*

[95] ACUA, MMBT, Washington, April 14, 1894, p. 45.

[96] ACUA, Report of Committee on Appointment of Father Hogan: Drs. Bouquillon, Shahan & Pace.

[97] BCA, 93-E-8, Committee (O'Gorman, Grannan, Pace, Peries, Bouquillon, Shahan, Quinn, Schroeder) to J. Card. Gibbons, Washington, April 27, 1894.

[98] BCA, 93-G-14, J. Card. Gibbons to Thomas O'Gorman, Baltimore, May 31, 1894, copy.

[99] ACUA, "Report to Board of Trustees," copy.

Archdiocese of Boston, who had won great honor during his two years (1890-1892) as a student of the university, was proposed to to the trustees' committe on professors and he met with the approval of the board. While Aiken was spending some time in Europe in further preparation for his work, the rest of the faculty filled the vacancy.[100] In consequence of the unpleasant situation created for Father Hogan while this matter was under considera- tion, the Superior General of the Sulpicians returned him to the honorable post of president of St. John's Seminary at Brighton, Massachusetts, which he had filled before coming to the uni- versity. Father Francis Louis Dumont, S.S., president of St. Charles College, Ellicott City, Maryland, was appointed to the university by his superior as Hogan's successor in Divinity College.[101]

During the sixth scholastic year seventy students followed the theological course given by the same professors as the year before. Only thirty-eight of these students resided in Caldwell Hall, the rest residing in the houses of studies of the Paulists and Marists. The thirty-eight students came from twenty-two dioceses, San Francisco having by far the largest representation with five students.[102] Maurice Francis Egan, prominent in the literary world and engaged in teaching English at the University of Notre Dame, had accepted the invitation to fill one of the chairs of English language and literature.[103] Robert Underwood Johnson, associate editor of the *Century Magazine*, had urged this ap-

[100] *Sixth Annual Report of the Rector of the Catholic University of America, September, 1895* (Washington, 1895), p. 4.

[101] *Ibid.*, p. 5. The matter concerning Hogan had come to the attention of the Holy Father who advised that the decision of the faculty be followed because of the weighty reasons they gave. While the decision was pending, Hogan wrote to Keane: "I am only concerned that the rest of my life shall not be thrown away as the last five years have been in a great measure" (ACUA, John B. Hogan, S.S., to John J. Keane, Washington, June 7, 1894). After the faculties' decision had been sustained, Hogan wrote to Keane: "The action of the University in my regard as a Sulpician will be felt by every member of the body who comes to know of it and will lessen infallibly the interest they would be disposed to take in the success of the great work" (ACUA, John B. Hogan, S.S., to John J. Keane, Brighton, Massachusetts, September 29, 1894).

[102] *Sixth Annual Report of the Rector*, p. 5. For the names of the students cf. *Year-Book of the Catholic University of America 1895-'96* (Washington, 1895), p. 29. Also cf. *CUB*, I (January, 1895), 92.

[103] NYAA, G-16, John J. Keane to M. A. Corrigan, Washington, May 22, 1895.

pointment on Cardinal Gibbons early in 1891 when he heard that Stoddard was likely to retire because of ill health. Johnson regarded his friend Egan as conspicuously qualified for the position:

He is par excellence a literary man.—a poet and a critic himself, and with a most extensive knowledge of literature in other languages besides his own. He has moreover the rare faculty of inspiring others with his own enthusiasm for letters. Moreover, he is recognized among literary men as a literary influence. What he says on literary topics is treated with consideration by men of his profession, and his capabilities are beyond his reputation.

Not only does Mr. Egan possess the standing necessary to give such a chair respect for the incumbent as well as for itself, but he is *persona grata* to men outside both of the church and of his profession. . . .[104]

After Egan had been appointed to the chair in 1895, Johnson wrote Gibbons to express his satisfaction with the work that his friend was doing at the university. He said: "He is already proving his capacity for the place, and his lectures on Shakespeare have aroused great interest."[105]

At the end of the sixth scholastic year, the first doctorates in theology were conferred upon Father George L. Lucas of the Diocese of Scranton, and Father Edmund Dublanchy of the Marist house of studies. Lucas' thesis, *Agnosticism and Religion*, and that of Dublanchy, *De Axiomate: Extra Ecclesiam Nulla Salus*, were accepted by the faculty as satisfactory. Both candidates had passed the trying ordeal of the six hour public examination, in two sessions of three hours each, which were attended by Archbishop Satolli, Monsignor Donatus Sbaretti, and Dr. Frederick Z. Rooker of the apostolic delegation, as well as by Fathers Aloysius Sabetti, René I. Holaind, and James W. Smith of the Society of Jesus, and Father Albert J. Stern of the Congregation of the Most Holy Redeemer.[106] During

[104] BCA, 88-H-1, R. U. Johnson to J. Card. Gibbons, New York, January 17, 1891.

[105] BCA, 94-E-6, R. U. Johnson to J. Card. Gibbons, New York, December 10, 1895.

[106] *Sixth Annual Report of the Rector*, p. 24. George L. Lucas entered the university in 1890. The New York *Sun* reported that he had taken the degree of doctor of divinity at St. Mary's Seminary before he entered the university (September 2, 1890).

the graduation exercises on June 20, 1895, when the apostolic delegate conferred the degrees on the two candidates for the doctorate, the seven candidates for the licentiate, and the nine candidates for the baccalaureate, Dublancy read the profession of faith of Pius IV and Lucas gave a brief inaugural lecture.[107]

In the first days of October, 1895, at the beginning of the seventh year of the university's work, the members of the Priests' Eucharistic League were welcomed to the university for their first eucharistic congress. Comparatively few of the members of the league could attend because the bulk of them lived in the central and western portions of the country. Nevertheless, twenty-five archbishops and bishops and 250 priests were present, "mostly eastern men and as yet unacquainted with the League." The directors pronounced that the congress was a success because it accomplished the two-fold purpose of calling the attention of the priests of the East to the eucharistic movement and of awakening the interest of the laity in it. The daily press was instrumental in drawing the attention of the country at large to the meaning of the congress and the directors were thankful to the news agents "for the prominence which they gave to an event so entirely religious and Catholic in its character."[108] Keane preached at the opening of the congress at the pontifical high Mass celebrated by the apostolic delegate in the presence of Cardinal Gibbons at St. Patrick's Church. The university campus was the scene of the two sessions of the congress and of the closing procession.[109]

On October 1, the day before the formal opening of the eucharistic congress, the alumni association of the Catholic University of America was formed. At the first meeting the Reverend William J. FitzGerald of Lamberville, New Jersey, was chosen president; Reverend William A. Fletcher of Baltimore, vice-president; Reverend Simon J. Carr, of the university, secretary, and Reverend William T. Russell of Baltimore, treasurer.[110]

After the distractions created by the eucharistic congress, class work began. Thirty-four students resided in Caldwell Hall and a number of the students of the Paulist, Marist, and Holy Cross

[107] "University Chronicle," *C UB*, I (July, 1895), 402-403.
[108] "University Chronicle," *C UB*, II (January, 1896), 102.
[109] *Ibid.*, 103-105.
[110] "University Chronicle," *C UB*, I (October, 1895), 566.

communities attended several of the courses with them.[111] The faculties of philosophy and of social sciences had been added that fall, but consideration of them will be deferred until later in this narrative. In Keane's last report towards the end of the seventh scholastic year, he told the board:

The work of the Faculty of Theology has gone steadily on in the lines made familiar by the experience of the six preceeding years. The organization of Academies, as adjuncts to class work, has now become complete, so that in every department of Divinity studies individual research is thus fostered and directed, and with the most useful results.

The need is still greatly felt of three additional professorships, and courses, namely, in New Testament Exegesis, in Thomastic Theology, and in Liturgy and Sacraments. Without these branches the Faculty cannot possibly have its due completeness, nor the body of instruction imparted its proper symmetry and fullness.[112]

Indeed, the work had gone on steadily under his patient guidance and the seed he had sown during these first years ultimately bore fruit.

Another professor was lost to the divinity faculty during the seventh scholastic year when Thomas O'Gorman was promoted to become second Bishop of Sioux Falls, South Dakota. Dr. O'Gorman communicated notice of his resignation from the chair of church history to the Board of Trustees, the faculty of theology, and the university senate through the rector on March 20, 1896.[113] In the same communication he requested the honor of being named "doctor emeritus" in accordance with the suggestion made in the *Constitutiones Facultatis Theologicae* (Cap. II, n. 111). The faculty of theology acted favorably on this request and by unanimous vote chose him as their first "doctor emeritus."[114] O'Gorman was consecrated on Sunday, April 19, in St. Patrick's Church, by Cardinal Satolli, assisted by Martin Marty, Bishop of St. Cloud, and by Bishop Keane. He chose his boyhood

[111] *Seventh Annual Report of the Rector of the Catholic University of America, March, 1896* (Washington, 1896), p. 22.

[112] *Ibid.*, pp. 5-6.

[113] Thomas O'Gorman to John J. Keane, Washington, March 20, 1896, cited in "University Chronicle," *CUB*, II (July, 1896), 428-429.

[114] Thomas J. Shahan to Thomas O'Gorman, Washington, April 6, 1896, cited in "University Chronicle," *CUB*, II (July, 1896), 429-430.

friend and companion, John Ireland, Archbishop of St. Paul, to preach the sermon at his consecration. [115]

On June 16, Keane witnessed the last graduation during his term of office. Seven received the degree of baccalaureate in theology and twelve received the licentiate.[116] The rector told the graduates:

The Catholic University is to be the University of the twentieth century. Its face is to the future. Its professors and its students must take into cognizance the studies of the past and present with eyes to the future. The University must be conducted on lines embracing the very highest ideals of the next century, and regard them in the influence they will have on speculative and practical learning.[117]

In his discourse at the end of the exercises the cardinal chancellor thanked God for the blessings that had attended their work. In retrospect, Gibbons declared: "We undertook this work in the firm conviction that it was God's work." In true prophesy, he added: "Difficulties, no doubt, await us, but they will not be the first that we have met and overcome."[118]

Besides their work of instruction and giving popular lectures, the rector and professors of the university had many demands made on their time and talent for public lectures and contributions to learned magazines. The many favorable reports on these lectures in the papers and the scholarly cast of the articles that appeared from their pens kept the name of the university before the public and gave it a popular standing in the minds of the American people whom it aimed to serve. Keane was particularly active in giving lectures throughout the country. Because of his position as rector of the university, his lordly bearing, his clear, logical, and inspiring presentation of many subjects, he was continually called upon both by the hierarchy and laity, Catholic and non-Catholic, to grace pulpits and platforms.

Shortly before the university had opened in 1889, Keane attended the National Educational Association's convention at Nashville, Tennessee. In his speech there he stressed the necessity of a Christian education if America's influence in the world was to

[115] "University Chronicle," *CUB*, II (July, 1896), 430. P. J. Garrigan represented the university at O'Gorman's installation (*North Western Catholic*, Sioux City, Iowa), May 9, 1896.

[116] "Graduating Exercises, 1895-'96," *CUB*, II (July, 1896), 444-445.

[117] *Ibid.*, p. 444.

[118] *Ibid.*, 454.

be directed in the right path. He also answered some attacks on the Catholic Church made by Mr. Edwin D. Mead of Boston, whose bias against Catholicism caused him to repeat slanders that had been answered many times before.[119] Likewise, the rector proposed some solutions to the school question before a large audience in Mechanics Hall at Worcester, Massachusetts, in January, 1890[120] and again at Baltimore in February, 1890.[121] The solutions proposed by the bishop were similar to those advanced by the Archbishop of St. Paul later in the year which ultimately culminated in the great "School Controversy."[122]

After a quick tour of the seminaries of the "north and east" in May of 1890,[123] Bishop Keane unveiled the University of Notre Dame dome figures on May 29 and gave a lecture on "Christian Patriotism" in which he advocated toleration as a watchword. He expressed the motto: "Union in essentials, tolerance in non-essentials, charity to all," a motto which was truly exemplified in his life.[124] Early in June, 1890, Keane administered the sacrament of confirmation in the university chapel to twenty-one candidates who had been prepared by the Paulists.[125] After the graduation exercises of the first scholastic year, Keane set out for New York and was involved in a railroad accident that resulted in slight

[119] *National Educational Association. Journal of Proceedings and Addresses. Session of the Year 1889, held at Nashville, Tennessee* (Topeka, Kansas, 1889), pp. 114-123, 147-152.

[120] Worcester *Spy*, January 24, 1890; *Republican* (Springfield, Massachusetts), January 26, 1890; Milwaukee *Sentinel*, January 29, 1890.

[121] New York *Observer*, March 6, 1890. In 1895 the *Western Watchman* (St. Louis) reported a talk delivered by Keane at Providence, Rhode Island: "The Bishop wants all public educational, reformatory and charitable institutions placed under Church control and management; and openly declares that he would rather see our public schools, hospitals, and prisons in the hands of Episcopalians, or Methodists, or Baptists, or Presbyterians, than have them purely secular and unchurched as they are. Against this all the Catholics of the country protest" (November 21, 1895).

[122] Cf. Daniel F. Reilly, O.P., *The School Controversy (1891-1893)*, (Washington, 1943).

[123] New York *Herald*, May 12, 1890.

[124] New York *Herald*, June 1, 1890; Indianapolis *Journal*, June 7, 1890; *Catholic News* (New York), June 8, 1890.

[125] ACUA, "St. Thomas Sunday School Record of Confirmation and First Communion." This record was kept until 1892. The new parish in Brookland took care of the children thereafter. Keane also administered minor orders in the chapel at St. Thomas College (PFA, "Students Book — St. Thomas College, 1890-1906").

injuries that necessitated a few weeks stay at Providence Hospital in Washington.[126] He spent most of July at Cape May, New Jersey, and after the meeting of the Board of Trustees at Boston (July 23-24), he preached on August 6 in St. Paul's Cathedral in Pittsburgh, at the opening of the twentieth national convention of the Catholic Total Abstinence Union of America.[127] The rector spent the rest of the summer in Europe,[128] returning in time for the opening of the second school year.

The second year was equally arduous for Bishop Keane. He had accepted an invitation to speak at the Catholic Young Mens' National Union Convention in Washington the first week in October.[129] On October 23 he gave the Dudleian lecture at Harvard University which elicited praise from some sources and wonderment from others. These lectures had begun in 1750 at the request of Judge Paul Dudley for the purpose of exposing the "damnable heresies" of the Catholic Church. They were continued without interruption until 1857, when the fund donated by Dudley for this purpose ceased to yield sufficient income from investment. The lapse continued until 1888 when the income revived.[130] After Keane had delivered the lecture on "The Obviousness of Christianity" at Harvard, the New York *Sun* reported:

The Bishop appeared in his sacerdotal robes and spoke from the pulpit [in Appleton Chapel] which Phillips Brooks, Andrew P. Peabody, and other Protestant leaders have adorned. He gave out the hymn, "Nearer my God, to Thee," at the beginning of the service, and "Rock of Ages" at the conclusion, and dismissed the congregation with the regular apostolic benediction. The discourse was a powerful and eloquent portrayal of the groping of humanity after the light which was in Jesus, and an incisive demonstration of the truth that

---

[126] BCA, 86-L-3, Patrick J. Ryan to J. Card. Gibbons, Philadelphia, June 21, 1890; New York *Tribune*, July 28, 1890; New York *Evening Telegram*, July 11, 1890. Some English and continental papers had reported that Keane was killed in the accident (ACUA, Thomas J. Shahan to John J. Keane, Berlin, June 29, 1890; D. J. O'Connell to John J. Keane, Paris, July 7, 1890).

[127] Boston *Pilot*, July 12, 1890. The rector visited his birthplace on this trip (ACUA, P. J. Ryan to John J. Keane, Philadelphia, October 7, 1890).

[128] New York *Tribune*, July 28, 1890.

[129] New York *Freeman's Journal and Catholic Register*, June 9, 1890.

[130] Boston *Herald*, May 11, 1891. The invitation to give the lecture was extended in June, 1890 (ACUA, Charles W. Eliot to John J. Keane, Cambridge, June 17, 1890).

all existing error is due to deviation from the principles of Christianity.[131]

The vice rector of the university wrote to Edward A. Pace in Europe that Keane's "visit and lecture in Harvard last month was a great success, and made a most favorable impression. The President and Faculty of Cornell have given him an invitation to do them a similar favor."[132] *L'Universe* of Paris took a different view:

Monsignor Keane, Rector of the Catholic University, was called upon to give a speech, October twenty-third, in the chapel of the Protestant University of Harvard, near Boston. Such strange scenes can be seen only in America, sometimes in England. . . .

The stranger who would have found himself that evening in that chapel full of Protestant ministers, among whom were some Catholics would have been surprised, perhaps even a bit scandalized, at seeing Monsignor Keane, dressed in his episcopal garments, mount the pulpit and speak to an audience of heretics. . . .

He received the congratulations of the reverend ministers, who will, no doubt, continue to accept but the gospel of free interpretation, and refuse submission to the Pope and the Church.[133]

---

[131] New York *Sun*, October 24, 1890. A reply to a Dudleian lecture delivered by the Reverend Brooke Herford on October 16, 1895, on "The Answer of Modern Liberalism to the Claims of the Roman Catholic Church," appeared in the *CUB* (Thomas Bouquillon *et al.*, "Catholicism vs. Science, Liberty, Truthfulness," *CUB*, II (July, 1896), 356-387).

[132] ACUA, P. J. Garrigan to Edward A. Pace, Washington, November 19, 1890. Garrigan stated further: "I do not know yet if he will accept [the Cornell invitation]. There is a 'dog in the manger' there! The Bishop of the diocese." The Bishop of the diocese, Bernard J. McQuaid, on a previous occasion had informed Keane that he did not want him to lecture at Cornell University (ACUA, Bernard J. McQuaid to John J. Keane, Rochester, February 25, 1890). Keane wrote to Garrigan: "I declined the invitation to Cornell Univ'y. It was only *to preach*, — and I cannot get into jobs of that kind, — totally different from the Harvard lecture" (ACUA, Garrigan Papers, John J. Keane to P. J. Garrigan, Kansas City, Kansas, November 21, 1890). A further indication of the rector's popularity as a lecturer before discerning audiences was given when the president of the Kent Club Lecture Committee of the Yale Law School extended an invitation to Keane to occupy a platform previously graced by Honorable Theodore Roosevelt, Honorable T. W. Higginson, and Professor Woodrow Wilson (ACUA, William A. McQuaid to John J. Keane, New Haven, November 11, 1891). The rector accepted the invitation and delivered a lecture on "The Church and the Social Problems of the Day," on February 26, 1892.

[133] *L'Universe* (Paris), November 29, 1890. In 1894, at a convocation that brought to Albany, New York, principals and teachers from the high schools of

The rector set out on a collection tour of the West following his appearance at Harvard, thus fulfilling a request made by the Board of Trustees at their meeting in Boston, July, 1890. The board in making the request had observed that it looked almost like an imposition on the rector, "who had done so much," yet they were convinced "that no person is capable of carrying through a successful canvass of the Country."[134] Despite his efforts, however, "owing to the stringency in the markets," Keane returned to the university nearly empty-handed on December 23.[135]

After Bishop Keane had been appointed to the Catholic University of America as its first rector he continued to be identified with the Catholic Total Abstinence Union. He worked tirelessly, as was his nature, to further the aims of the Union, just as others worked unstintingly to counteract the influence and aims of the total abstainers. Keane's identification with the total abstainers caused the university to be identified with the same aims and this provoked antagonism to the institution on the part of those who were not sympathetic with the rector's views on the question. In August, 1891, the rector attended the twenty-first annual convention of the total abstainers held at the Academy of Music in Washington. In his sermon at the high Mass in St. Patrick's Church at the opening of the convention, he told the members of the Union: "It is a noble thing this fighting valiantly for the

---

the state, a Dr. Hall, from Boston, told Father Sylvester Malone, a Brooklyn priest who had defeated Bishop McQuaid in seeking an appointment as a state regent in New York, that: "He could sit at the feet of such a man as Bp. Keane and learn as he had heard him lecture at Harvard" (BCA, 93-K-5, Sylvester Malone to J. Card. Gibbons, Brooklyn, August 30, 1893). T. C. Trueblood, a professor of oratory and elocution who had heard Keane lecture at Ann Arbor, wrote: "I have had occasion several times since your excellent address here to commend your style of oratory to my classes as being the most finished and most direct of any we have had since I came, and I am desirous to know in a word what value you set upon the study of oratory, and what your own course has been" (ACUA, T. C. Trueblood to John J. Keane, Ann Arbor, Michigan, June 10, 1891). When Keane preached on the fiftieth anniversary of the death of Daniel O'Connell, "The Cardinal Archbishop of Westminster pronounced the discourse of Archbishop Keane to rank with the masterpieces of Ventura, Lacordaire and Dupanloup" (*Ancient and Modern Masterpieces of Leading Lights of the Catholic Church* (New York, 1906), II, 593).

[134] ACUA, MMBT, Boston, July 24, 1890, p. 31.

[135] ACUA, P. J. Garrigan to Edward A. Pace, Washington, November 19, 1890; *Ibid.*, December 16, 1890.

love of humanity with this one sin that is the parent of thousands and tens of thousands of other sins."[136] A few years later (1895) he addressed a mass-meeting of the convention of the Catholic Total Abstinence Union at Carnegie Hall, New York, when the audience called for him at the completion of an address given by the Honorable Theodore Roosevelt.[137] Because of his active participation in temperance work and his outstanding ability as an orator, Keane was invited in September, 1895 by the citizens of Buffalo, New York, to address a mass-meeting in Music Hall there in an endeavor to check the spread of intemperance and arouse public opinion so that the Sunday liquor law would be enforced.[138] The rector accepted this invitation through Stephen V. Ryan, Bishop of Buffalo,[139] and once again he shared the platform with Theodore Roosevelt[140] and moved his audience with a discourse entitled, "The Catholic Church and the American Sunday," which was a logical presentation of the purpose of civil legislation.[141]

In the spring of 1892, Keane suffered an attack of grippe that required a few weeks of hospitalization.[142] His recovery was sufficiently advanced by May to allow him to deliver a funeral oration "in a round sonorous voice and with all the graces and emotions of a great pulpit orator," at the services in the chamber of the United States Senate over Senator John S. Barbour of Virginia.[143] This was the first time in the history of the United States that the services for the dead prescribed by the Catholic Church were performed in the senate chamber. The senator was not a Catholic, but he had signified his intention of embracing the

[136] Washington *Evening Star*, August 5, 1891; Washington *Post*, August 7, 1891.

[137] George Zurcher, "Foreign Ideas in the Catholic Church in America," *Roycroft Quarterly* (November, 1896), 23-24.

[138] Washington *Post*, August 7, 1895. Archbishop Ireland, with whom Keane was closely associated in the temperance movement, had addressed the citizens of Buffalo some years before on a similar movement.

[139] *Ibid.*

[140] *Catholic Union and Times* (Buffalo), September 19, 1895.

[141] J. J. Keane, *The Catholic Church and the American Sunday* (Buffalo, 1895).

[142] ACUA, Garrigan papers, John J. Keane to P. J. Garrigan, Norfolk, April 9, 1892; *Ibid.*, April 22, 1892; RDA, John J. Keane to John Ireland, Washington, April 29, 1892.

[143] New York *Herald*, May 17, 1892.

faith. The senator's wife, who was a Catholic, had requested that Keane deliver the sermon and the request was granted.[144] Michael Cardinal Ledochowski, Prefect of the Congregation of the Propaganda, wrote Gibbons inquiring whether the article in the New York *Herald* for May 17, about Keane's participation in the funeral services for the senator, was true; if so, under what circumstances?[145] Gibbons informed the cardinal prefect that Keane had taken particular care to explain the Church's discipline on catechumens and that both the sermon and the prayers said by Father Cornelius Gillespie, S.J., had been previously approved by him.[146]

Keane left for Europe soon after classes had adjourned in June, 1892, and a doctor in London advised him to go to Switzerland—rather than "to the relaxing climate of Arcachon [France]" —to rid himself of the symptoms of the grippe which still clung to him. He spent nearly a month with his friend, the Honorable R. J. Hemmick, the American consul, at his home just outside of Geneva.[147] After a summer of comparative rest in the enjoyable climate and amid pleasant surroundings, the bishop returned by the Anchor Line from Glascow to begin the new school year.[148]

Once more he was called upon to deliver lectures and take an

---

[144] *Ibid.*

[145] BCA, 89-Y-9, M. Card. Ledochowski to J. Card. Gibbons, Rome, June 27. 1892 (French).

[146] BCA, 90-A-8, J. Card. Gibbons to M. Card. Ledochowski, Baltimore, July 10, 1892 (French), copy.

[147] RDA, John J. Keane to D. J. O'Connell, London, July 20, 1892; BCA, 90-C-6, P. J. Garrigan to J. Card. Gibbons, Washington, August 19, 1892. Otto Zardetti, Bishop of St. Cloud, then in Europe, kept Corrigan informed as to the whereabouts of Keane. He received this information from Salvatore M. Brandi, S.J. He also informed Corrigan that Keane was visited by O'Connell and both in turn visited Cardinal Ledochowski at Lucerne (NYAA, C-44,Otto Zardetti to M. A. Corrigan, Bad Jordan, August 4, 1892; NYAA, C-44, Otto Zardetti to M. A. Corrigan, Jorambad, August 14, 1892). Garrigan was being considered as a possible candidate for the Diocese of Springfield during this time. When another was appointed, Keane wrote: "No one could be to the work what you have so devotedly been these past years. . . . therefore do I thank God most devoutly for our escape" (ACUA, Garrigan Papers, John J. Keane to P. J. Garrigan, Paris, August 21, 1892). Gibbons wrote: "I rejoice exceedingly that you are spared to the University for some time yet" (ACUA, Garrigan Papers, J. Card. Gibbons to P. J. Garrigan, Baltimore, August 20, 1892).

[148] BCA, 90-C-6, P. J. Garrigan to J. Card. Gibbons, Washington, August 19, 1892.

66

active part in public gatherings. On January 18, 1893, he gave a lecture on "The Great Lessons Taught by History," to the members of the Brooklyn Institute of Arts and Sciences in Association Hall.[149] On February 10, he lectured at Cambridge on "The Wisdom of the Ages" for the benefit of St. Paul's Church fund. President Eliot of Harvard presided at the latter meeting and introduced Keane to the audience,[150] and later that year (June 28, 1893) Charles W. Eliot conferred the honorary doctorate in laws on Keane at Harvard University.[151]

The bishop was particularly active in the preparatory work for the Parliament of Religions that was held in connection with the World's Columbian Exposition in Chicago. Keane had received the first notice of the object of the World's Congress Auxiliary in 1890.[152] In 1891 and again in 1892 he had declined an appointment as a member of the Advisory Council on Religious Missions of the World's Congress Auxiliary.[153] When the directors of the World's Columbian Exposition requested Keane to make the bishops aware of the objects of their organization, the rector sent a letter to each archbishop just before their meeting on November 16, 1892, in which he explained that, besides the series of religious congresses in which the archbishops had already decided to participate, a parliament of religions was to be held as a central feature. The bishop explained that "the Parliament of Religions is not meant for *discussions*, but *for exposition*." After stating objections to the plans and reasons for carrying them out, he added: "It is not in our power to hinder the Parliament from taking place. It is already certain that all the other forms of religion will be ably represented. *Can the Catholic Church afford*

[149] New York *World*, February 3, 1893. The rector had lectured before this body on "Leo XIII and the Social Problems of the Day" on January 21, 1892 (ACUA, Franklin W. Hooper to John J. Keane, Brooklyn, December 21,1891).

[150] New York *Tribune*, February 24, 1893.

[151] Archives of Mount Saint Mary's College, Emmitsburg, Maryland. John J. Keane to E. P. Allen, Washington, June 16, 1893. Keane had promised Allen to be present for the commencement but the cardinal had told the rector that he should receive the Harvard degree. Since these two occasions fell on the same day, Keane sent his regrets to Allen.

[152] ACUA, Printed form giving the original announcement of the objects of the World's Congress Auxiliary of the World's Columbian Exposition.

[153] ACUA, Benj. Butterworth to John J. Keane, Chicago, June 11, 1891; Charles E. Young to John J. Keane, Chicago, March 22, 1892. On the latter Keane wrote: "Appointment declined, J. J. K."

not to be there?"[154] The archbishops approved of participation and appointed Keane to be their representative in the preparatory work that would assure the Catholic Church a prominent place in the proceedings.

Cardinal Gibbons then sent a cordial letter to the Reverend John Henry Barrows, the chairman of the Committee on Religious Congresses, in which he said:

I deem this movement you are engaged in promoting worthy of all encouragement and praise. If conducted with moderation and good-will, such a congress may result, by the blessing of Divine Providence, in benefits more far-reaching than the most sanguine could dare to hope for.[155]

Keane's name was then added to those of Cardinal Gibbons and Archbishops Ireland, Ryan, and Janssens on the advisory council. There followed considerable correspondence between the rector and the chairman of the committee which gave evidence of a desire to please the representative of the Catholic Church.[156] At the Catholic Congress, one of the denominational congresses held just before the Parliament of Religions, attended by Cardinal Gibbons, Archbishop Corrigan, and many others, Keane talked on "Education and the Catholic Church."[157] The rector was on the speakers' platform at the opening of the Parliament of Religions on September 11 along with Cardinal Gibbons, Archbishop Patrick A. Feehan of Chicago, Archbishop Patrick J. Ryan of Philadelphia, Archbishop Francis Redwood, S.M., Archbishop of Wellington, New Zealand, and Bishop Joseph B. Cotter of Winona.[158] Besides delivering his own papers on "The Incarnation Idea in History and in Jesus Christ" on the eighth day[159]

[154] BCA, 90-P-6, John J. Keane to the Most Reverend the Board of Archbishops of the United States, Washington, November 12, 1892.

[155] ACUA, John Henry Barrows to "Dear Sir," Chicago, January 27, 1893.

[156] ACUA, John Henry Barrows to John J. Keane, Chicago, December 20, 1892; *Ibid.*, January 4, 1893; *Ibid.*, January 20, 1893; *Ibid.*, January 9, 1893; *Ibid.*, February 17, 1893; *Ibid.*, March 1, 1893; Charles A. Schaeffer to John J. Keane, Iowa City, March 14, 1893; John Henry Barrows to John J. Keane, Chicago, April 5, 1893; William Pipe to John J. Keane, Chicago, May 16, 1893.

[157] John Henry Barrows *The World's Parliament of Religions* (Chicago, 1893), II, 1407-1416.

[158] *Ibid.*, I, 64-66.

[159] *Ibid.*, I, 123.

and on "The Ultimate Religion" on the seventeenth day,[160] the rector read papers contributed by Cardinal Gibbons, Professor Thomas Dwight of Harvard, and Father Charles F. Connelly of Boston, on the fourth, ninth, and eleventh days[161] and presided as chairman of a number of the sessions.[162] At the close of the Parliament of Religions Keane was on the platform with John Moore, Bishop of St. Augustine, and he ended it with "a prayer of benediction delivered in great earnestness."[163]

Participation in this type of religious meeting was tolerated until 1895 when Leo XIII informed the bishops of the United States, through the apostolic delegate, that "although these promiscuous conventions have unto this day been tolerated with prudent silence, it would nevertheless seem more advisable that the Catholics should hold their conventions separately."[164]

At the invitation of Archbishop Riordan, the university's rector went to California in February, 1894.[165] He preached a week's mission at St. Mary's Cathedral in San Francisco which received excellent publicity and was attended by large numbers. The SanFrancisco *Chronicle* reported: "His Grace is an eloquent speaker, logical in his statements, forcible in his comparisons and convincing in his conclusions. He enunciates clearly . . . he holds

---

[160] *Ibid.*, I, 151.

[161] *Ibid.*, I, 116, 125, 136.

[162] *Ibid.*, I, 120.

[163] *Ibid.*, I, 186. Barrows related that on the last day, "President [Charles C] Bonney [President of the World's Columbian Exposition] presented the popular and tolerant Bishop Keane, of the Catholic University of America, who, as always, was received with the most cordial enthusiasm" (*Ibid.*, I, 182). Barrows also related: "Those who saw the Greek Archbishop, Dionysius Latas, greeting the Catholic Bishop Keane, with the apostolic kiss on the cheek and words of brotherly love, those who heard Bishop Keane relate how Archbishop Ireland and himself, finding that they were unable to enter the Hall of Columbus on account of the throng, went to the Hall of Washington and presided over the Jewish Conference; . . . and the scores of thousands who beheld day after day the representatives of the great historic religions joining in the Lord's Prayer, felt profoundly that a new era of religious fraternity had dawned" (*Ibid.*, II, 1559-1560).

[164] *Catholic Union and Times* (Buffalo), October 24, 1895, cited in George Zurcher, "Foreign Ideas in the Catholic Church in America," *Roycroft Quarterly*, (November, 1896), 50. For the letter of Leo XIII to Satolli, dated September 18, 1895, cf. Frederick J. Zwierlein, *The Life and Letters of Bishop McQuaid* (Rochester, 1927), III, 328.

[165] RDA, John J. Keane to D. J. O'Connell, Washington, January 5, 1894.

69

the attention of his hearers all through his discourse." The same paper reported that "fully 6000 people crowded and pushed their way into the cathedral in the evening to listen to Bishop Keane's closing sermon of the week," and the account continued with a sketch of the history of the university and its need of money.[166]

The early summer of 1894 found Keane at Atlantic City recovering from an acute attack of hay-fever.[167] When classes were dismissed for the year his steps were once more directed to Europe. First he went to Rome, where he transacted his business, and then he visited Pegli, Lourdes, Paris, and Brussels.[168] While in Brussels, the rector attended the third assembly of the International Scientific Congress of Catholics and "at their earnest request explained, first in the Section of Religious Studies, and later before the united assembly, the history and significance of the Parliament of Religions."[169] His discourse received a sympathetic echo in the *Journal de Bruxelles*, the *Voce della Verità*, the *Bulletin Critique*, and the *Revue Catholique de Bordeaux*. A writer in the latter was especially lavish in his praise of the American bishop:

Very rarely have I had the opportunity of hearing such a magnificent speech. It is not that you meet therein sonorous, emphatic passages with which so many so-called orators bore their listeners. The eloquence of Monsignor Keane is essentially *real*. The deep impression it makes comes from the *things* said with simplicity, all the more perfect since those things are most important in themselves. And what a surprising command of our language! Were it not for the accent which is strongly American, sentence structure is such, the appropriateness of diction so excellent, that one would think he were listening to the loftiest national eloquence. And beneath that distinguished demeanor marked

---

[166] San Francisco *Chronicle*, February 12, 13, 15, 19, 1894.

[167] NYAA, G-9, John J. Keane to M. A. Corrigan, Atlantic City, May 26, 1894.

[168] RDA, John J. Keane to D. J. O'Connell, Pegli, August 3, 1894.

[169] "University Chronicle," *CUB*, I (January, 1895), 78. Thomas J. Shahan stated the purpose of these congresses as follows: "These congresses, then, perform, in a measure and temporarily, one part of the work of the medieval universities. They bring together men of all nationalities, one in Catholic faith, and one in devotion to truth and science. ... They make common property the results of grave, close study in many departments of knowledge, and they tend to create public opinion in scientific matters — something by no means to be rejected, since it is one of the deadliest weapons of our adversaries" ("The Catholic Congress of Brussels," *CUB*, I (January, 1895), 82).

with cold reserve, we feel the beat of a generous heart and the radiation of our faith in all its splendor. The success of His Excellency Monsignor Keane's addresses has been wonderful.[170]

After this congress was over he attended the meeting of Catholic Truth Societies near Liverpool and then set sail from there on September 15.[171]

The rector spent the next year in much the same way, traveling and lecturing. In January, 1895, the university faculty began the publication of the *Catholic University Bulletin*. Keane had reported to the Board of Trustees in 1894 that the faculty regarded the publication of a university bulletin four or five times during the scholastic year as a real necessity. O'Gorman told Ireland the real story behind its origin:

Speaking of Reviews, we—Bouquillon, Shahan, Pace & myself,—have made up our minds to go into the business. We shall form a partnership & issue a Review on the first of January next. We are keeping the thing a secret for fear Corrigan may set the Jesuits at the revival of their project in the same line, that died this summer for want of unity among themselves. We also fear lest Archb. Ryan might oppose our plan, if we submitted it to the Board of University Directors. It is to be our own property and venture. It will be a severe lesson to Ryan & Hewitt & show the Jesuits we can do what they failed to do. The Card. & Bp. Keane are delighted with our project & Fr. McMahon says we can command his purse. What do you think of it? Every avenue of Catholic thought has been shut to us. We must have one of our own.[172]

Thomas J. Shahan was appointed editor-in-chief of the project and Bouquillon, Pace, and O'Gorman gave him splendid co-operation in preparing the first issues.[173] The object of the journal was announced in the initial issue:

[170] *Revue Catholique de Bordeaux*, October 10, 1894 cited in "University Chronicles," *CUB*, I (January, 1895), 90-91.

[171] RDA, John J. Keane to D. J. O'Connell, Pegli, August 3, 1895.

[172] RDA, O'Connell Papers, Thomas O'Gorman to John Ireland, New York, April 15, [1894]. The private nature of the venture explains the reluctance of Hyvernat, Pohle, and Schroeder to contribute to its success until they were commanded to do so. Cf. *infra*, p. 152.

[173] ACUA, John J. Keane to Thomas Shahan, Cape May, New Jersey, July 22, 1895. After Bouquillon's death it was reported: "His pen and his counsel were always at the disposition of the Editor-in-Chief; indeed, he was one of the original five who pledged themselves to execute the work" (ACUA, "Third Annual Report of the Board of Editors of the Catholic University Bulletin, January 13, 1903, submitted to the Rector and Academic Senate").

71

The BULLETIN is to convey to all who are interested in the Catholic University of America a full knowledge of what is being done by its professors and students, and to act as a hyphen between the academic corps on the one hand, and the world of American thought and action on the other. It does not undertake to add to the number of general reviews, but to be a means of communication with the great Catholic body and the scientific world in general, whereby the aim, the plans, the methods, the work, and the spirit of the University may be better and more wisely appreciated.[174]

After receiving the first issue, Placide L. Chapelle, Archbishop of Santa Fé, wrote: "I received yesterday the "Bulletin" & after reading it through carefully I may safely say that your Programme & the manner of carrying it out are both admirable. I enclose my subsctiption."[175] Others found the magazine equally interesting and during its first year it was self-supporting, its paying subscribers numbering over 1000.[176] Naturally, the rector contributed his share to this important undertaking.[177]

The professors of the university were also quite active in lecturing outside the university and publishing articles in the *University Bulletin* and other learned magazines. During the great school controversy of Archbishop Ireland, Bouquillon wrote four pamphlets and an article on education.[178] O'Gorman and Schroeder also wrote on education during that same period.[179] O'Gorman's greatest contribution during his stay at the university was his *History of the Roman Catholic Church in the United States*.[180] His aid to Pope Leo XIII in preparing the Encyclical *Longinqua*

---

[174] "Prospectus," *C UB*, I (January, 1895), i.

[175] ACUA, P. L. Chapelle to Thomas Shahan, Santa Fé, January 27, 1895.

[176] *Sixth Annual Report of the Rector*, p. 24.

[177] J. J. Keane, "The Financial Side of the University," *C UB*, I (April, 1895), 149-164; J. J. Keane, "International Arbitration," *C UB*, II (July, 1896), 305-309.

[178] Thomas Bouquillon, *Education: To Whom Does It Belong?* (Baltimore, 1891); *Education: To Whom Does It Belong? A Rejoinder to Critics* (Baltimore, 1892); *Education: To Whom Does It Belong; A Rejoinder to Civiltà Cattolica* (Baltimore, 1892); Thomas Bouquillon, "The Catholic Controversy About Education. A Reply," *Educational Review*, III (April, 1892), 365-373.

[179] Thomas O'Gorman, "The Educational Policy of Archbishop Ireland," *Educational Review*, III (May, 1892), 461-471; Jospeh Schroeder, "American Catholics and European School Legislation," *A ER*, VI (May, 1892), 366-393.

[180] Thomas O'Gorman, *History of the Roman Catholic Church in the United States* (New York, 1907).

oceani gave him a special place in the esteem and affection of the Holy Father and may have been instrumental in his elevation to the episcopacy in 1896.[181]

During Keane's administration the vice rector was kept busily engaged in caring for the institution during the frequent absences of the rector and in maintaining account of the finances of the university, for which he had to submit a report in writing every three months to the academic senate and every year, and as often as they called for it, to the Board of Trustees.[182] After the university had developed and new faculties were added, the rector invited Garrigan's attention to the clause in the general constitutions which read:

Under the authority of the rector he [the vice rector] shall see that officials, professors, and students faithfully discharge their respective obligations, that academic and other appointed duties are properly fulfilled, and that all things proceed in the prescribed way.[183]

Keane advised him to "study this matter carefully, and to devise such plan as to you seems best for keeping the discipline and the studies of the institution under proper direction and control."[184]

There were numerous changes in the personnel of the Board of Trustees of the Catholic University of America between the time of their incorporation on April 21, 1887, and the dismissal of Bishop Keane on September 15, 1896. When the university opened, Casper H. Borgess, Bishop of Detroit, and Bernard N. Farren, of Philadelphia had been replaced by Camillus P. Maes, Bishop of Covington, and Kilian C. Flasch, Bishop of La Crosse.[185] Of the original group authorized by the board to collect funds for the university, consisting of Keane, Spalding, Ireland

[181] For the Latin and a good English translation of the encyclical *Longinqua oceani*, cf. "Encyclical Letter," *CUB*, I (April, 1895), 231-247. The Pope had told O'Connell: "O'Gorman helped me a great deal: he gave me many notes but now I must go over them myself and make them my own, I shall give them another coloring, but the sense will be there." O'Connell also told Gibbons: "The Pope took a great fancy to O'Gorman and attaches much weight to his opinions" (BCA, 93-K-7, D. J. O'Connell to J. Card. Gibbons, Grottaferrata, September 9, 1894).

[182] *Constitutiones*, Cap. V, n. 5.

[183] *Ibid.*, Cap. V, n. 3.

[184] ACUA, John J. Keane to P. J. Garrigan, Washington, March 10, 1896.

[185] [Philip J. Garrigan], "The First Lustrum of the Catholic University," *AER*, (September, 1889), 345. Cf. ACUA, MMBT, Baltimore, September 7, 1887, p. 17.

and Marty[186] — Maes and Flasch were added later — [187] Keane and Spalding were the most active and they obtained the best results. The work of the board was facilitated by the appointment of various committees according to their needs. After the university was launched the committees on studies and discipline, finance, organization, and professors became permanent. These committees studied the rector's annual report, in which he made recommendations affecting the welfare of the university, and they in turn made recommendations that were acted upon by the board. When the university was functioning smoothly the board met once each year on the second Wednesday after Easter.[188] In 1892 Ignatius F. Horstmann, Bishop of Cleveland, was chosen to fill the vacancy created by the death of Bishop Flasch. The same year Thomas S. Lee, pastor of St. Matthew's Church in Washington, was appointed secretary of the board upon the resignation of the office by John M. Farley, the first secretary of the trustees.[189] The board acted favorably on Keane's recommendation in 1894 to invite all the archbishops of the country to become *ex officio* members of the trustees.[190] All the archbishops accepted the invitation and, when it was found to be inexpedient to increase the incorporated board beyond seventeen, they were constituted as an advisory board without legal status and without a vote at the meetings.[191]

The trustees lost their first treasurer and one of their original members by the death of Mr. Eugene Kelly, of New York, on December 11, 1894.[192] Kelly had been appointed treasurer at the fourth meeting of the university committee[193] and he had attended every meeting save the last one before his death. Thomas E. Waggaman of Washington was elected to the office of treasurer in his place and Joseph Banigan of Providence, Rhode Island, was appointed to succeed him as a member of the board.[194] The same

[186] ACUA, MMBT, Baltimore, November 11, 1885, p. 11.

[187] ACUA, MMBT, Baltimore, September 7, 1887, p. 18.

[188] ACUA, MMBT, Boston, July 24, 1890, p. 31.

[189] ACUA, MMBT, Washington, April 27, 1892, p. 37.

[190] ACUA, MMBT, Washington, April 4, 1894, p. 47. Cf. *Fifth Annual Report of the Rector*, p. 9.

[191] ACUA, MMBT, Washington, October 1, 1895, p. 49.

[192] "Mr. Eugene Kelly Esq. (A Necrology)," *CUB*, II (January, 1895), 99.

[193] ACUA, MMBT, Baltimore, May 7, 1885, p. 9.

[194] ACUA, MMBT, Washington, October 1, 1895.

year Thomas S. Lee resigned as secretary and Ignatius F. Horstmann was elected in his place.[195] Four days after Keane received notice that his holding of the office of rector had been terminated by the Holy See, Bishop Marty of St. Cloud died and the board appointed Patrick W. Riordan, Archbishop of San Francisco, to be his successor as a legal member of the board.[196]

Thus was the university organized during the first rector's administration. The number of students was disappointingly few, the faculty of theology was slow in reaching its full development, and the over-all results were not as promising as those who conceived the idea had hoped for and predicted. Yet, through it all, Bishop Keane gave unsparingly of his talents and energies in the hope that the future would bring a realization of his vision and an answer to his prayers. The faculty strove uncomplainingly and unceasingly to fire the few young minds entrusted to them with an all-consuming love of study, and the Board of Trustees solicitously watched over their charge.

[195] *Ibid.*
[196] ACUA, MMBT, Washington, October 21, 1896, p. 61.

CHAPTER III

FINANCES AND ACADEMIC GROWTH

Among the many problems that confronted the committee appointed by the Third Plenary Council of Baltimore to carry out the commission of establishing a university, finances occupied almost a leading place. The fathers of the council recognized the need of generosity on the part of clergy and laity if the undertaking was to be a success. Hence they urged:

In order that the undertaking may the more speedily and safely be brought to a happy issue, let not the Bishops grow weary of exhorting and entreating the chief personages of their dioceses, whether in the ranks of the clergy or of the laity, who possess wealth and are animated with zeal for the Church's welfare, that following the example given by the Bishops themselves and others, they may gladly consecrate some part of their means to a work so full of advantage to the Church and of utility to the people.[1]

This appeal was sorely needed, for of the $300,000 donated by Miss Mary Gwendoline Caldwell to the university project, $100,000 was to be used for the endowment of the Shakespeare Caldwell chair of dogmatic theology and the Elizabeth Brekenridge Caldwell chair of philosophy.[2] This left the committee only $200,000 on hand for erecting a suitable building to house the first faculty and student body, for defraying the salaries of the rector, vice rector, faculty, and Sulpicians, for creating a suitable library, and for meeting the ordinary expenses of the institution they contemplated. Hence there was a necessity for a vigorous campaign for funds to meet these needs and to provide for the needs of the future. At the very first meeting of the committee the question of the endowment of professorships was discussed.[3] After Miss Caldwell had actually placed her promised gift in the hands of the council's committee, John Lancaster Spalding, John Ireland, John J. Keane, and Martin Marty were designated by

[1] *Acta et Decreta Concilii Plenarii Baltimorensis Tertii,* Tit. V, cap. III, cited in J. J. Keane, "The Financial Side of the University," *C UB,* I (April, 1895), 151. For the Latin text, cf. *Acta et Decreta Concilii Plenarii Baltimorensis Tertii* (Baltimore, 1886), p. 94.

[2] *Solemnities of the Dedication,* p. 85.

[3] ACUA, MMBT, New York, January 26, 1885, p. 3.

the committee as collectors for the university.[4] Due to the appeals of these men, as well as to those made by Camillus P. Maes and Kilian C. Flasch, who were added to the collecting committee later, wealthy Catholics throughout the country contributed fairly generously to the project, thus enabling the rector to tell Cardinal Gibbons ten months before the university opened that "sufficiency of funds is now secured for all needs at our start."[5] Seven chairs had been endowed by this time. Besides the two chairs provided for by Miss Caldwell, the Misses Andrews of Baltimore had endowed the Andrews chair of scriptural archaeology in memory of their father, Dr. Thomas Francis Andrews; the Misses Drexel of Philadelphia had founded the Francis A. Drexel chair of moral thoelogy; Eugene Kelly of New York had endowed the Eugene Kelly chair of ecclesiastical history, and his wife, a relative of the former Bishop of New York, John Hughes, had founded the Margaret Hughes Kelly chair of scriptural exegesis; and a donation from Honorable Myles P. O'Connor of San José, California, had been used to endow the O'Connor chair of canon law.[6] Besides these endowments, which amounted to $350,000, since $50,000 was considered the minimum for such donations, there were many smaller contributions in amounts from $20,000 to $1,000 that enabled the Board of Trustees to bring Caldwell Hall to completion and meet the current expenses.[7] Besides the purchase of the university grounds, which cost $39,899.90, and the building of Caldwell Hall and the chapel, which cost $399,242.78, the board had to care for the farm house, barn, and outbuildings that required repairs amounting to $5,000.[8] Moreover, it had to meet the immediate expenses of the rector and his salary of $3,000, the salary of the vice rector, $1,500,[9] and

[4] Ellis, *op. cit.*, p. 157. Cf. *Ibid.*, pp. 158-173; 177; 243-248; 282; 342; 382 for material on the finances of the university before its opening.

[5] BCA, 85-P-9, John J. Keane to J. Card. Gibbons, Rome, January 22, 1889. Keane announced that six chairs were endowed (ACUA, MMBT, Washington, May 24, 1888, p. 20).

[6] *Solemnities of the Dedication*, pp. 85-92.

[7] *Ibid.*, p. 93.

[8] ACUA, *Statement of the Financial Condition of the Catholic University of America from its Beginning to November 1, 1903* (Washington, 1903), Personal and Private.

[9] ACUA, MMBT, Baltimore, November 13, 1888, p. 24. The salary of the vice rector was increased to $2,000 in 1895 (ACUA, MMBT, Washington, October 11, 1895, p. 53).

the expenses of three young priests studying in Europe in preparation for their work at the university.[10]

The first professors were assured their salary, $2,000 and board, by the endowments that brought six per cent interest.[11] The expenses entailed in providing for the students were met by the tuition paid for them, $250 a year, or by the scholarships that were established for various dioceses.[12] Keane gave a very practical justification for charging student fees at the university in an article that appeared in the *Catholic University Bulletin* in later years:

It is recognized that fees must be charged, lest even the foolish should seem justified in supposing that learning is of no value; but it is also recognized that practically the requirement of fees should be so minimized by free scholarships and other such methods, that the poor man's son can have just as good a chance in the noble strife for intellectual superiority and for all the success and preeminence in life which this implies, as the son of the rich man has. This is the best antidote to communism and anarchism, and all the forms of social discontent which seethe and ferment for the world's mischief. The more we place equally within the reach of all the best advantages which give success in life, the more we take away all reason for complaint, disarm violence, and make the foundations of society impregnable.[13]

After the university's first year it was evident that the tuition charged for the student was sufficient to meet the expenses incurred for their food and domestic services.[14] During the first few years much of the food for the professors and students was supplied by the cultivation of the land around the university by a farmer hired for that purpose by the board.[15] At the end of the first year the vice rector's report showed an indebtedness of

[10] ACUA, MMBT, Baltimore, November 13, 1888, p. 24; ACUA, MMBT, Baltimore, November 12, 1889, p. 27. The men studying in Europe were not to receive more than $700 a year.

[11] ACUA, MMBT, Baltimore, November 12, 1889, p. 27. Investments were realizing an income of $19,000.

[12] *Official Announcements of the Catholic University of America, September, 1889* (Baltimore, 1889). This six-page leaflet has no pagination. The university would, as far as practical, supply all the needed textbooks.

[13] J. J. Keane, "The Financial Side of the University, *C UB*, I (April, 1895), 155.

[14] ACUA, "First Annual Report of the Rector of the Catholic University of America, July, 1890" (Typewritten, no pagination).

[15] *Second Annual Report of the Rector*, p. 5.

78

$50,203.14 at six per cent.[16] This indebtedness still remained at the end of the second year due to the financial depression from which the country generally had been suffering.[17]

Keane began his campaign for general diocesan collections for the university just before the institution opened. It was his plan to use these collections to establish scholarships and he felt that if a collection were taken up once he could accomplish his aims. He told Gibbons: "I hope Your Eminence may think well of encouraging the idea & recommending it in conversation with Bishops."[18] The Board of Trustees did not favor this idea, adhering rather to the original plan of soliciting contributions only from individuals of means. Accordingly, in 1890, when there was a need for strong efforts to raise funds, they asked the rector to canvass the country so their depleted treasury could be filled and a surplus created to meet the expenses that would result from the contemplated additions to the university.[19] This tour met with only scanty success,[20] so once more the rector recommended a general collection throughout the United States. He told the board:

It has been suggested by Bishops and priests that if one general collection were ordered by the Bishops of the country, say on the first Sunday of Advent, there would be a willing and generous response from the masses of the people, who take an interest in the work and are proud of it, but have thus far had no opportunity given them of taking part in it according to their means.[21]

Once more the board refused to endorse the rector's plan. They

[16] "First Annual Report of the Rector."
[17] *Second Annual Report of the Rector*, p. 6.
[18] BCA, 85-P-9, John J. Keane to J. Card. Gibbons, Rome, January 22, 1889.
[19] ACUA, MMBT, Boston, July 24, 1890, p. 31.
[20] ACUA, P. J. Garrigan to Edward A. Pace, Washington, November 19, 1890; *Ibid.*, December 16, 1890. These letters in ACUA, Garrigan Papers, John J. Keane to P. J. Garrigan, indicate the extensive tour made by the rector at this time to secure funds: Boston, October 25, 1890; Worcester, October 27, 1890, in which he mentions Albany and Buffalo as his next stops; Detroit, November 7, 1890; Chicago, November 12, 1890; in which he mentions St. Louis and Denver, as his next stopping places; Kansas City, Kansas, November 21, 1890, in which he says: "I am resigned to be a tramp, even with the scanty return to be expected at present;" Denver, December 1, 1890, Lincoln and Omaha to be visited next; Omaha, December 11, 1890, Dubuque, Notre Dame, and New York next.
[21] *Second Annual Report of the Rector*, p. 29.

may have been partially influenced by the gift of real estate, valued at $400,000, from Father James McMahon, pastor of St. Andrew's Church, New York.[22]

In 1892 the vice rector's report showed that there had been no deficit for the year; that the university had increased its capital; that many necessary additions and improvements had been made; and, in general, the university had enjoyed a most prosperous year.[23] Yet an indebtedness of over $63,000 remained and the board found it necessary to authorize the negotiation of a loan.[24] By the next meeting of the trustees (1893) the indebtedness had been decreased by more than half and the vice rector made the following recommendations for further economy:

After much inquiry, close examination and advice with other institutions who have had experience, we have decided to commit the domestic affairs of the house to the care of a religious community, Sisters of Providence from the diocese of Covington, Ky. While we praise the present management of our domestic department, which has been very satisfactory, yet, because of the difficulty of securing and retaining reliable help near Washington, we think that a religious community will be both more efficient and economical. We hope that the matter may commend itself to the members of the Board.[25]

The board was favorable to this recommendation, but once more it refused to second the rector's plan for a general collection, although it was strongly endorsed by the trustees' finance committee, which reported that they "do not see their way clear to do what they are asked" if a general collection was not made in all the churches of the country in 1894. The board had been asked to authorize the construction of a students' hall in anticipation of the needs that would certainly arise from the addition of faculties

[22] ACUA, MMBT, Washington, April 8, 1891, p. 32. McMahon's letter making the donation was read and accepted at this meeting. The board agreed to grant his request to live at the university for life and Keane so notified him (ACUA, John J. Keane to James McMahon, Washington, April 9, 1891). According to the New York *Sun* he made over the deeds to his property on April 10 (April 11, 1891).

[23] *Third Annual Report of the Rector*, p. 20.

[24] NYAA, CUA file, "Finance Meeting of the Board of Directors, 1892."

[25] ACUA, "Report of the Vice-Rector." Ten pages, no pagination. Mrs. Theresa Lamb of London, was given charge of the housekeeping arrangements when the university opened. She had been employed in St. Mary's Seminary, Baltimore, for five years previous to her engagement by the university (New York, *Evening Telegram*, May 16, 1889).

for lay students when McMahon Hall was completed. But the board authorized the rector to proceed with this addition provided only that "he does not encroach upon the university fund."[26] Hence, the project was tabled until a later date.

The next year's report showed that the total assets of the university had increased by nearly $20,000, while the liabilities were only about $1,400 greater than the year before.[27] Keane thanked Mr. Waggaman, the treasurer, for the fact that their income had not fallen short, especially since "educational institutions in many places have been embarrassed by the diminution of their resources."[28]

In the five years that followed the opening of the university two more chairs in the School of Theology were endowed; the one, created by the will of Patrick Quinn of Philadelphia, was called the Quinn chair of ecclesiastical history; the other, endowed by the Catholic Total Abstinence Union of America, was designated the Father Mathew chair of psychology.[29] By this time ten scholarships or burses had been created: three for the Archdiocese of Baltimore, two for the Archdiocese of New York, two for the Diocese of Alton, one each for the Archdiocese of Milwaukee and the Diocese of Pittsburgh, and one at the disposal of the university.[30] Since no provision had been made for the salary of the rector, the vice rector, the Sulpician fathers, the professor of English literature, and the professor of elocution by endowments, Keane began two organizations, which were called the Divinity Fund Association and the University Fund Association, with the object of creating a general fund of $200,000 to meet these expenses. The former was made up from the ranks of the clergy and the latter from the laity. Each member pledged to give $100 for ten years or during life and the goal of each association was 100 members. By January, 1893, the Divinity Fund Association had

[26] ACUA, MMBT, Washington, April 11, 1893, p. 42.

[27] *Fifth Annual Report of the Rector*, p. 15.

[28] *Ibid.*, p. 7.

[29] J. J. Keane, "The Financial Side of the University," *CUB*, I (April, 1895), 159-160. The Board of Trustees accepted $25,000, in lieu of the full endowment, for the Father Mathew chair of psychology (ACUA, MMBT, Washington, April 11, 1893, p. 43). For the beginnings of the movement to endow the Father Mathew chair cf. Ellis, *op. cit.*, pp. 307, 369. Also cf. *Freeman's Journal*, September 7, 1889 and Washington *Post*, August 7, 1891.

[30] *Year-Book of the Catholic University of America, 1895-'96* (Washington, 1895), p. 6.

fifty-one members and the University Fund Association had thirty-three members, all of whom had fulfilled their pledge.[31] The rector appealed to the members of these associations in January of each year and he gave them an account of the membership and the amount received in fulfillment of their pledges. Both these organizations failed to reach full membership during Keane's administration, there being only fifty-six in the Divinity Fund Association and forty-five in the University Fund Association in 1895. Over half of the members failed to honor their pledges during that year. The receipts from the former amounted to $2,400 and those from the latter amounted to $3,100 in the year before he was relieved of his position as rector.[32] In 1894 the nucleus of the Chapel Fund Association was formed from the University Fund Association. The members of this association contributed ten dollars a year to provide for the expenses of the chapel. They hoped to raise sufficient funds to endow the chapel permanently and, possibly, to erect "the future University Chapel or Church."[33] By the end of 1895 this association numbered 170 members who that year contributed $1,900.[34]

The library, "one of the first cares of every institution of learning," was among the main concerns of Bishop Keane. A year before the university opened he had requested the Board of Trustees to make an appropriation for and to authorize the purchase of books. The board named Archbishop Corrigan as chairman of a committee on the library and it authorized him to choose other members from the trustees or outside the board to aid in the judicious expenditure of $5,000 to assure a properly equipped library for the purposes of the university.[35] The chairman chose

[31] NYAA, CUA file, John J. Keane to the Members of the Divinity Fund Association and of the University Fund Association, Washington, January 2, 1893. Also cf. J. J. Keane, "The Financial Side of the University," *CUB*, I (April, 1895), 160-161.

[32] ACUA, John J. Keane to the Members of the Divinity Fund Association and of the University Fund Association, and to all the Friends of the Catholic University of America, Washington, January 2, 1894; *Ibid.*, January 29, 1895; John J. Keane to the Members of the Divinity Fund Association, of the University Fund Association, of the Chapel Fund Association, and to all the Benefactors of the Catholic University of America, Washington, January 15, 1896.

[33] ACUA, John J. Keane to the Members, Washington, January 2, 1894.

[34] ACUA, John J. Keane to the Members, Washington, January 15, 1896.

[35] ACUA, MMBT, Baltimore, November 13, 1888, p. 23.

four men who were acquainted with the needs of such a library. They drew up appropriate lists separately and then met in joint counsel to decide what books would be the most useful in view of their limited budget. The Archbishop of New York contracted for the books that they decided to obtain and then resigned his charge of the committee after the university opened.[36] During the first year the crypt, or lower floor of the chapel in Caldwell Hall, housed the library of about 8,000 volumes.[37] Alexis Orban, S.S., the librarian, "greatly aided especially by Dr. Bouquillon," began the work of organization and cataloging at once.[38] During the first year the library committee, consisting of the rector, the librarian, John B. Hogan, and Thomas Bouquillon, met regularly each month in the rector's room to draw up the rules of the library, to determine the choice of periodicals, and to consider measures for the improvement of the library.[39] The space alloted to the library was found to be inadequate after the first year, so the whole basement was given over to it by improvements during the summer of 1890 which increased its capacity to 60,000 volumes.[40]

Since the board did not make any appropriation for the library in the beginning, the accessions were largely limited to the donations of friends of the university,[41] and particularly by the generous gift of about 3,000 volumes from Michael J. O'Farrell, Bishop of Trenton.[42] In 1893 the librarian begged the board to appropriate a regular fund so the library committee could meet current and prospective needs in a systematic way.[43] In answer to his plea, the trustees appropriated $1,750 for the following year and it did the same for the succeeding year.[44] By September, 1896, the library had a total of over 17,000 volumes. The inauguration of the new faculties the year before necessitated some changes in the library. The books that pertained especially to the

[36] Ellis, *op. cit.*, pp. 329-331; 380; 396-397.

[37] *Fifth Annual Report of the Rector*, p. 27.

[38] ACUA, "Chronicles," p. 48.

[39] *Second Annual Report of the Rector*, p. 14. Cf. *Fifth Annual Report of the Rector*, p. 27.

[40] *Fifth Annual Report of the Rector*, p. 27.

[41] *Fifth Annual Report of the Rector*, p. 27.

[42] ACUA, "Chronicles," p. 48.

[43] *Fourth Annual Report of the Rector*, p. 16.

[44] ACUA, MMBT, Washington, April 14, 1894, p. 54.

83

subjects taught in the new schools were moved to McMahon Hall to more spacious reading rooms. Only about 1,800 volumes were transferred at that time and the Caldwell Hall library remained the chief depository for books.[45] An unexpected donation came to the library shortly after the inauguration of McMahon Hall from Mr. Joseph Banigan, one of the trustees. On the day of the inauguration Keane had remarked to him about their need of books. Shortly thereafter he informed the rector that he had made an investment of $50,000 at eight per cent and he would send the dividends from that investment semi-annually for the library until the amount of $50,000 had been paid up.[46] The holdings of the library were described in the first issue of the *Catholic University Bulletin* as follows:

Besides the Latin and Greek patrologies, the principal scholastic theologians, the *Acta Sanctorum,* the reprint of Baronius, and several other great collections, the library possesses a goodly number of the best modern works on the sciences taught at the University. Over one hundred theological reviews, American and European, are received, and there are complete sets of the *Civiltà Cattolica* and the *Dublin Review.*[47]

As we have already seen, the Board of Trustees and the rector of the university had extended an invitation to religious congregations to establish houses of study around the university. The Paulists were the first to accept the invitation, making use of a building on the grounds. Since many of the orders had few students to send to a graduate school at one time and since most of them had already established houses of study elsewhere for their undergraduates, it was natural that they would be slow to vote a large expenditure for a house of studies near the university until there was reasonable assurance that the university project would be a success. After the university had completed its first year, Father Aloysius Spencer, O.P., Provincial of the Dominicans, conferred with Cardinal Gibbons about establishing a house of studies in his archdiocese. The cardinal then wrote to the Master General of the Dominicans, telling him: "Aprés en avoir conféré avec le Provincial de votre ordre, je suis heureux de vous proposer d'établir une maison d'études pour vos subjets, dans mon

---

[45] *Seventh Annual Report of the Rector*, p. 39.

[46] *Ibid.*, p. 11.

[47] "University Chronicle," *CUB*, I (January, 1895), 94.

diocèse et auprès de notre Université Catholique."[48] The rector reported to the Board of Trustees in 1891 that formal negotiations had been opened by the Dominicans and the Marists with a view to establishing houses of studies similar to the one already prospering under the Paulists. He requested the board "to give instructions as to the nature of the contract to be made on these and similar occasions."[49] The board then empowered Cardinal Gibbons to make contracts with religious orders in its name.[50] When the Dominicans had received word from their vicar general in Rome that they could proceed with the foundation of a house at Washington,[51] they were presented with the following terms of agreement:

TERMS OF AGREEMENT BETWEEN THE CATHOLIC UNIVERSITY OF AMERICA AND RELIGIOUS BODIES ESTABLISHING HOUSES OF STUDY IN CONNECTION THEREWITH

1. The orders and congregations of religious men in the United States are cordially invited to establish houses of study or scholasticates in connection with the Catholic University of America.

2. In so doing, it is presumed that their purpose is to give their students the advantages offered by the University, and to co-operate for the attainment of the ends which the Bishops of the country had in view in establishing it.

3. In these houses of study the courses of ecclesiastical education shall be up to the level required by the Plenary Councils for the colleges and seminaries of the country.

4. Each religious order or congregation is free to give in its house of study such superior courses as are required by its Constitutions; but, in order that the occasions of undue rivalry may be as far as possible precluded, it is agreed that these courses shall be for its own students only, no outside students being admitted thereto, unless with explicit consent in each case of the Rector of the University.

---

[48] BCA, 87-B-10, J. Card. Gibbons to General of the Dominicans [Andreas Fruhwirth], Baltimore, October 9, 1890 (French), copy.

[49] *Second Annual Report of the Rector*, p. 24.

[50] ACUA, MMBT, Washington, April 8, 1891, p. 34.

[51] BCA, 88-P-3, Aloy. Spencer, O.P., to J. Card. Gibbons, New York, May 12, 1891. The approval of the Sacred Congregation was required before a new foundation could be made (ACUA, Aloy. Spencer, O.P., to John J. Keane, Tarrytown, April 28, 1891).

5. Their students, when duly prepared, may become matriculated students of the University and candidates for its degress, on the same terms as other students, and subject to the rules of the University.

6. For the maintenance of harmony and good order the supervisory authority of the University, in regard to matters above specified and matters similarly relating to the external scholastic relations of the houses of study with the University and with one another, is recognized and accepted.

I————————————being authorized to act in the name of————————————do hereby, in the name of said———— ——————————, sign and agree to the above conditions, this———— day of————, in the year of Our Lord————.
                                                                                              _____52

The Dominicans considered this proposed agreement at a meeting of the intermediate congregation, or chapter, of the province, held at St. Rose, Kentucky, on February 6, 1892. After mature deliberation they made the following decision:

"Ordinamus novam studiorum domum aedificandam esse in civitate Novi Portus loco civitatis Washington, in qua civitate Patres Provinciae olim statuerunt domum istam esse locandam." (Ex. Act. Cong. Intermed. 1892)[53]

Father Spencer communicated this decision to Cardinal Gibbons who, in turn, informed the rector. Keane wrote the chancellor immediately:

I am surprised indeed that Father Spencer should have found any fault to find with the terms of agreement now proposed to him. We have

---

[52] BCA, 89-P-4, John J. Keane to J. Card. Gibbons, Washington, February 22, 1892. The terms were attached to this letter. In the meeting of the board the next year the terms of agreement were approved by the committee on organization with these changes:

"1. Terms approved
"2. Terms approved
"3. Terms approved but omitting 'by Plenary Councils'
"4. Terms approved add 'with the explicit consent of Senate of Univ. on the condition that he not be a student of the house.'
"5. Terms approved
"6. Substitute for the words 'the supervisory authority of the University etc' words 'the Board of Directors' " (NYAA, CUA file, Committee report (rough draft), April 27, 1892; ACUA, MMBT, Washington, April 27, 1892, p. 35).

[53] Cited in ACUA, Lawrence F. Kearney, O.P., to Thomas J. Conaty, Zanesville, Ohio, February 4, 1902.

endeavored to shape them in as perfect accordance as possible with the views which he expressed. Least of all can I see any reasonableness to his objection to the last clause. Common sense dictates that the observance of such an agreement calls for the supervision of some authority, and surely it is only reasonable that, since these houses are connected with the University, the central authority of the University should have the power in question. The very terms of the article clearly show that no power is claimed or thought of, extending beyond these merely external relations between the houses of study and the University.

I fear your Eminence is right in supposing that some outside influence must be at work prejudicing those who at first showed only friendliness in this matter.[54]

Meanwhile the decision of the chapter had been communicated to the master general in Rome, who concurred with their judgment:

Placeat tibi, Admodum R. [everende] P. [ater] Prior Provincialis, Eminentissimo Domino Cardinali Gibbons, omni sua par est, reverentia significare, nos grato animo benevolentiam suam recolere et nonnisi majoris libertatis causa erectionem Colegii in Civitate Novi-Portus faciendam decrevisse. Si plena vobis conceditur libertas in civitate Washintonopoli et Vos in Consilo Provinciae vel in Capitulo Provinciali hanc erectionem decernitis, promptum animum habemus, talem decisionem satisfaciat. Sed, stantibus rerum circumstantiis actualibus, non potuimus aliam sententiam ferri, quam ipsa Congregatio Intermedia Ordinatione secunda tulit.[55]

When the provincial received the master general's decision he sent the substance of the letter to Gibbons and concluded: "If we came to Washington we would have to be, as regards the University, at full liberty and free from all conditions."[56] The rector communicated this decision to the Board of Trustees at their next meeting (1893), adding, "this, of course, ends the negotiations."[57]

[54] BCA, 89-P-4, John J. Keane to J. Card. Gibbons, Washington, February 22, 1892.

[55] Andreas Fruhwirth to Admodum Reverende Pater Prior Provincialis (Aloy. Spencer), Romae, 19 Maji, 1892, cited in ACUA, Lawrence F. Kearney, O.P., to Thomas J. Conaty, Zanesville, Ohio, February 4, 1902.

[56] BCA, 89-W-10, Aloy. Spencer, O.P., to J. Card. Gibbons, New York, June 9, 1892.

[57] *Fourth Annual Report of the Rector*, p. 6. For negotiations with the Dominicans during Conaty's administration cf. Peter E. Hogan, S.S.J., "Thomas J. Conaty, Second Rector of the Catholic University of America, 1896-1903" (Unpublished Master's thesis, Department of History, Catholic University of America, 1947), pp. 98-100.

Later the negotiations between the university and the Order of Preachers were resumed and ended successfully with the Dominican House of Studies being erected in 1903.

The Marists, meanwhile, had signed the agreement. They purchased a residence in Brookland and had it prepared for occupancy in the fall of 1892.[58] In 1894 an addtion was made to their house under the direction of their provincial, B. Forestier, S.M., which enabled them to accommodate some thirty students.[59]

In the fall of 1895 the Congregation of the Holy Cross was welcomed to the university. Their coming was attributed to "the enlightened foresight of Fr. Francais, the superior of the Congregation, and to the efforts of V. Rev. Fr. Corby and Rev. Dr. Zahm." During their first year they had thirteen students under the direction of Father P. J. Franciscus, C.S.C.[60]

During the sixth scholastic year (1894-1895) the first signs of the fulfillment of a desire of James O'Connor, Bishop of Omaha, came too late for him to see its realization.[61] In the "Chronicles of the Catholic University of America," Keane related an event that took place just before he sailed for Europe in 1888 to have the statutes of the university approved:

In New York I met Bp. O'Connor, of Omaha, who told me he had taken that long journey in order to confer with me about the practicability of having the University exercise some sort of supervision & direction over the Seminaries & Colleges of the country, in order to, as it were, coerce them into elevating the standard of their studies. The need of such improvement he considered deplorable, and unless it came from *outside* coercion, it seemed to him hopeless. I showed him the many difficulties & the inevitable resistance in the way of such supervision. But I promised to use my influence to induce the Holy See to at least plant the germ of it, by recommending affiliation of those institutions with the University. This explains a sentence to that effect in the Holy Father's Brief of March 7th, '89.[62]

The papal brief of March 7, 1889, *Magni nobis gaudii*, contained this sentence:

We exhort you all that you should take care to affiliate with your

---

[58] *Third Annual Report of the Rector*, p. 8.

[59] "University Chronicle," *C UB*, I (January, 1895), 93.

[60] "University Chronicle," *C UB*, I (October, 1895) 566.

[61] James O'Connor, Bishop of Omaha, died May 27, 1890 (Theodore Maynard, *The Story of American Catholicism* (New York, 1946), p. 636).

[62] ACUA, "Chronicles," pp. 28-29.

88

university, your seminaries, colleges, and other Catholic institutions, according to the plan suggested in the Constitutions, in such manner, however, as not to destroy their autonomy.[63]

In the fall of 1894 the St. Paul Seminary, St. Paul, Minnesota, placed itself under the indirect influence of the leading Catholic institution of the land. By virtue of their affiliation, the university had the right to preside over and pass upon the examinations for degrees held in the seminary; and the seminary had the privilege of having the baccalaureate of the university conferred on those students who passed the examinations satisfactorily.[64]

Among the many indications of the interest of the clergy and laity of Europe and America in the new university during its first years, were the generous donations of works of art. While Keane was in Rome in the winter and spring of 1888-1889, he had preached a series of sermons in the Church of San Silvestro. The Roman correspondent for the *Catholic Mirror* reported that "the announcement of each sermon attracted to the church a vast congregation of auditors, who manifested their interest by the closest attention to the luminous words that fell with such ease and power from the lips of the Bishop."[65]   As a sign of their appreciation of the university rector's work in Rome and as an indication of their interest in the great institution that he was founding in America, the Catholics of Great Britain and Ireland in Rome presented a marble bust of St. Thomas Aquinas sculptured by Luigi Guglielmi on the day the university opened.[66] The university received another precious work of art from Rome, namely, the Ugolini portrait of the Holy Father presented by Leo XIII himself.   Keane told how this came about:

I asked him[Leo XIII] to give a few sittings, in order that a suitable portrait of him might be painted by a distinguished artist whom I

---

[63] ACUA, "Apostolic Letters of His Holiness Pope Leo XIII to The Most Eminent and Most Reverend James Cardinal Gibbons", p. 2. This is a portion of the translation of the constitutions of the university which includes a translation of the rescript of March 23, 1889, the general constitutions, and the special constitutions of the School of Sacred Sciences. This material is printed but not bound. It has nineteen pages. The Latin text of Leo XIII's letter, *Magni nobis gaudii,* may be found in *A ER,* I (June, 1889), 223-226.

[64] *Sixth Annual Report of the Rector,* p. 6.

[65] *Catholic Mirror* (Baltimore), March 9, 1889.

[66] ACUA, Committee on behalf of the Catholics of Great Britain and Ireland in Rome to John J. Keane, November 13, 1889 (printed).

had selected. "No," said he, "I prefer to present to the University a portrait which I possess, and which presided, as it were, over my Golden Jubilee Exposition. That is, if you consider it good enough for the University." And in spite of my protest, he insisted on having the large portrait & its immense frame carried & set up in one of the halls of the Vatican, that I might, a couple of days later, see it & judge "whether it would be good enough." Of course I declared that it was excellent, and far more precious, as his own gift, than any other could be. —It was judged not advisable to attempt to transport the immense frame; the frame it now wears was made by Myers & Hedicen, Balto.[67]

When the frame was completed the portrait was placed in the public lecture hall.

Portraits of Washington (after Stuart) and Archbishop Carroll by Signor Luigi Gregori, a Florentine artist, were placed in the parlors of the university during its first days,[68] as well as portraits in oil of Myles P. O'Connor and Francis A. Drexel, whose names were perpetuated by two chairs in the university.[69] Mrs. C. S. Hewit, a sister-in-law of Augustine F. Hewit, C.S.P., gave a handsome painting of Orestes A. Brownson, originally presented to her husband, Dr. H. S. Hewit, by Brownson, and this was installed in the lecture hall.[70]

The most valuable work of art presented to the university during its early years was a huge statue of Leo XIII, the gift of Mr. Joseph F. Loubat, a wealthy gentleman from New York City, who was later raised to the dignity of a Roman count by the Holy Father. Loubat had written to Archbishop Corrigan in the spring of 1889 about the statue of Leo XIII that had been exhibited in the Vatican during the jubilee of the Holy Father. He had learned that a duplicate was to be erected at Carpineto Romano, the birthplace of Leo XIII, and he thought that "it would be a graceful act on my part to have a triplicate one made and erected in the U. S., wherever your Grace should suggest. I presume either the grounds of the Catholic University at Washington or in the Central Park at New York." Loubat asked

[67] ACUA, "Chronicles," p. 33.

[68] ACUA, Luigi Gregori to John J. Keane, Notre Dame, October 23, 1889; *Harper's Weekly*, New York, November 16, 1889.

[69] New York *Tribune*, July 28, 1890.

[70] ACUA, [Mrs.] C. S. Hewit to John J. Keane, Bridgeport, June 4, 1890. Cf. New York *Tribune*, July 28, 1890.

Corrigan: "Does it not strike your Grace that the most appropriate place for the Statue of Leo XIII would be in the grounds of the Catholic University at Washington?"[71] After correspondence between the New York prelate and the count had established the fitting character of such an act and when it was determined that the university would be the logical recipient, Corrigan wrote the rector about the statue and told him that "acting under my advice, Mr. Loubat has determined to offer the statue to the Catholic University."[72] The statue was made by Guiseppi Luchetti from Carrarra marble representing the Holy Father seated in the *sedia gestatoria*, crowned with the tiara, and in the act of giving his blessing *urbi et orbi*.[73] When the sculpture was finished, the count informed Corrigan that the inscription on the front of the pedestal had been composed by the Holy Father himself. On the right hand side, there was the Pope's coat of arms, and on the left hand side, those conferred on the count by His Holiness. In the same letter he informed the archbishop that the Sovereign Pontiff had permitted him to erect the duplicate statue at Carpineto Romano in the principal church, and he had ordered a third statue for Perugia.[74] After considerable correspondence in which the progress of the masterpiece was discussed,[75] the statue finally arrived in Washington in July, 1891,[76] and the unveiling took place in the "divinity prayer hall" on September 28.[77] Later it was moved to the place it now occupies in the foyer of McMahon Hall in acquiescence to the expressed wish of the donor.[78]

Another interesting ceremony took place at the university in

[71] NYAA, CUA file, J. F. Loubat to M. A. Corrigan, Nice, April 8, 1889.

[72] NYAA, CUA file, M. A. Corrigan to John J. Keane, New York, September 19, 1889, copy.

[73] *Ibid.*

[74] NYAA, CUA file, J. F. Loubat to M. A. Corrigan, Rome, May 26, 1891.

[75] NYAA, C-18, M. A. Corrigan to J. F. Loubat, New York, January 16, 1891, copy; NYAA, C-18, M. A. Corrigan to J. F. Loubat, New York, January (n. d.), 1891, copy.

[76] NYAA, CUA file, P. J. Garrigan to M. A. Corrigan, Washington, July 7, 1891.

[77] Washington *Post*, August 3, 1891. This paper reported that the statue cost $10,000. Corrigan had accepted Keane's invitation to "say a word on the occasion" (ACUA, M. A. Corrigan to John J. Keane, New York, September 9, 1891).

[78] ACUA, J. F. Loubat to John J. Keane, Paris, August 11, 1892.

the winter of 1892 when a bronze bust of John Boyle O'Reilly, presented by friends of the famous Boston man of letters, was unveiled. The presentation address was made by William Byrne, the vicar general of the Archdiocese of Boston, as the representative of a committee from Boston that included the Governor of Massachusetts.[79]   After the presentation ceremonies Mr. Samuel Kitson, the artist who had fashioned the bust of O'Reilly, went to Baltimore to begin work on a bust of Cardinal Gibbons that was intended for the ornamentation of the library.[80]

During the same winter of 1892 there occured an event that must have saddened the heart of the rector of the university and the intimate friends of Mr. Merwin Marie Snell, who, until then, had been the rector's secretary and a lecturer on comparative religions in the university.[81] The story is inserted in this study, mainly with a view of exhibiting a letter that presented Mr. Snell's attitude towards the Catholic Church in direct contradiction to the statements that appeared in the papers at the time.

On December 30, 1892, the New York *Tribune* had reported from Washington:

Dr. Merwin Marie Snell, private secretary to Bishop Keane and lecturer on comparative religion in the Catholic University here, has made something of a stir in religious circles by announcing at the same time his defection from the Roman Catholic Church and his marriage to the daughter of a Protestant clergyman. The marriage took place on Christmas Eve, the Rev. Mr. Rankin, president of Howard University performing the ceremony. The bride is Miss Minnie Gilbert

---

[79] Washington *Evening Star*, February 4, 1892; Washington *Post*, February 4, 1892.

[80] Washington *Post*, February 6, 1892.

[81] This biography of Snell was given in the New York *Mail* & *Express*: "Mr. Snell is well known in Catholic circles, especially in the literary world, and he held a high place in the Church of Rome [sic]. Mr. Snell was not born into the Catholic Church. On the contrary, his father was a Congregationalist minister in New Haven, a descendant of Jonathan Edwards, and one of a family which has heretofore been identified closely with that church.

"His most important paper, perhaps, was upon "The Duality of Primitive Tradition," which was in French, and was read before the International Scientific Congress, which met in Paris in 1888. Another paper upon "Methods of the Science of Comparative Religion" was read before the American Association for the Advancement of Science two years ago" (December 29, 1892). After Snell left the university he became the editor of the *Oriental Review* and he took an active part in the World's Parliament of Religions.

Sprague Andrews, daughter of Rev. L. W. Andrews, a Presbyterian minister.[82]

The New York *Sun* added:

"This step excommunicated me from the Catholic Church, *issue facto* [*sic*]," said Dr. Snell tonight. "I do not anticipate any formal excommunication from the powers that be. My decision was made at the point where my study of religions made it possible for me to no longer remain an honest communicant of the Catholic Church. I am not prepared to talk about my religious attitude now. I will soon define my position in a public address." [83]

The following long letter which Snell sent to Thomas J. Conaty, presiding officer of the Catholic Summer School, in the summer of 1893, explained his true position:

As I had the honor of participating last year in the work of your body, in which I still take an enthusiastic interest, I feel it a duty which I owe to the Catholic faith, as well as to the science of comparative religion which I represent, to make through you, to the attendants of the Catholic Summer School, especially to those who have a personal knowledge of me, a public denial of the statements which have gone the round of the newspaper press of the country since its last meeting, to the effect that I had become convinced, through my scientific studies or otherwise, of the falsity of the Catholic Religion, or at least had come to place upon it a lower estimate than formerly.

Permit me to say, on the contrary, that my studies of all religions and philosophies, ancient and modern, Christian and non-Christian, in the fullest light of the most rationalistic modern science, have only served to day by day strengthen my conviction that the Catholic religion is the summing up of the whole heritage of the world's religious truth, and the Catholic Church is not only the grandest possible confederation of human energies, but the Supreme Organon of the Divine Spirit, and the veritable Kingdom of God upon earth.

There is not a single element of any religion, even the lowest forms of paganism, that is not essentially a reminiscence or a prophesy of something which in its perfected glory is to be found in the Catholic Church. The Catholic religion is the great white light of Divine Truth, of which other religions are the colored and refracted rays; it is the cosmic symphony, of which other creeds are broken and discordant strains; it is the vast ocean of supernatural grace and power, of which all other benificent activities are the stagnant pools. It is the central

---

[82] New York *Tribune*, December 30, 1892.
[83] New York *Sun*, December 29, 1892.

stream of evolution, the condensed record of the immeasurable past, the consummation of the living present, the germ and prophesy of a wonder-teeming futurity.

I believe that the world is in the throes of a sublime parturition, from which will issue an age of spiritual triumphs beside which all her material achievements will be as nothing; and I believe that over these triumphs Rome will preside, and that they will be preeminently the triumphs of the Church.

The Catholic Church, one, holy and apostolic in her essential nature, and Roman, more and more dutifully and unswervingly Roman, in her allegiance, will be the Church of the New Era. All the kingdoms of the world will bring their honor and glory into it; all the religions of the world, which are to meet in brotherly conference at Chicago next month, in the first Universal Parliament of Religions, will pour into it all the treasures of their centuries of aspiration and endeavor, and will find in its unchanging teaching the solution of their problems, the goal of their desires, the fruition of their labors.

A new generation of teachers will arise to instruct the thirsting nations in the Everlasting Faith. The heresies of negation are dying, sinking into nothingness by the weight of their own utter sterility; the Church will now have to face the far higher and more fecund religions of the pagan world, the progeny of prehistoric schisms. With the new seed the method of evangelization changes. The world-wide structure of the Divine Hierarchy is now firmly established; the Christian influence is now dominant throughout the planet. And now, just as the Fathers of the Church made all that was best in the Greek thought their own, and used it as a lever by which to lift up the populations of the Levant into the higher light, so will the new champions of immortal truth bring into the service of their Divine Master, the Theanthropos, the God of man, and *the* Man of God, all the philosophies of the Occident and the Orient which have hitherto refused his sovereignty, all the religious ideals in the remotest corners of the earth which have ever been placed in rivalry with Him; all the methods which have not yet received the baptism of His mysteries. Thus, by the irresistible efficacy of light and love, will all nations turn to the Incarnate Truth, accept the ministry of the Eternal Priesthood, and become united to the visible center of the world's unity, the radiating focus of all celestial influences, the Holy Roman Church, the See of Blessed Peter, the triple-crowned Pontiff of a Redeemed humanity.

This is my firm hope; my well-justified conviction, based upon most significant facts. But if the future of the Church were, as some fear, to be, on the contrary, a renewal of the bloody baptisms of the Apostolic Age; to whatever depth of outward humiliation she might be brought, I trust that, God helping us, I, and every one of you to whom my words come, will still be able to say: "I believe in one holy, Catholic, Apostolic and Roman Church. In this hope & faith I live, and in it, by God's grace, I hope to die."

Regarding myself I need say nothing; I write neither to excuse nor to accuse myself for my personal shortcomings, the judgment of which can belong only to the authorized ministers of the Divine justice and mercy; but to partly undo the harm which may have been done to some, and to mitigate the grief which must have been caused to many, by the use to which my name has often been put during the past months by the enemies of God and His holy Holy [*sic*] Church.

Yours in deep humility,

s/ Merwin Marie Snell[84]

The irregular marriage attempted by Snell, which was sensationally reported by the press and which was accompanied by unfounded speculation as to his future religious affiliations, was validated later. He continued his studies in comparative religion and contributed serious papers on hierological subjects to the publications of the University of Chicago. In 1902, when he was president of Albertus Magnus College, in Wichita, Kansas, he wrote Denis J. O'Connell, then rector of the university, requesting that he would be considered for a teaching position in that institution if a vacancy in his specialty should occur.[85]

The most important sign of the prosperity and growth of the Catholic University of America during Keane's administration was the inauguration of two new schools on October 1, 1895. This action came in response to the hopes of the fathers of the Third Plenary Council of Baltimore, the Holy Father, the Board of Trustees, the rector, and the friends of the new institution. On April 21, 1887, the Board of Trustees had provided for the establishment of all the faculties of a complete university in the certificate of incorporation. By law they were allowed to teach theology, philosophy, natural sciences, mathematics, history, belles-lettres, ancient and modern languages, law, and medicine.[86] In the brief by which Leo XIII had given his solemn approbation to the establishment of the university, he had proposed as models "the universities which, in the middle ages and in the centuries

---

[84] ACUA, Merwin-Marie Snell to Thomas J. Conaty, Chicago, July 28, 1893.

[85] ACUA, O'Connell Papers, Merwin-Marie Snell to D. J. O'Connell, Wichita, May 25, 1903.

[86] ACUA, *By-Laws of the Board of Trustees of the Catholic University of America* (Washington, 1900), Appendix A.

following, enriched church and state with multitudes of men of learning." He also indicated that, although he approved the laying of the foundations of the university in the faculty of theology, it was his wish that as soon as possible the laity should be given a place in the new institution.[87] The Sovereign Pontiff also indicated his hopes for the university in the apostolic letter of March 7, 1889, by which approval was given to the constitutions of the university. He said:

We give, therefore, to your university, power to confer academic degrees on students who shall have passed satisfactory examinations and likewise to bestow the doctorate in philosophy, theology, pontifical law, and in those other studies in which the different degrees and the doctorate are usually conferred, whenever the teaching of these branches shall have been established. . . . We desire, in addition, . . . that all departments of the University may be so ordered that young clerics and laymen may have an equal opportunity of fully satisfying their laudible desire for science. We wish that among these departments there should be founded a school of Pontifical law and public ecclesiastical law, since we realize the great importance of these studies, especially at the present time.[88]

Almost a year before this papal letter the rector had expressed his sanguine hopes and the hopes of the Catholic people for the institution that he was so instrumental in founding in the *Catholic World* when he wrote:

They [the Catholic people] rejoice that the throne of sacred science should be erected first, and that the aspirants to the ministry should first be provided for; but they are no less solicitous for the highest welfare of their other sons, to whom Providence does not grant a vocation to the ecclesiastical state, but whom they are anxious to fit for the best and noblest usefullness in their future career, whatever it may be, by the deepest and broadest and purest learning that can be bestowed upon them. Very many parents are now asking whether the university will not be ready for their boys when they are sufficiently advanced to be fit for it; and from our hearts we answer that we hope it may be.[89]

In the same article the rector had indicated how the development and expansion of the university would be effected when the time

[87] ACUA, "Apostolic Letters of His Holiness Pope Leo XIII to the Most Eminent and Most Reverend James Cardinal Gibbons," p. 1.

[88] *Ibid.*, p. 2.

[89] John J. Keane, "The Catholic University of Louvain," *CW*, XLVI (January, 1888), 525-526.

96

came. The University of Louvain would be its model because "it is actively and successfully engaged in meeting all the intellectual demands of the age we live in." When Louvain reopened in 1834 it began with the faculty of theology and then added the faculty of philosophy and letters during the first year. Other faculties were added later, and thus it advanced towards a complete development. Louvain taught a practical lesson in the fact that "it lost no time in throwing open its academic halls to lay students." The rector found it particularly noteworthy that the first faculty for lay students at Louvain was not the faculty of law or medicine but that of philosophy and letters. The same was also true of the Johns Hopkins University which the bishop admired.[90] Hence, copying these excellent models the Catholic University of America would open its doors to lay students by the inauguration of the faculty of philosophy and letters.

Before the university had opened provision had been made in the plans of Caldwell Hall for the construction of an extensive south wing. The rector found that such an addition was desirable shortly after the university work had begun. He proposed the construction of the wing provided for in the original plans of Caldwell Hall so that space could be provided for the library and museum and additional accommodations for the professors and students. "It has been suggested," he said, "that they [the quarters thus provided] might temporarily be occupied by the first lay students of the University, to provide for whom is the object which the Directors now have the nearest at heart."[91]

Bishop Keane's ambitious plans for expansion were not realized during the first years of the university's existence because of the lack of funds. Nevertheless Keane did not lose sight of the goal. Hogan told his friend, Father Rex, during the first year, that the rector hoped to have the philosophical department organized within a couple of years.[92] At the end of the second year the rector urged the Board of Trustees to provide temporary accommodations for a school of philosophy by the erection of a south wing on Caldwell Hall since the erection of a new building was

[90] *Ibid.*, 531-532.

[91] *Solemnities of the Dedication*, p. 6.

[92] SMSA, John B. Hogan, S.S., to Charles B. Rex, S.S., Washington, June 9, 1890.

beyond their means.[93] That same year Providence provided for the lack of funds through a gift of real estate, valued at about $400,000[94] from Father James McMahon of New York.[95] With this gift in hand, there was no delay in beginning the construction of the building that was to house the new schools. The cornerstone was laid on the afternoon of April 27, 1892, following the meeting of the Board of Trustees.[96] As originally proposed the building was to be much larger and erected only in part, but new plans had been drawn up and approved by Cardinal Gibbons and the chairman of the board's building committee.[97]

The actual building of a suitable structure to house the new school was the least of the rector's worries. His greatest and most important task was the proper organization of the school of philosophy, science, and letters (only one school was contemplated at first), and the recruiting of competent professors to initiate the work. Besides the valuable advice given by the faculty of theology, the rector sought the counsel of prominent educators, and he studied other institutions as to the best method of having the new school grow out of the School of Theology.[98] At the same meeting of the board at which the gift of Father McMahon was accepted, the rector was empowered to negotiate with professors for the new faculty "if funds permit."[99] Three months later Bishop Keane wrote to Judge William C. Robinson, professor of law at Yale University, requesting a consultation concerning the establishment of a school of social sciences "for the broad, deep, and carefuly study, by both lay and ecclesiastical students of the great social questions which the march of events is bringing more

[93] *Second Annual Report of the Rector*, p. 28. Mr. E. Francis Baldwin submitted preliminary working plans for an addition, intended to complete the south wing of the Divinity Building, that would have cost about $92,000 (ACUA, E. F. Baldwin to John J. Keane, Baltimore, April 7, 1891).

[94] ACUA, MMBT, Washington, April 8, 1891, p. 32.

[95] James McMahon was born in Ireland in 1816. He received his education at Maynooth, at the Sulpician seminary in Paris and in Montreal. He came to New York in 1843 and he was ordained by Bishop John Hughes (New York *News*, September 27, 1895).

[96] RDA, John J. Keane to John Ireland, Washington, April 29, 1892.

[97] *Third Annual Report of the Rector*, p. 2.

[98] *Supra*, pp. 8, 21.

[99] ACUA, MMBT, Washington, April 8, 1891, p. 34.

and more to the surface."[100]   A few days later, in a personal interview, the rector requested Judge Robinson to take charge of the work of organizing and conducting the school of social sciences embracing the departments of sociology, economics, politics, and jurisprudence. The judge told the rector that he would "hold the matter under consideration and would certainly give him all the assistance in my power."[101] A few months later Keane wrote to Robinson:

While not pushing your words farther than you meant, I am counting on it as the will of Providence that you shall have the legal branch and be the chief of our School of Sociology. America and the Catholic Church can alone give the world the social science of the future. How noble a work to organize and head the first School established for that purpose.[102]

Robinson could not resist such an appeal and accordingly he entered upon the preparations necessary for the establishment and direction of the school.[103]

Meanwhile the first public announcement of the plans for the opening of the school of philosophy, science, and letters appeared in 1891,[104] and a permanent committee on the new faculty, consisting of Archbishop Ryan, Bishop Maes, and Monsignor Farley, had been appointed by the board in 1892.[105]   In 1893

[100] John J. Keane to William C. Robinson, Washington, April 18, 1891, cited in ACUA, William C. Robinson to the Rector and Senate, and by reference if necessary, to the Board of Trustees of the Catholic University of America, Washington, October n.d., 1900. William Callyhan Robinson (July 26, 1834 — November 6, 1911) was ordained for the ministry in the Episcopal church. After he was converted to Catholocism, he studied law. In 1869 he was one of three elected to take charge of Yale Law School. Cf. Charles Sumner Lobingier, "Robinson, William Callyhan," *DA B*, XVI, 56-57.

[101] ACUA, William C. Robinson to the Rector and Senate, and by reference if necessary, to the Board of Trustees of the Catholic University of America, Washington, October n.d., 1900.

[102] John J. Keane to William C. Robinson, Washington, August 1, 1891, cited in ACUA William C. Robinson to the Rector and Senate, and by reference if necessary, to the Board of Trustees of the Catholic University of America, Washington, October n.d., 1900.

[103] ACUA, William C. Robinson to the Rector and Senate, and by reference if necessary to the Board of Trustees of the Catholic University of America, Washington, October n.d., 1900.

[104] *Official Announcements for the Scholastic Year, 1891-'92* (Washignton, 1891). No pagination.

[105] NYAA, CUA file, MMBT, Washington, April 27, 1892.

Keane reported the progress that had been made toward the organization of the new school and the faculty. He proposed the names of some men with whom he requested authorization to make formal contracts and he asked particularly to have permission to negotiate with Father L. C. Casartelli, president of St. Bede's College, Manchester, England, "noted scholar in Comparative Religions and the Sacred Literatures of the East."[106] The rector was unusually firm about the necessity of establishing the new school immediately in his report to the Board of Trustees that year. He told the members:

I beg leave to impress on the Board of Directors that this is a question of vital and urgent importance, and that to ignore it, to leave it to solve itself, is to condemn to comparative sterility the institution whose care has been entrusted to them. If the University is to become what the Holy Father and the people of America expect it to be, energetic efforts need to be made both in order to encourage, solidify, and perfect the Faculty already in existence, and in order to render practicable and successful the Faculty which we have promised to shortly open for the laity.[107]

Plans were made for the inauguration of the new faculty in the fall of 1894. It was announced that the McMahon Hall of philosophy would be completed early in 1894 and the school for the laity would open on Tuesday, October 2.[108] Owing to the financial embarrassment consequent on the panic of 1893 the opening of the new school was postponed another year. The academic senate believed that the opening could not be delayed any longer than that without causing grave injury to the reputation of the university.[109]

While the rector was seeking a suitable faculty for the new school, the apostolic delegate was attempting to detach the schools of law and of medicine from Georgetown University and to attach them to the Catholic University of America. When the rector heard that Archbishop Satolli was attempting this without

[106] *Fourth Annual Report of the Rector*, pp. 10-12. Keane had corresponded with Father Casartelli in 1890 with a view to obtaining him. At that time Casartelli said that "the bishop would not want to part with him" (ACUA, L. C. Casartelli to John J. Keane, Manchester, June 19, 1890).

[107] *Ibid.*, p. 13.

[108] *Year-Book of the Catholic University of America, 1893-'94* (Washington, 1893), pp. 39-40.

[109] *Fifth Annual Report of the Rector*, p. 8.

consulting any of the authorities of either university, he asked him if it were true. Keane reported:

He told me it was true; that the relation of said Schools to Georgetown College, making of it a university, was the chief plea for the rivalry between the two institutions, the chief occasion for the charges that our institution was an unjust encroachment on the field already occupied by the other. He said that the Jesuits had no right to have such Schools, according to their rules, and the transfer of them to our Univ'y would put all in order and assure peace.

I replied that, in the first place, he would not succeed in his attempt; that there were too many parties concerned, too many interests involved, and the negotiations would fail; and that then the odium of the attempt would be attached to the Univ'y, that we would assuredly be accused of a shameful attempt to rob Georgetown and the Jesuits of what belonged to them and would have not only the odium of the attempt, but also the disgrace of the failure.

In the next place, I explained to him that the schools in question were not the kind of schools of Law and Medicine that we hoped to organize; as they were *night-schools,* frequented mostly by young men who were government employees during the day & had only the evening hours to fit themselves for professions, whereas our institution was to have true university-schools, working their students all day long. I urged that they would not suit us, because of their being located in the heart of the city, whereas our schools, it was thought, ought to be all grouped together & form a unity. I told him, moreover, that the Faculties of those schools were composed almost entirely of Protestants, and would therefore not be acceptable to us.[110]

The delegate persisted in his attempt to detach the Georgetown schools in spite of the weighty reasons advanced by the rector. After the consent of the Holy Father and the Father General of the Jesuits had been obtained, the delegate wrote to the deans of the two Georgetown faculties in question. After a preliminary statement about the history of the Catholic University of America and the hopes of Leo XIII for its development into a complete university at an early date, he said:

And now I deem it an honor to make known to you, and through you to the Professors of your Faculty the desire of the Holy Father in this matter, as I am commissioned to do. The opinion and the wish of the Holy Father is, that your Faculty should aggregate to the Catholic

---

[110] ACUA, "Chronicles," This was a letter written by Keane from San José, California, October 25, 1896, inserted at the end of the "Chronicles" at his request.

University through an amicable arrangement between the two parties. The General of the Society of Jesus has already given to the Holy Father his written consent to such a transfer. It is meant by His Holiness, that your Faculty should have with the Catholic University such business and academic relations as it has enjoyed formerly with the University of Georgetown, in accordance with the Constitutions granted by the Holy See to the University. The Holy Father puts the highest trust in your wisdom, that both parties be willing and interested in having one grand complete institution in Washington; which would turn to the greater progress of your Faculty and to the glory of science and of the Church itself.[111]

The dean of the law school, Mr. George E. Hamilton, answered within a week. He told the delegate that he was surprised that the communication came to him direct rather than through the president of Georgetown. After consultation with the professors on the faculty, the following decision had been reached:

Speaking, therefore, for myself and all the Professors, I wish to assure you that the contemplated transfer will never be consented to or permitted by us to be carried into effect. It cannot be carried into effect whether the President and the Directors of Georgetown University or the Jesuit organization, is willing or unwilling. It cannot be carried into effect by a direct mandate from Pope Leo XIII.

The Law Department of the University of Georgetown was organized by the graduates of the Academic Department, and through love for the old and honored institution. The Faculty serves not because of monied considerations or salaries, but because of their affection for, and interest in, the University of Georgetown; and the proposition of transfer is not only impracticable but borders close upon an offense.

. . . . The transfer is, therefore, out of the question.[112]

The dean of the medical school, G. L. Magruder, M.D., answered the delegate the next week. Besides telling him that he had seen Hamilton's reply in the name of the faculty of the law school, in which he heartily concurred, he said:

I have frequently and carefully considered the subject, and am now positively of the opinion that a purely sectarian medical school would not prosper in this country. Consequently I would not be willing to serve as a member of such a Faculty. As there are but few Catholics in the Medical Faculty the wishes of the Catholic University or even

---

[111] ACUA, "Letter of the Most Rev. Apostolic Delegate to Deans of Law & Medicine Faculties of Georgetown University, March 1, 1894, copy."

[112] ACUA, G. E. Hamilton to Most Rev. & "Dear Sir" [Satolli], Washington, March 6, 1894, copy.

102

His Holiness Leo XIII, would not have the slightest influence upon them.[113]

After the deans of the two faculties had written their reply to the apostolic delegate, Keane wrote to Denis O'Connell:

I am greatly relieved by this decision. From the beginning I told him the project would not work,—the schools could not suit us,—it would bring on accusations of trying to rob the Jesuits, etc. All in vain. He thought it would be a great "colpo di stato", and so he persisted. The result has put those schools & their connexion with Geotn. in their true light,—and we are saved from relations with them;—but the odium of the attempt will be surely thrown on us by the Jesuits & their friends.[114]

The rector harbored grave doubts about the practicality of opening the department of social sciences in the fall of 1895. There was the great difficulty of finding Catholic teachers in these fields due to the fact that there had never been a demand for them. There was the added problem of the uncertainty of being able to interest sufficient students to attend the courses even if the teachers could be obtained.[115] Judge Robinson, in his usual thorough manner, gave Keane the pros and cons on the matter, stating that he believed that the supply of Catholic teachers would not be any more plentiful ten or twenty years later unless a demand for them was created then. As far as students were concerned, Yale, even with persistent advertising, had only eleven students take their doctorate in sixteen years, and of the eleven five were Japanese. Yet, he had designed the course with the prospect of having both sexes represented. He said he had attended a summer school "where I met many earnest females *and no males*" interested in the subject that the school would present. He advised that if the school were opened it should be with the prospect of permanency since professors would be obliged to give up positions in which they were assured permanent employment and to move to Washington with their families. As for himself, the judge had not broken his ties with Yale as yet, therefore, they could make their decision without any prejudice to him or anyone else.[116] The committee on organization of new schools

[113] ACUA, G. L. Magruder to Very Rev. & "Dear Sir" [Satolli], Washington, March 12, 1894, copy.

[114] RDA, John J. Keane to D. J. O'Connell, Washington, April 13, 1894.

[115] ACUA, W. C. Robinson to John J. Keane, New Haven, December 9, 1894.

[116] *Ibid.*

(Pace, Bouquillon, and Shahan) considered Robinson's letter and they reported to Keane that:

1. It is advisable to open these schools in Oct. 1895, according to announcement.
2. No distinction should be made in regard to color or sex. . . .
3. All students should be admitted who evince the intellectual capacity.[117]

There was some difference of opinion in the committee as to the manner in which the work of the new school should be announced to the public. Shahan favored a formal announcement that they were going to give undergraduate studies while Bouquillon and Pace favored another plan:

Bouquillon and Pace believe that the best plan is so to word our announcement as to lay stress on the superior quality of our teaching, without however, frightening away students by loudly insisting on "postgraduate" work. We ought to come down just far enough to encourage those who hesitate; then when we get them here, the professors will soon find out what is to be done in each case. To formally announce undergraduate courses would embroil us with the colleges; whereas, by accepting their graduate *tales quales,* we can quietly *foro interno,* supply the defects of their training; and if the colleges object to such a course as encroachment on their field, we will have an answer ready for them.[118]

The same committee had previously recommended:

As concerns admission of students, prudence demands that we should not be too exacting at first. The const. provide that a student may be received either by passing examination or by presenting a diploma. We advise that for the time being diplomas given in Catholic Colleges be accepted, and if the previous training is found to be deficient, these institutions can gradually be brought to the proper level.[119]

With regard to the hiring of professors, the committee recommended that the conditions should be based upon the principle that they were being engaged for a Catholic institution, therefore:

a. Ordinarily, the professors shall be Catholics. Exceptions to this rule should be more difficult in proportion as the science in question has

---

[117] ACUA, Edward A. Pace to John J. Keane, Washington, December 16, 1894. This is a committee report.

[118] *Ibid.*

[119] ACUA, "Report of the Committee on New Schools, December 5, 1894." The committee consisted of Pace, Bouquillon, and Shahan. It was appointed November 8, 1894.

104

closer relations with Catholic truth, and should be less frequently made in favor of young men than in favor of experienced teachers whose views and character have reached a certain stability.

b. While assuming the obligation to respect the teachings of the Church, professors must also understand that they enjoy the freedom of investigation which the Church secures them. But their rights and obligations extend to their publications as well as to their lectures and intercourse with the students.

c. Non-Catholic teachers who may be employed in our schools and cannot make a profession of faith, should make a formal promise, as men of honor, not to antagonize in any way the doctrines of the Church.

d. Should reasonable doubt arise as to whether a conclusion or an opinion conflicts with Catholic faith, the matter should be referred, in the first instance, to the Faculty of Theology of the University.[120]

The professors who were to teach in the new school held a meeting at the university on December 23, 1894, at which they decided:

The standard of our teaching is to be the highest attainable in a University, its essential feature being original research. It will, however, be of such a character that while the end in view is the most thorough scientific work, the beginnings, or requisite for taking up our courses, will not be determined by hard and fast regulations. The ability of each applicant and his mental development, rather than previous studies and class requirements will be taken into consideration.[121]

All the professors at this meeting were in favor of the admission of women to the courses, but it was decided that no announcement would be made to that effect, although if any women applied and had the necessary qualifications they were not to be refused admission.[122] The tuition was fixed at $100 a year.[123]

On January 21, 1895, the academic senate resolved to inaugurate two faculties, the faculty of philosophy and the faculty of

[120] ACUA, "Second Report of the Senate Committee on the Organization of Schools." No date.

[121] ACUA, "Report of Professors' Meeting, December 23, 1894."

[122] *Ibid.*

[123] ACUA, "Acts of the Senate Relative to Schools and Departments." Session of January 21, 1896. The sessions of the academic senate on February 11, 1896, June 4, 1896, and November 10, 1896 made decisions affecting the relations of faculty members to one another and to other faculties.

105

social sciences, rather than the one faculty of philosophy, science, and letters, as had previously been announced. These faculties would work in two schools divided into departments. The School of Philosophy was subdivided into the departments of philosophy proper, mathematical sciences, physical sciences, biological sciences, and letters. The School of Social Sciences was subdivided into the departments of sociology, economics, political science, and law. With the addition of the department of technology to the School of Philosophy, it was thus that the new schools were opened on the first Tuesday of October, 1895.[124]

The search for suitable professors engaged the rector for some time before the new schools opened. Among those obtained for the School of Philosophy was Father William J. Kerby, of the Archdiocese of Dubuque, a former student of the university. The young priest's superior, Archbishop John Hennessy, did not want to release him at first. Later he waived his objections and he told Gibbons: "Grave as these reasons are they are now put aside and what I certainly would have done neither for the Rector nor the University I shall now do most cheerfully."[125] At the same time, Edmund T. Shanahan, a priest of the Archdiocese of Boston, then studying in Rome accepted the invitation to an associate professorship in higher metaphysics.[126] By the middle of March, 1895, the rector had nearly all the professors either under contract or he had approached them with a view to obtaining the necessary approval of the board's committee on professors.[127] In the announcements relative to the opening of the new schools, the School of Philosophy had a faculty of about fifteen members including some of the professors in the School of Theology, under the direction of Edward A. Pace, as dean.[128] The School of the Social Sciences was under the

[124] *Year-Book of the Catholic University of America, 1895-'96* (Washington, 1895), pp. 33-56.

[125] BCA, 93-Q-5, John Hennessy to James Gibbons, Dubuque, January 20, 1895.

[126] ACUA, Edmund T. Shanahan to John J. Keane, Rome, January 25, 1895. Father Charles F. Aiken of the Archdiocese of Boston, a former student, accepted an invitation to teach at the university the same year.

[127] NYAA, G-16, John J. Keane, to M. A. Corrigan, Washington, March 13, 1895.

[128] *Year-Book of the Catholic University of America, 1895-96* (Washington, 1895), pp. 33-47.

direction of William C. Robinson, who was to be aided by three associate professors and several special lecturers.[129]

The recruiting of a student body for the new schools was another cause of great anxiety to the rector. Keane told the members of the board in 1894:

The awakening and fostering of popular interest in the matter, in order to procure the necessary funds, and especially to secure students, is a task which, I beg leave to say, will call for the energetic action of every member of the Board during the next eighteen months.[130]

The rector spent the months of May and June visiting a large number of Catholic colleges and other educational institutions in which he explained in detail the special advantages offered by the program of studies that was to be inaugurated at the university that fall.[131] It had been announced that no religious qualifications would be required of those seeking entrance to the new schools, but "morality, decorum, and devotion to study will be imperatively demanded."[132] A month before the new faculties were inaugurated, the secular press contained the announcement that women would be admitted "save only that they will not matriculate or take degrees. The university degree is of no advantage to man or woman except as an aid to securing employment in certain cases."[133] A number of women applied for entrance and the rector was obliged to announce:

The University would be glad if it were in her power to grant them the educational advantages which they desire. But the question of co-education is too important to be settled hurriedly; it has not yet been consid-

---

[129] *Ibid.*, pp. 49-56. Also cf. "University Chronicle," *CUB*, I (April, 1895), 248. When the new schools were opened the following men were added to the faculty: Edmund T. Shanahan, associate professor of philosophy; Daniel Quinn, professor of Hellenic literature; Rene deSaussure, associate professor of mathematics; John J. Griffin, professor of chemistry; Frank K. Cameron, associate professor of chemistry; Edward L. Greene, professor of botany, John A. Robinson, associate professor of law. Cf. *Inauguration of the Schools of Philosophy and the Social Sciences and Dedication of McMahon Hall, Catholic University of America, October 1, 1895 — Official Report* (Washington, 1895), pp. 39-40.

[130] *Fifth Annual Report of the Rector*, p. 8.

[131] "University Chronicle," *CUB*, I (July, 1895), 401.

[132] "University Chronicle," *CUB*, I (January, 1895), 89. Also cf. *Year-Book of the Catholic University of America, 1895-'96*, p. 34.

[133] New York *Evening Sun*, September 10, 1895.

ered by the Board of Directors, and nothing will be done except as they decide; so that for the present scholastic year at least women cannot be admitted to the courses.[134]

There were three colored men among the students who presented themselves for admission to the new schools. Keane said: "They were simply tested as to their previous education, and this being found satisfactory, no notice whatever was taken of their color. They stand on exactly the same footing as other students of equal calibre and acquirements."[135] As the authorities had expected, the number of applicants for admission were not many. Philosophy and law had the greatest number of students, the former with twenty-two, the latter with twenty-one. There were only two students for the course in economics and one each for sociology and political science. The department of technology began with eight students.[136] Only two chairs in the new schools were endowed before the fall of 1895; the one, called the James Whiteford chair of common law, had been provided for in the will of Mrs. Celinda B. Whiteford of Baltimore; the other, called the Banigan chair of political economy, was donated by Mr. Joseph Banigan of Providence, Rhode Island, one of the trustees of the university, on the occasion of the dedication of a working-girls' home at Providence, which was erected through his munificence. Three scholarships, known as the Joseph D. Peabody scholarship in chemistry and physics, had been placed at the disposal of the university by the will of Miss Mary D. Peabody of Washington.[137]

The work of building and planning having been completed, the McMahon Hall of Philosophy, built entirely of granite from Port Deposit, Maryland, with carved granite trimmings, at a cost of $310,969.33,[138] was solemnly blessed and dedicated by Cardinal Gibbons, the chancellor, on October 1, 1895. After the dedi-

[134] J. J. Keane, "Inauguration of McMahon Hall," *C UB*, I (October, 1895), 540.

[135] *Ibid.*, pp. 539-540.

[136] *Year-Book of the Catholic University of America, 1896-'97* (Washington, 1896), p. 80.

[137] *Ibid.*, pp. 8-9. Also cf. J. J. Keane, "The Financial Side of the University," *C UB*, I (April, 1895), 162.

[138] ACUA, *Statement of the Financial Condition of the Catholic University of America From its Beginning to November 1, 1903* (Washington, 1903). Personal & Private. For a description of McMahon Hall, cf. Edward A. Pace, "The McMahon Hall of Philosophy," *C UB*, I (January, 1895), 53-64. Also cf. New York *News*, September 27, 1895.

McMAHON HALL

cation, the inaugural exercises were held in the assembly room of the new building. On the stage there were the apostolic delegate, the trustees of the university, the professors of the three faculties, many prelates from every part of the country, the presidents of Georgetown University, the John Hopkins University, and the Columbian University, and the generous donor of the funds for the new structure, Monsignor James McMahon. The auditorium and adjacent corridors were crowded with those who came to witness the inaugural ceremonies, some of whom were to participate in the first Priests' Eucharistic Congress that opened the next day.[139] After the rector had welcomed the guests, he read the brief of Leo XIII of June 29, 1895, in which the Sovereign Pontiff declared: "We wish, therefore, that the university may, through this new development, more and more advance, wax strong, and flourish, for the advantage and honor both of religion and of the Republic."[140] The apostolic delegate then spoke for an hour in Latin on "Philosophia et Facultas Philosophiae."[141] This was followed by a short discourse given by Edward A. Pace, the dean of the faculty of philosophy, in which he discussed the scope of the School of Philosophy.[142] The dean of the School of Social Sciences, William C. Robinson, then treated the scope and guiding principles of the faculty which he directed.[143] The chancellor closed the inaugural exercises with words of praise for the tireless zeal of the rector and for the generous donor of the new building. He called upon others to imitate Monsignor McMahon in his generosity to so worthy a cause, and he ended by welcoming the new students and wished them success in their important work.[144] After the festivities the cardinal reported the inauguration of the new faculties to Rome and he received a reply from the Cardinal Prefect of the Congregation of the Propaganda in which he expressed his pleasure at the work that had been accomplished

[139] J. J. Keane, "Inauguration of McMahon Hall," *C UB*, I (October, 1895), 540-541.

[140] *Benevolentiae testandae*, cited in "Inauguration of McMahon Hall," *C UB*, I (October, 1895), 541-542. The brief is given in Latin and in an English translation.

[141] "Inuaguration of McMahon Hall," *C UB*, I (October, 1895), 543-548. A synopsis of the discourse is given in Latin.

[142] *Ibid.*, pp. 548-552.

[143] *Ibid.*, pp. 552-561.

[144] *Ibid.*, pp. 561-564. Also cf. ACUA, "Programme — Dedication of McMahon Hall."

and he assured the chancellor that there was no longer any doubt that the university would flourish.[145]

During the first year three students received the baccalaureate of laws and five received the master of laws.[146] Since two of the students were sufficiently advanced by January, 1896, they were given their degrees on March 7 and at the same time the first honorary degrees in the University's history were conferred on George M. Searle, C.S.P. (Ph.D.) and Charles Warren Stoddard (LL.D.). This was done in conformity with the established rule of the university that no honorary degrees would ever be conferred "as a compliment, but solely in due recognition of distinguished knowledge possessed and work done in the very lines indicated by the degrees conferred."[147]

It became evident almost from the very beginning that the department of technology was out of place in the School of Philosophy, so an institute of technology was organized with Daniel W. Shea as its director.[148] Although this made the former department a separate subdivision of the university, it did not give the members of the institute official representation in the academic senate. At the end of the first year the director of the institute recommended that it be raised to the dignity of a school, but this recommendation was not favorably decided until January 11, 1898.[149]

With the addition of new schools it became necessary to increase the administrative personnel of the institution. The rector employed Philip N. Robinson, a relative of the dean of the School of Social Sciences, to be the bursar. He was charged with the registration of the lay students, the financial accounts that had to be kept with the lay students, the supervision and editing of various publications, and the care of a store for textbooks, stationery, and other items.[150]

[145] BCA, 94-C-5, M. Cardinal Ledochowski to J. Card. Gibbons, Rome, November 16, 1895 (Latin).

[146] *Year-Book of the Catholic University of America, 1896-'97*, pp. 81-82.

[147] *Seventh Annual Report of the Rector*, p. 10.

[148] *Ibid.*, p. 9.

[149] ACUA, "Institute of Technology." This is a written collection of reports from the director of the institute and the committee appointed to study and report on the institute to the senate.

[150] J. J. Keane to William C. Robinson, Washington, April 27, 1895, cited in ACUA, "Report of the Rector on Philip N. Robinson's Appointment, May 14, 1901."

One of the important problems that faced the Board of Trustees and the rector when the new schools were contemplated had been the provision of suitable quarters for the professors and the students. Judge Robinson had applied to the university authorities for a residence within the university grounds when it became evident that he would accept the direction of one of the new schools. The chancellor and the rector considered it to be wise to grant this request as well as to provide suitable residences for the other professors on the three faculties if they would desire them. Since the Board of Trustees had decided not to sell any of the land purchased for the university,[151] they were asked to vote favorably on the plan for building three or four "cottages" at a cost of $5,000 apiece to be rented to the professors.[152] The board authorized this expenditure with the stipulation that the rent charged should be equal to six per cent of their cost and that the occupant should be responsible for the ordinary repair.[153] Only one building was erected under this plan at a cost of $7,876.38,[154] and it was occupied by Professor Robinson and his family a month after the new schools were inaugurated.[155] The other members of the new faculties were given accommodations in Caldwell Hall or they found a residence in the vicinity of the university.[156]

The erection of a hall for lay students had been part of the rector's plans for a number of years before the new schools were opened. He had been authorized to build a dormitory in 1893 "provided that he does not encroach upon the University Fund."[157] Again in 1894, a student's dormitory for fifty was authorized by the board to be built on Bunker Hill Road.[158] Yet nothing had been done up to the time when the new schools were launched. After the first year's work with the lay students Keane

[151] ACUA, MMBT, Washington, April 8, 1891, p. 34.

[152] NYAA, CUA file, P. J. Garrigan to M. A. Corrigan, Washington, March 22, 1895.

[153] ACUA, MMBT, Washington, October 1, 1895, p. 52.

[154] ACUA, *Statement of the Financial Condition of the Catholic University of America From its Beginning to November 1, 1903* (Washington, 1903). Personal & Private.

[155] *Seventh Annual Report of the Rector*, p. 19.

[156] *Year-Book of the Catholic University of America, 1896-'97*, pp. 5-8.

[157] ACUA, MMBT, Washington, April 11, 1893, p. 42.

[158] ACUA, MMBT, Washington, April 4, 1894, p. 48.

once more urged that dormitories be provided for them "not that there is any evidence of pernicious results following their residence with private families but it would increase their efficiency."[159] The board then gave their approval to the erection of "a dormitory building to contain an oratory, parlor, small play room, and about fourty-five rooms . . . at a cost of not more than $50,000."[160] The committee appointed by the board to see to the construction of the new building finally determined on a structure that would accommodate thirty-nine students and three professors. Since the vice rector had been dissatisfied with the work of E. Francis Baldwin, the architect, and Edward Brady, the superintendent, on McMahon Hall, the new structure was entrusted to the contractor who was at that time erecting the Corcoran Art Gallery in the city.[161] The ground for the new building had been broken late in June, 1896, with the prospect of having it ready for occupancy that fall,[162] but it was not opened until January 30, 1897.[163] At the time the new building was under construction the city decided to run a street between the university property and the B. & O. tracks. This cut off about ninety feet of the university's ground but it was considered to be an improvement.[164]

With the addition of new faculties greater financial burdens were created for the university. Endowments for the chairs were very slow in coming in due to the long-continued financial depression throughout the country. Other donations were not sufficient to meet the regular expenditures. The rector told the board:

We have in hand the creation of a University, and the world expects and demands of us that it shall be up to the University level of the times, and shall be an honor to the Church. But a glance at the statistics of the

[159] *Seventh Annual Report of the Rector*, p. 5.

[160] ACUA, MMBT, Washington, April 15, 1896, p. 55.

[161] NYAA, G-23, John J. Keane to M. A. Corrigan, Washington, June 12, 1896.

[162] "University Chronicle," *C UB*, II (July, 1896), 422-423.

[163] *Year-Book of the Catholic University of America, 1897-'98* (Washington, 1897), p. 12.

[164] NYAA, G-23, John J. Keane to M. A. Corrigan, Washington, June 12, 1896. The new road also separated the B. & O. University Station that had been built in 1890 by the railroad on ground donated by the trustees (ACUA, C. K. Vord to John J. Keane, Baltimore, November 29, 1889; *Ibid.*, January 13, 1890; *Ibid.*, January 31, 1890).

universities of the country shows that our income and our expenditures are very small indeed in comparison with theirs. Work cannot be done without expenditure, and both the utility and the reputation of the University will be seriously imperiled unless its resources be made adequate to present conditions and urgent needs, and that at once. To leave this to chance, or to the efforts of any one man, especially of a man whose time could all be profitably taken up in the work of the interior administration, does not seem reasonable, and can assuredly not make a success of the undertaking. Moreover, it is most undesirable that any show of reason should be given for the insinuation of certain parties who speak of the institution as "Bishop Keane's University." Every consideration seems plainly to demand that some concerted action should be taken to secure the welfare of the University.

At the last meeting of the Board, it was voted that the question of a general collection, then strongly recommended by the Committee on Finances, should be deferred till the following meeting. I most earnestly beg that this provision, whose reasonableness is so manifest and whose need is so urgent, should be no longer delayed.[165]

This plea was sympathetically seconded by the board but it was deferred until the next meeting because Archbishop Ireland thought that such a collection would be a failure unless it was thoroughly discussed and approved in the next annual meeting of the archbishops scheduled for October.[166] A month after Keane's administration had come to an end the board decided that the prelates attending that meeting and the bishops of the country should be requested to take up a collection for the benefit of the university within a year.[167] The treasurer reported at that meeting that the university was free from all debt but that there would be a deficit of about $29,000 in the current running expenses for the year.[168] The same day the Ancient Order of Hibernians gave the funds to endow the chair of Celtic languages and literature.[169] Keane had been authorized to accept the offer of the chair in 1893.[170] At that time some doubted the propriety of

---

[165] *Seventh Annual Report of the Rector*, pp. 12-13.
[166] ACUA, MMBT, Washington, April 18, 1896, p. 59.
[167] ACUA, MMBT, Washington, October 21, 1896, p. 62.
[168] *Ibid.*
[169] *Ibid.*
[170] ACUA, MMBT, Washington, April 11, 1893, p. 43.

113

the gift and the probability of its realization. Bishop McQuaid of Rochester told Denis O'Connell:

Bp. Keane's calling on the A.O.H. to found a chair in his University is another added to the many scandals growing out of the shocking liberalism spreading over the country. Another specimen was given by Bp. Foley, when he allowed himself to be dubbed Chaplain of this miserable secret society. Such men as Kenrick of Baltimore, Wood of of Philadelphia, Hughes of New York condemned these societies. That the Mollie Maguires of Pa. & the A.O.H. are even one and the same society cannot be denied. This fact was demonstrated beyond gainsay at the trials of the Mollie Maguires for brutal murders. This new University Chair ought to be labeled the "Murderers' Chair." This well-earned appellation will never be given to it because the chair will never exist. The Father Matthew Chair, with the help of many good people, and the labor of many zealous priests, did not realize over $20,000, instead of $50,000.[171]

During Keane's administration over $640,000 was invested from emdowments for twelve chairs and thirteen scholarships. Three buildings had been erected and another was in the process of construction. The university was free from all debt. The former public lecture hall in Caldwell Hall had been divided into three rooms for the use of the librarian after a more spacious public lecture hall was provided in McMahon Hall.[172] The university had its own eletric light plant after McMahon Hall was built and a boardwalk was built from the new building to the Brookland entrance to the university grounds.[173] A city gas main was laid through the grounds and connected with the chemical laboratories and with some lighting fixtures.[174] A branch post office had been opened by the government in Caldwell Hall in 1894 and moved to the basement of McMahon Hall the next year.[175]

[171] RDA, Bernard J. McQuaid to D. J. O'Connell, Rochester, January, 16 1892. The Rochester prelate later changed his views about the Ancient Order of Hibernians. Cf. Zwierlein, *op. cit.*, II, 466 ff.

[172] "University Chronicle," *C UB*, I (October, 1895), 565.

[173] *Ibid.*

[174] *Seventh Annual Report of the Rector*, p.19.

[175] "University Chronicle," *C UB*, I (April, 1895), 265. Cf. "University Chronicle," *C UB*, I (October, 1895), 565. Also cf. ACUA, S. H. Merrill to P. J. Garrigan, Washington, August 31, 1894. "University Station" was established on September 15, 1894, a sub-station of the post-office at Washington, D. C.

At the end of Bishop Keane's administration it became necessary for him to begin negotiations for a new contract between the university and the Sulpicians due to the fact that the vice rector wished the office of procurator to be transferred to them.[176] Cardinal Gibbons had requested the Superior General of the Sulpicians, J. H. Icard, S.S., to have his society take over the direction of the university priest-students a year before the institution opened and a contract had been entered at that time between the Sulpician superior and Bishop Keane.[177] The Sulpicians assigned to the university found their position far from ideal, principally because the contract was not specific enough about the position of the president of Divinity College. Orban complained to Maignen that Hogan was introduced as "disciplinarian" when he should have some title of honor, such as "President of the Ecclesiastical Department" or "Superior of the Students."[178] This lack of outward titles of prestige tended to weaken the students' respect for his authority. The Sulpicians charged with the direction of the students experienced another difficulty from the fact that professors and students all resided in the same building. In the summer of 1894 the Superior General of the Sulpicians had discussed the situation with Bishop Keane, who promised to remove the causes for complaint. In writing to his confrères in America, Captier, the Superior General, told them: "The state of affairs at the University Seminary is always worrying me."[179]

In March of 1895, the rector asked Father Dumont, who was then president of Divinity College, to take over the administration of the house. The bishop told him that buildings would be put up for the professors and all would leave Caldwell Hall, only the rector, vice rector, and one or two of the professors remaining for a time.[180] When Father Rex heard about the request that had

[176] ACUA, MMBT, Washington, October 1, 1895, p. 43.

[177] BCA, 85-A-1, J. Card. Gibbons to J. H. Icard, S.S., Baltimore, September 2, 1888 (French), copy. A copy of the contract may be found in SMSA. This contract is in French.

[178] SMSA, A. Orban, S.S., to A. Magnien, S.S., Washington, May 16, 1890 (French).

[179] SMSA, A. Captier, S.S., to "Bien Cher Ami," Paris, January 4, 1895 (French).

[180] SMSA, L.F. Dumont, S.S., to Charles B. Rex, S.S., Washington, March 18, 1895. (Fr. Dumont usually signed his name, L.F. Dumont, whereas the *Year Books* use Francis Louis).

been made, he told his friend that this would afford them an opportunity to bring about a more satisfactory position for the Sulpicians at the University. The president concurred with this view and he told Rex:

The rt. rev. rector had referred me to the vice-rector. I went to see him last evening, he is a *finasseur,* he aims at making of us his clerks, but under cover of the higher authority of the rector. He is far from being in a hurry as the rector, though *he* especially sighs after his deliverance from drudgery work; I am on my guard, & he understood me yesterday.[181]

Garrigan gave Dumont a copy of the conditions on which the rector and himself were agreed if the Sulpicians were to accept the domestic administration of Divinity College. The president sent this to his friend, commenting: "1st you will notice that it refers exclusively to the Treasureship as such, it is the vice-rector *part.* With regard to disciplinary management of community the arrangement depends on the rector who is now absent."[182] Dumont was particularly apprehensive about the fact that such an agreement would place the Sulpicians under the surveillance of the vice rector since he was responsible for all the finances of the university. Dumont told his friend that it would be "well if he proves the right man, numberless annoyances if he is not."[183] If the Sulpicians were to accept the domestic administration someone who was capable of its proper management would have to be assigned the responsibility. The president told Rex that Father Orban could not do it. "It would be a failure in more than one way: he has no aptitude, no spirit of order & economy, is very impulsive & excited easily, would become wretchedly miserable & his health might be imapired." He also told his friend that his own health was not so good and that if he would be required to assume the added burden he would ask for an increase in salary.[184]

Before April 15, 1895, Father Dumont had not seen the contract entered into between the Sulpician superior general and the

[181] SMSA, L. F. Dumont, S.S., to Charles B. Rex, S.S., Washington, March 20, 1895.

[182] SMSA, L. F. Dumont, S.S., to Charles B. Rex, S.S., Washington, March 25, 1895. The conditions were attached to this letter.

[183] *Ibid.*

[184] SMSA, L. F. Dumont, S.S., to Charles B. Rex, S.S., Washington, n.d. "Fr. Orban has left us for Paris, not to return. This change the rector insisted on with Fr. Capther [*sic*]. It is a good move" (BCA, 94-P-5, P. J. Garrigan to J. Card. Gibbons, Washington, August 1, 1896).

university; in fact, he was not certain that there was a formal contract. The rector did not show him the contract until he said that he was going to write to Paris to find out if there was one. When the contract was produced and read, Dumont told Rex:

Of course he [Orban] is loud in proclaiming bad faith he knew it for 5 years. I do not make chorus with him & I told him I could not judge so. . . .

I am very much tempted to see bad faith in the late transactions of the authority *here* with us.

Why to propose conditions prepare them & word them carefully & call on us to examine them, refer them to others for consideration, when there is an explicit clause in contract bearing on the point.

Why to delay communicating contract till I morally force them to do so.[185]

Dumont then told the rector that the Sulpicians could not accept the domestic administration of the house that year. In his usual rocky English he reported to Rex:

I asked him how it was that a report circulated in the house that *we* were to take the *economic* at the end of June, that *he* the vice-rector and Mgr. McMahon would take their meals with the students under my presidency, I added the question is under consideration not solved, it has to be referred to Paris, though practically solved in the contract, that I could not be treasurer. The administration of the Sulp. would effectually turn all the professors out of the house, and hearing of it all without an exception had formed their plans. Let the rector and vice-rector turn them out & we step in next, this I said to the rector, & I gave reasons affecting both the interests of the University and ours.[186]

After considerable correspondence on the subject, Captier, the Superior General of the Sulpicians in Paris, made the following suggestions to his Sulpician confrères and to Bishop Keane:

1° that the semy may be, as soon as practicable, isolated in the building assigned for its use, from persons not belonging to the community which it is understood to constitute, & not observing the same rules. The absence of that condition is the cause of our delaying to take charge of the treasurer's office, as too difficult

---

[185] SMSA, L. F. Dumont, S.S., to Charles B. Rex, S.S., Washington, April 15, 1895.

[186] SMSA, L. F. Dumont, S.S., to Charles B. Rex, S.S., Washington, April 15, 1895.

to be administered & alien from our mission, if it had to be extended to other persons than members of the Community.

2° That the authority of those who have to enforce the rule, especially the President, be so raised in the eyes of the students, that he may feel equal to his work. Some means to that end would be:

    a) that in the semy chapel, the 1st rank should be assigned to him, unless in the presence of the rector & vice-rector.

    b) that he should be invited *ex-officio* to be present at the students' examinations & should occupy there an honorable place, after the rector, vice-rector, or other eventual president of the Committee on examinations.

These distinctions which may seem unimportant in themselves, are certainly not so in the practical appreciation of the students.

3° that the president should have control of whatever takes place in the semy with the exception of studies. Nothing, for instance, ought to be appointed as to the time & other circumstances of meals, religious services, or other exercises except through his agency, or at least, in consequence of an understanding with him.

4° that it should also be his office to admit the students in the semy, so that if the rector or any other officer has to deal with a case of admission the name of the candidate & information about him should be communicated to the President, & it should be for him to notify the administration, unless want of time or some other urgent reason would, in a given case, require a departure from that rule. . . . It should also belong to him, at the close of the scholastic year to report to the students' bishops about their conduct & success at the University.[187]

The matter was finally settled shortly after the close of Keane's administration when a new agreement was signed that embodied many of the suggestions made by the superior general:

Agreement between the Catholic University of America and the Sulpician Fathers with Regard to the Presidency and the Procuratorship of the Divinity College.

President of the Divinity College

I. The relations of the President of the Divinity College with the Board of Directors of the Catholic University and with the University are such as stated in the (a) Constitutions of the University,

---

[187] SMSA, A. Captier, S.S., to Very Rev. Dear Sir, n.d. This long letter was probably written to Thomas J. Conaty, the second rector of the Catholic University of America. The superior of the Sulpicians said he had communicated the same to Bishop Keane previously.

Chapter VIII, section V, VI, (b) Const. Fac. Theo. Chapter V, section II, (c) in contract between Bishop Keane and Father Icard.

II. It shall be the duty of the President to receive the students of the Divinity College, assign them to their rooms, and admit them to the Community. All information concerning the students at the time of their admission will be communicated to him by the Rector or Vice-Rector who may have admitted them.

III. It shall be his duty to make an annual report to the Bishops as to the conduct and application of their students at the University and these reports will be countersigned by the Rector; hence the monthly reports of the Faculty will be communicated to him by the Registrar. According to the Constitutions, Chap. V, sec. IV, he will also report to the Senate in writing such matters as may be of general interest to the University.

IV. He will have the control of whatever pertains to his Community, with the exception of studies. The hours for meals and religious exercises should be determined by him after consulation with the Rector or Vice-Rector.

V. On all occasions when the University is present as such, within the Divinity College or elsewhere, the President will take rank as provided for in the Senate Rules. On all occasions in Divinity Building, for instance in Refectory or in the Chapel when neither the several Faculties as Faculties nor the University as such takes part in the ceremony, the President will rank after the Rector and Vice-Rector.

The Sulpician Procurator of Divinity College

1. The Procurator shall have the care and management of the Divinity building, supplies and domestic service; as for extraordinary repairs he is subject to Chap. V, no. 4 of Gen. Constitutions.

2. The Sisters and all the help of the Divinity College shall depend on him, unless in the case of help whose occupation is of such character as to demand portion of their time in other Departments of the University, and those latter shall be arranged for by consultation with the Vice-Rector.

3. He shall have charge of what pertains, not only to the refectory of the students, but also of that of the Rector, Vice-Rector and professors, as long as circumstances necessitate their residenece in the Divinity building.

4. He shall keep accounts of all the receipt and expenditures, and have them transferred regularly to the University accounts kept by the University bookkeeper.

5. In the discharge of his office, the Procurator will depend upon his immediate superior alone, through whom will be communicated all the directions which the Rector and Vice-Rector may see fit to give.

119

6. He shall collect all fees for board of students and receipt all bills for same. As such resources may be insufficient to meet the expenses pertaining to the household economy of Divinity College, all deficits shall be provided for by the University administration.[188]

Signed: The Catholic University of America

Thomas J. Conaty, Rector

Signed: A. Captier,

Sup. S.S.

[188] SMSA, "Agreement between the Catholic University of America and the Sulpician Fathers with regard to the Presidency and the Procuratorship of the Divinity College," copy. The ACUA also have a copy of these documents. Keane had talked to the Sulpician superior in Paris when he was on his way to Rome after his dismissal from the university. It was then that Captier promised to make satisfactory arrangements for managing the domestic department (ACUA, Garrigan Papers, John J. Keane to P. J. Garrigan, Rome, January 22, 1897).

CHAPTER IV

THE UNIVERSITY AND THE CONTROVERSIES
OF THE DAY

The Catholic University of America came into being at a time when the hierarchy of the United States was divided into opposite camps, each of which apparently was convinced that their point of view on devisive issues was the more orthodox and, therefore, necessary to be maintained at all costs. One group was referred to in the secular press of the period as the "liberal" or progressive party with John Ireland, Archbishop of St. Paul, as its recognized leader. The other group was often termed the "ultramontane" or conservative party with Michael A. Corrigan, Archbishop of New York, directing its destinies. During its formative years the university suffered because of this peculiar situation, not so much that any single bishop was opposed to the university idea as such, but because the first rector of the university, John J. Keane, was so strikingly identified with the liberal group. As a result the university project naturally received its greatest support from that wing of the hierarchy and it suffered its principal opposition at the hands of the so-called conservatives.[1]

A month after the university opened, Bishop McQuaid of Rochester, one of the conservative opponents of the university, wrote to his friend, Archbishop Corrigan: "The university is lapsing into quietness, & quietness precedes death. Time will tell who was right. My convictions are stronger now than ever."[2] But the quietness was soon disturbed when the seemingly insoluble school question flared into the public view, lining the liberals and conservatives against each other in a struggle for supremacy.[3] It is necessary to a full understanding of the university history in these years to expand on some matters to show how the controversy affected the institution's life.

[1] For a treatment of the problems during the formative years, cf. Ellis, *op. cit., passim.*

[2] NYAA, C-16, Bernard J. McQuiad to M. A. Corrigan, Rochester, December 30, 1889.

[3] The controversy has been treated extensively by Daniel J. O'Reilly, O.P., in his book, *The School Controversy (1891-1893)* (Washington, 1943).

121

The university became involved in the battle between Ireland and the opponents of his Faribault-Stillwater school plan through a pamphlet that was published by Thomas Bouquillon, professor of moral theology at Washington. Bouquillon's brochure was attacked by the conservatives as a vindication of the St. Paul prelate's plan, which they wholeheartedly opposed as contrary to their understanding of the Church's mind on the subject. According to Bishop Keane the professor's pamphlet originated in this manner:

Early in 1891, the question of the relation of the State to Catholic schools had become a burning one in the country, owing first to the teachings of Bishop McQuaid of Rochester and Judge Dunne, who both insisted that the State had nothing to do with education or schools, & that to so assert is State-Socialism,—and secondly to the action of Dr. Quigley of Toledo, Ohio, in resisting State supervision of schools, a resistance in which he was repeatedly worsted by the courts of Ohio.— About that time our Prof. Dr. Bouquillon treated this very question in the natural course of his class work. The students were greatly interested, & begged him to prepare two special lectures on the subject. He did so. These were spoken of in the Seminary at Baltimore & Rev. Dr. Magnien asked to see the MS. After reading it, he spoke of it to the Cardinal [Gibbons], who urged its publication in the Catholic Quarterly in Phila. It came too late for the April no. and was held over for the July no. But before July came, it was returned to Dr. B. with a curt note from Dr. Horstmann, then assistant editor. To Dr. B's protest against his really impertinent strictures, he replied apologetically, but persisted in refusing to publish it in the Quarterly.[4] The Cardinal then advised that it sh'd be published in pamphlet form,—& so it was entrusted to Murphy & Co. The proofs were not corrected til the end of vacation, & the pamphlet appeared in November '91.

Meantime, Abp. Ireland had arranged that the schools at Faribault, Minn., should be accepted by the State as public schools & supported from the public funds. Similar arrangements had existed for years in 13 other dioceses, dating from "the Poughkeepsie plan" which had long existed under the administration of Card. McCloskey & Archbp. Corrigan. But as soon as the same arrangement was entered into by Abp. Ireland his enemies within the Catholic fold throughout the country

---

[4] After a decision had been rendered by Rome in the case, Archbishop Ryan of Philadelphia wrote Denis O'Connell: "so the 'great controversy' is over!...

"I foresaw and foretold that this war would arise if Dr. Bouquillon's Article was published in the 'Quarterly' & hence declined to publish it. Its appearance in pamphlet form opened the battle" (RDA, P. J. Ryan to D. J. O'Connell, Philadelphia, June 21, 1892).

assailed him bitterly, & denounced the arrangement as anti-Catholic. The controversy thus started was raging when Dr. Bouquillon's pamphlet appeared, and it was instantly pounced upon as a defence of Abp. Ireland. The principles exposed in it were indeed virtually a vindication of Abp. Ireland; but, as the above facts show, its composition & publication were quite independent of his action.[5]

As far as the present writer can determine, it has never been clearly brought out by previous publications on this subject that Bouquillon was not alone in the preparation of the first pamphlet, nor in formulating the answers to the attacks that followed its publication. In the first report of the chancellor of the university to Rome made in 1892 under the title "De Scriptis Professorum Aliorumque Universitatis Membrorum," it was declared:

R. professor Bouquillon . . . praeteria (collaborante R. professore O'Gorman) opusculum edidit de iuribus et obligationibus, auctoritate et libertate in materia scholarum; quod opusculum cum, praeter omnem

---

[5] ACUA, "Chronicles," pp. 50-52. According to archival sources this account is substantially correct. Magnien returned the manuscript on January 9, 1891, and told Bouquillon that an article on the subject, signed by such an outstanding authority, would have a salutary effect (ACUA, Bouquillon Papers, A. Magnien, S.S., to Th. Bouquillon, Baltimore, January 9, 1891 (French)). Horstmann informed Bouquillon in March that all of his manuscript had arrived but that it was too late for the April number. He added: "Of course you give me permission to make such changes in the language of the article to make it read smoothly as I judge best" (ACUA, Bouquillon Papers, Ign. F. Horstmann to Th. Bouquillon, Philadelphia, March 31, 1891). Bouquillon received a letter from Horstmann in May in which reasons were advanced for refusing to publish the article (ACUA, Bouquillon Papers, Ign. F. Horstmann to Th. Bouquillon, Philadelphia, May 11, 1891). This was answered by Bouquillon. The French draft and the English translation, in O'Gorman's hand, are to be found in ACUA, Bouquillon Papers. In reply to this, Horstmann indicated that the action taken in refusing to publish Bouquillon's article was "more that of his Grace who marked with lead pencil all those lines in the application you find in the manuscript and said he would not approve of those pages as they stood" (ACUA, Bouquillon Papers, Ign. F. Horstmann to Th. Bouquillon, Philadelphia, May 15, 1891). Bouquillon also made a thorough reply to this letter (ACUA, Bouquillon Papers, copy). On June 3, Magnien conveyed the cardinal's wishes that the university professor publish the rejected article in the form of a brochure (ACUA, Bouquillon Papers, A. Magnien, S.S., to Th. Bouquillon, Baltimore, June 3, 1891 (French)).

123

expectationem, fuisset variis nominibus impugnatum, auctores aliis opusculis sinceritatem doctrinae suae vindicarunt.[6]

If Thomas O'Gorman, professor of church history in the university, had a hand in the preparation of the pamphlet usually attributed solely to Bouquillon—and according to Gibbons' report to Rome he certainly did—it would explain his keen interest throughout the controversy that followed on a basis broader than his personal affection for the Archbishop of St. Paul.

The first to launch an attack upon Bouquillon was René I. Holaind, S.J. Father Holaind, a former professor of ethics in the Jesuit Scholasticate at Woodstock, Maryland, then stationed at St. Francis Xavier's Church in New York, was a friend of Archbishop Corrigan, who had previously engaged him as an ally in his struggle against Henry George and Father McGlynn. Holaind and Corrigan likewise shared a suspicion concerning the orthodoxy of the teaching at the university. Before the school controversy had opened Holaind had written to Corrigan:

The teachers expressly and repeatedly say that the holding of land in severalty is a natural right. . . .

I have already insisted on this in my first paper, but in treating of family rights I shall have another occasion. It is very distressing to refute a person so much my superior in every sense, but the obedience due to the Church is in jeopardy. Come what may truth must be vindicated. I shall begin my second paper immediately, and will send it before publication. I am very sorry Mgr. Schroeder is away; he would have been a powerful ally. I am sorry to say that liberalism has crept into the University, but it is a fact. Probably Dr. Pohle could help us, but I do not know him personally.

---

[6] ACUA, "Beatissimo Patri Leoni Papae XIII Catholicae Universitatis Americae Cancellarius," p. 15. This is a twenty-five page printed document giving a report on the university and its work from 1889-1892. The document was not dated but it was sent to Rome in May, 1892, in care of D. J. O'Connell to be presented to the Holy Father by John Ireland, who was to give all needed explanations (RDA, John J. Keane to John Ireland, Washington, April 29, 1892). For further evidence on the date of the document's composition, cf. *Third Annual Report of the Rector*, p. 14. The English translations of Bouquillon's replies to the Horstmann letters are in O'Gorman's hand (ACUA, Bouquillon Papers, copies). Bouquillon must have submitted his response to Holaind's pamphlet to O'Gorman before having it published, for a letter written by O'Gorman gives the professor some advice as to changes to be made in a number of paragraphs of his reply (ACUA, Bouquillon Papers, Thomas O'Gorman to Th. Bouquillon, St. Paul, n.d. (French)).

124

My arguments will not convince those men for they are like the Schoolmaster of Goldsmith.[7]

A few months later, in a letter that contained marked news items from the New York *Mail and Express* and the information that similar articles had appeared in the New York *Staats Zeitung* on September 16 and 18, the Jesuit writer told Corrigan: "I hope some explanation will come from Faribault."[8] It must have been shortly thereafter that he began to collect material for his pamphlet since he told Corrigan:

The papers have been collected by F. Hughes. They show how unscrupulous the defenders of the Faribault transaction must be. It would be advisable to get several copies of F. John Conry's letter in the Mail and Express.

I am sketching rapidly a few propositions covering the general principles, and I am getting some passages of Hammerstein and Jansen translated.

Could I get the text of the instruction sent by the S. Cong of the inquisitions [*sic*] to the Bishops of the United States, dated June 30, 1875.

Although my hands are full already I shall do everything in my power to help in this emergency. The future of the Catholic Schools is in the balance. Should the hierarchy decide to press the Poughkeepsie plan, then let us have their instructions and obey them implicitly, but let us not divide, and especially let us not fight under a false flag.[9]

[7] NYAA, C-34, R. I. Holaind, S.J., to M. A. Corrigan, New York, July 1, 1891. Another Jesuit had written Corrigan in 1888: "As the chief defender of Catholic teaching in the recent controversy on the ownership of land you will be pleased to see the articles on the same subject by F. Victor Cathrein, S.J., which appeared in the N. Y. Freeman's Journal from Febr. 18th-March 10th. . . .

"Your Grace will accept these articles translated by a member of the Faculty of Woodstock College as an acknowledgement of what you have done for a cause which is of the highest importance for the welfare of this great country, and as an assurance that the Fathers of the Society of Jesus will ever stand by your side" (NYAA, C-19, J. W. Heinzle, S.J., to M. A. Corrigan, Woodstock, Maryland, March 29, 1888).

[8] NYAA, C-34, R. I. Holaind, S.J., to M. A. Corrigan, New York, September 22, 1891.

[9] NYAA, C-34, R. I. Holaind, S.J., to M. A. Corrigan, New York, n.d. (In 1891 file).

The New York prelate, who had requested the Jesuit to prepare the pamphlet and had paid for the printing of it,[10] had informed his friend, Bernard McQuaid, about the plans that had been made, for the Bishop of Rochester wrote:

I am pleased that Dr. Bouquillon is to be answered seriously. Since the Professsors of the U have no students to teach, they take to the writing of pamphlets. They cannot let the U die of inanition; they must bury it with contempt.[11]

Keane described the pamphlet published by Holaind as "a lie in its very title." He continued:

Dr. B's was entitled "Who shall educate?" Father Holaind's title repeated the question & added: "The Parent first." This was an intimation that Dr. B. had taught the contrary,—which was absolutely false. And the whole attack was devoted to proving what Dr. B. had not questioned, and refuting what Dr.B. had not asserted.[12]

After Bouquillon's pamphlet had been subjected to public rebuke the rector gave an interview to a representative of the New York *Globe Democrat* in which he defended his professor:

The pamphlet is nothing more than a quotation from the ecclesiastical authorities, theological and philosophical, in all ages. The only new thing about the matter is that people should so far forget this fact as to misrepresent the writer's views. It has always been understood that there are two forms of human society, the civil and the religious, and it has also been understood that these two forms of society should co-operate for the welfare of mankind. . . . Education is considered to be

---

[10] ACUA, "Chronicles," p. 52. It was stated there: "It was interesting news to be informed later on, by Civiltà Cattolica itself, that it had been prepared at the request & printed at the expense of Archbishop Corrigan." A. Magnien wrote to Ireland: "The Jesuits of the South American College speak the truth when they say that Archbishop Corrigan has induced them to go into the fight on the school question. Fr. Holaind himself has said that the Archbishop asked him to write his pamphlet & that he paid for the printing of it" (RDA, A. Magnien, S.S., to John Ireland, Baltimore, March 31, 1892). Patrick Hennessy, pastor of St. Patrick's Church, Jersey City, New Jersey, wrote Gibbons at that time: "It is well known that he [Corrigan] urged Father Hollaind [*sic*] to attack Prof. Bouquillon, and it is little concealed that he has instigated Judge Dunne & the Catholic Herald of New York to decry the Archbishop of St. Paul & his plan" (BCA, 89-T-6, P. Hennessy to J. Card. Gibbons, Jersey City, April 9, 1892).

[11] NYAA, C-16, Bernard J. McQuaid to M. A. Corrigan, Rochester, November 26, 1891.

[12] ACUA, "Chronicles," p. 52.

126

one of the essentials of human welfare; and sound philosophy teaches us, as sound theologians have always understood, that here also civil and religious authority should cooperate for the teaching of men in all relationships toward this world and toward the world to come. The Church and State, therefore, should be united in education just as in everything else. This, Dr. Bouquillon shows, has been the teaching of the leading authorities of the Church in all ages. Therefore there is nothing new in his position. The only novelty is the short-sighted people with their false philosophy or their exaggerated ideas of either State or Church authority who wish to keep education exclusively in the hands of either one or the other, whereas both ought to cooperate for its protection.[13]

After the first round in the battle of pamphlets had been fought, Robert Fulton, S.J., President of Boston College, wrote to J. Havens Richards, S.J., President of Georgetown University, concerning their confrére:

Well, he has been [sic] and done it! Plucky man he has ranged against himself the Americanizing Bps., the University, the Paulists, etc. We shall have a lively time. May it not be that we Jesuits suffer as we are wont—quidquid delirant reges, plectuntur Achivi [The people suffer for the mad acts of their kings].

But in my poor judgment Fr. Holaind has gained the victory and Bouquillon proved himself an inferior man.[14]

The "lively time" was just beginning. Holaind informed Corrigan that he had heard that Bouqillon was correcting the proofs of another pamphlet "somewhat abusive with regard to myself and others." Since "His Eminence the Cardinal [Gibbons] has persuaded my superiors to prevent me from answering," the "plucky man" placed his honor and reputation in charge of his episcopal protector.[15]

The Jesuit was right. Bouquillon prepared and published a second pamphlet entitled, *Education: To Whom Does It Belong? A Rejoinder to Critics.* Thomas J. Campbell, S.J., superior of the New York-Maryland Province of the Society of Jesus, wrote Gibbons: "It has given me great pain to hear that Dr. Bouquillon

[13] New York *Globe Democrat*, November 29, 1891.

[14] Georgetown University Archives, Robert Fulton, S.J., to J. Havens Richards, S.J., Mobile, December 18, 1891.

[15] NYAA, C-34, R. I. Holaind, S.J., to M. A. Corrigan, Washington, December 23, 1891.

has issued a new pamphlet. After the agreement entered into by all those interested I am sure this must be an error."[16] After the second pamphlet appeared McQuaid wrote to Denis O'Connell:

Just now, Bouquillon, in the name of his Superiors, has set the American Catholic World agog on the school question, apropos of the Fairbuillt [sic] arrangement. If these imported Europeans, with the old world motives, would only keep quiet, until they had found out where they were, it would conduce to their comfort. In his reply to critics, Boquillon [sic] loses his temper.[17]

The Rochester prelate was also concerned about the newspaper reports that Archbishop Ireland was soon to leave for Rome. "As it is not his visit *ad limina*," he said, "we wonder what takes him there. He is the head and front of the new liberalistic party in the American Church."[18]

While there were some who thought that the university professor was getting the worst of it in the battle of pamphlets—the standard had been snatched up by the co-workers of the stricken Holaind—there were others who praised him and wished him well. Placide L. Chapelle, the Coadjutor Archbishop of Santa Fé, wrote to Abbé Magnien:

In this question of education I think the Jesuits have been extremely over-eager and I would not be surprised if they got a bit dizzy. It is a deplorable thing to see an order which is capable of doing so much good to our churches, obstinately set upon causing disunion in the church by carrying on a disloyal war against the hierarchy. And that for fear of being surpassed.[19]

---

[16] BCA, 89-H-8, T. J. Campbell, S.J., to J. Card. Gibbons, New York, January 11, 1892. It was enlightening to note this statement in the preface to the second edition of W. Wilmers, S.J., *Handbook of the Christian Religion*, written on January 1, 1892: "The third appendix [The *Syllabus* of Pius I X] particularly will be found opportune at a time when liberalism, albeit unwittingly, crops out at times even in Catholic circles, and necessarily calls forth adverse criticism in the more conservative portion of the Catholic press. In such circumstances it is well that the educated Catholic laity should have a standard by which to judge what is, and what is not, liberalism in the odious sense of the word" (W. Wilmers, S.J., *Handbook of the Christian Religion* (New York: 1892), p. vi).

[17] RDA, Bernard J. McQuaid to D. J. O'Connell, Rochester, January 16, 1892.

[18] *Ibid.*

[19] SMSA, P. L. Chapelle to A. Magnien, S.S., Tucson, Arizona, January 24, 1892.

Among the Jesuits who carried on the war begun by Holaind's reply to Bouquillon, Salvatore M. Brandi, S.J., was the most influential. He had taught at the Jesuit Scholasticate at Woodstock, Maryland, and at the time he was one of the editors of the *Civiltà Cattolica*, an important fortnightly review published in Rome by the Society of Jesus. After his pamphlet had appeared, in which he took issue with Bouquillon's second brochure, Chapelle told Gibbons:

I have just received Fr. Brandi's pamphlet. I am astounded. So it appears that the Society has taken up in earnest the cudgels against the University & a portion of our Hierarchy, for it seems to me that the educational question is only a pretext. Dr. Bouquillon's reply is very strong & written in excellent taste. There ought not to be any weakening on any side. Our interests as Catholics, bishops & American citizens are too precious to be jeopardized by men who see nothing beyond the prestige of their society.[20]

A priest from St. Louis, stationed at Sacred Heart Church, was also pleased with Bouquillon's second pamphlet. He told Magnien:

Dr. Bouquillon's latest gave me genuine pleasure for it is a clear, eloquent, and to my mind, convincing statement of the State's rights in the case, rights which I have always "felt in my bones" to be undeniable. The doughty Doctor is a heroic figure standing alone in the field against "all comers"—may his right hand never forget its cunning. [21]

About the same time the Sulpician rector of St. Mary's Seminary told Denis O'Connell that the school controversy was going along a little more peacefully than at the beginning. He said: "Dr. Bouquillon is more than a match for all of them."[22] Later Keane wrote about the second round of pamphlets:

Dr. B. issued a reply in which he plainly showed the unfairness & sophistry with which he had been assailed. This was attacked by

---

[20] BCA, 89-H-8, P. L. Chapelle to J. Card. Gibbons, Tucson, Arizona, February 1, 1892.

[21] SMSA, J. T. Foley to A. Magnien, S.S., St. Louis, February 22, 1892. Bouquillon also received words of encouragement and admiration from his former companions at Maredsous. Dom Laurent Jannens advised him, however, to discontinue the polemics with *Civiltà Cattolica* (ACUA, Bouquillon Papers, Laurent Jannens, O.S.B. to Th. Bouquillon, Maredsous, July 17, 1892 (French); Basile DeMeester, O.S.B., to Th. Bouquillon, Maredsous, July 18, 1892 (French).

[22] RDA, A. Magnien, S.S., to D. J. O'Connell, Baltimore, February 22, 1892.

several Jesuits, & especially by the Civiltà Cattolica, which assailed with vehemence not only Dr. B., but Abp. Ireland, and the Cath. Univ'y of America, which were evidently the chief objects of animosity.

Again Dr. B. replied with trenchant logic to the cunning sophistries of these various attacks. The press everywhere in Europe as in America, was full of the controversy. The enemies of Abp. Ireland & of the University made things very hot for them both.[23]

Human nature being what it is, the professors of the university were divided on the school issue. Keane said: "The great bulk of them agreed with Dr. B. But Dr. Schroeder wrote against him, and with him sided Dr. Pohle. Dr. Messmer also wrote against him."[24] Among those active in the support of Bouquillon on the university faculty, O'Gorman was the most outspoken. The chancellor told Bishop Maes of Covington, who had protested to the cardinal against the continued activity of Bouquillon and O'Gorman in the school controversy, that "Dr. O'Gorman may be excused for his utterances owing to his former relations with Abp. Ireland and his warm friendship for him."[25] Another prefessor, Thomas J. Shahan, expressed sympathy for his colleague to Denis O'Connell:

My classes take up all my time. I only wish I had more, to take a hand in these controversies, such bad faith, secret tyranny, double-dealing, and distortion of the plain truth were seldom witnessed in the Church,—never in our American Church History has there been such a spectacle. The motives of action on the part of our opponents are so clearly ambition, personal jealousy, and order-interests, that every non-Catholic sees it now.

I trust the right views will prevail at Rome, and the Church not be saddled with a burden that a century of efforts will not rid her of.

The Catholics of the English-speaking race have toiled for three centuries to break down the accusations of disloyalty to government, intolerance, slavish submission to Rome, impure politics, and the like. Though a minority, we have worked wonders, and now here comes the German mediaeval priest, and the members of an order, whose powers for harm are great, to upset the whole. May they reap confusion.[26]

[23] ACUA, "Chronicles," pp. 52-53.

[24] *Ibid.*

[25] BCA, 89-Y-4, J. Card. Gibbons to Camillus P. Maes, Baltimore, June 16, 1892. Copy.

[26] RDA, Thomas J. Shahan to D. J. O'Connell, Washington, March 3, 1892.

The rector held practically the same view on the question, for he later wrote:

While trying to be friendly to all, my convictions were entirely on the side of Dr. B. & Mgr. Satolli,—and my feelings totally against the unfairness, the interested politics, the sophistry by which they were assailed.[27]

As a result of the divided allegiance of the faculty of the university the friendly feelings and unity that had existed previous to the controversy suffered to a certain degree.[28]

When Ireland went to Rome to explain his challenged school experiment, he also defended Bouquillon against those who had written to Rome denouncing the professor's teachings. The St. Paul prelate wrote Gibbons about his first opportunity to present a defense of the university professor before the Pope:

Toward the end [of the audience], he mentioned Bouquillon. He evidently had been spoken to by an enemy. I argued mildly, & asked permission to write for him some memoranda. He said that he would gladly read them, & then talk to me again of the contents. I am sure I will dispel all unfavorable ideas, & come out the victor.

Rampolla is all right—knows Dr. Bouquillon personally. . . .

Mgr. Cadagnis, the rector of the Appolinare, endorses all Dr. Bouquillon's ideas, cordially and fully.

All the papers, owned or controlled by Jesuits in Italy, are writing fierce articles against Dr. Bouquillon & myself.[29]

The Archbishop of St. Paul was given an opportunity to defend Bouquillon's teachings in a more thorough manner later when he was called before the cardinals of the Sacred Congregation of the Propagation of the Faith. He told the cardinals: "This pamphlet, which saw the light of day by reason of the formal desires of ecclesiastical superiors, answers both a need and a state of mind." Then, after he had shown how the pamphlet satisfied the Church's needs in America, he concluded:

Dr. Bouquillon has thus rendered a service both to his country and to his Church. The success of his brochure will contribute to the success of the Catholic cause. It will bring to a close a period of prejudices, and will render accessible to Rome's influence this young Republic

---

[27] ACUA, "Chronicles," p. 55.

[28] *Ibid.*

[29] BCA, 89-P-1, John Ireland to J. Card. Gibbons, Rome, February 21, 1892.

whose future opens out on such beautiful and unanticipated perspectives.[30]

The friends of the university were extremely anxious that Bouquillon's writings should be entirely cleared of any suspicion of heresy and, incidentally, that Ireland's school experiment should not be condemned. While Ireland was in Rome the Abbé Magnien wrote to him: "You must by all means get a clear and strong letter of positive approval for yourself & Dr. Bouquillon. For God's sake do not leave Rome until every difficulty has been solved, & the path is clear."[31] After it seemed evident that the Bouquillon pamphlets would not be censured, Magnien wrote to O'Connell:

There is another point about which the Cardinal is much concerned. He was grealy rejoiced when he knew that neither the Inquisition nor the Index were to touch Dr. Bouquillon's brochures but he fears that later on his enemies may find means to do what they were prevented from doing this time, & hence he greatly desires that Archbishop Ireland and you should see that all possible danger for the future is averted. After all the war against Dr. Bouquillon is a war against the University, & if the professor's doctrine is censured in any form the Institution would suffer.[32]

Fortunately for the welfare of the university, Bouquillon's brochures were in no way censured. On the contrary, he continued to hold a high place in the esteem of the Holy Father who addressed him as "Our most Beloved Son," in a reply to a letter which the university professor sent at the approach of Christmas, 1892, in the name of the School of Theology in his capacity as its dean.[33] When he went to Rome in the summer of 1893 he was "received everywhere with honor" and he had a cordial audience with the Sovereign Pontiff.[34]

Simultaneously with the school controversy there was also

[30] Reilly, *op. cit.*, pp. 267-270.

[31] RDA, A. Magnien, S.S., to John Ireland, Baltimore, March 31, 1892. Rampolla wrote to Bouquillon in March, 1892, telling him that the brochures had been submitted to the Sacred Congregation of the Propaganda for examination and that there was no doubt about the orthodoxy of his teachings (ACUA, Bouquillon Papers, M. Card. Rampolla to Th. Bouquillon, Rome, March 23, 1892 (French)).

[32] RDA, A. Magnien, S.S., to D. J. O'Connell, Baltimore, April 22, 1892.

[33] Baltimore *Catholic Mirror*, January 21, 1893. The letter was written by Leo XIII on December 30, 1892.

[34] BCA, 91-T-4, D. J. O'Connell to J. Card. Gibbons, Rome, August 1, 1893.

132

considerable discussion about the possibility and probability of Corrigan and Ireland being created princes of the Church. Magnien wrote O'Connell at the time:

The appointment of the other candidate [Corrigan] would, in the present circumstances, be a true misfortune. It would give power and strength to the opponents of the University, which is as much the work of Leo XIII as of the American episcopate, & confer authority to those views & principles which in America & for America are fraught with mischievous consequences, because they have no other effect than to make Americans consider the Church as narrow minded & more or less inimical to the institutions of the country.[35]

Rome had probably been fully informed by both parties about the consequences of singling out the leader of either group in the American hierarchy for special honors. At any rate, neither received the red hat, whatever were their merits for the high honor.

When the news about Rome's decision on Ireland's school experiment appeared in the American press, Keane was among the first to rejoice with him. He wrote:

How can I sufficiently congratulate you on the *glorious* news given us by yesterday's paper! It is a triumph which marks an epoch. It opens up a future of harmonious relations between America and the Church, and crushes the hindrances which would fain have barred the portals. Now let us have a pronouncement from the Pope, clear and unmistakable in meaning which, while reasserting Catholic principles, as of course it is sure to do, & thus closing the mouths of those who are ready to assert that the Church is being committed to a false policy, will above all give the country clearly to understand that we recognize & admit civil rights & are ready to cooperate fairly in education as in all else that concerns the public welfare.[36]

There was no mistaking the university rector's allegiance during the whole controversy. He was a member of the liberal party and he saw eye to eye with that party's leader in the matter of education.

It was inevitable that the university should suffer from these sharp differences of opinion between its representatives and some members of the hierarchy, so thoroughly aired in the press.

[35] RDA, A. Magnien, S.S., to D. J. O'Connell, Baltimore, April 17, 1892.
[36] RDA, John J. Keane to John Ireland, Washington, April 29, 1892.

During the controversy Camillus Maes wrote to Cardinal Gibbons:

My interest in the present welfare and in the future of the university prompts me to again call your attention, as Chancellor of it, to the effect which the continued harping on terms of Drs. Bouquillon & O'Gorman is producing on the majority of the Rt. Rev. Bishops, on almost all the priests and on the whole laity of the Country. The impression is distinctly this: "The Catholic University, by direction of its Ecclesiastical Superiors, is deliberately posing before the Country as the champion of the Faribault system, and favors the application of that System wherever it is possible to do so, even when not necessary."

I do not enter into the merits of the controversy; that would be out of place in this instance. Just now, I am only concerned as a member of the Board with the best interests of our beloved Institution, and I wish to state emphatically that the action of these Professors is ruinous to the University.[37]

The chancellor answered the Bishop of Covington immediately:

I fully agree with you that everything should be averted which would weaken the confidence of the Bishops of the country in the University.

On receipt of your letter, I wrote immediately to the Rt. Rev. Rector, calling his attention to the subject of your letter, adding that the University must do nothing which would make its professors suspected of partisanship. The Bishop entirely accords with these views. I requested the two professors of whom you write, to call to see me.[38]

The impression, mentioned by Bishop Maes, about the university being considered as the champion of the Faribault plan, and, therefore, damaging to the cause of Catholic schools, was answered later by Keane:

The damage was done by those who, for interested & unworthy motives, had falsely represented Satolli & the Univ'y & Dr. B. as opposed to the Catholic school system, & had thus led many to conclude that if these distinguished authorities were really opposed to the system, then the system was probably not worthy of support. The remedy must be that they who made the change should acknowledge that they misrepresented & that the above authorities have never been the enemies of Catholic

---

[37] BCA, 89-Y-1, Camillus P. Maes to J. Card. Gibbons, Covington, June 11, 1892.

[38] BCA, 89-Y-4, J. Card. Gibbons to Camillus P. Maes, Baltimore, June 16, 1892, copy.

education & Catholic schools, but their best friends.—That the Univ'y had to suffer somewhat from these unjust attacks, is obvious.[39]

The great controversy was finally silenced by papal intervention, although the effects of it were harmful to the university for a number of years thereafter. Before considering the effects of the school controversy upon the university during the years that immediately followed, it is necessary to consider related problems that plagued the Catholic Church in the United States during the same years. Because these problems were closely allied to the school controversy, they contributed to the bitterness with which that disagreement was carried on, as they also contributed to the intensity of the opposition to the university.

In 1891, Cahenslyism, a movement described as the "demand for a greater degree of ecclesiastical autonomy by foreign language groups within the American Church,"[40] revived in time to complicate further the trouble over the schools. John J. Meng has summarized the issue thus:

It became one of the weapons in the struggle over "Americanization" of the Church in this country. The proponents of "Americanization" viewed Cahenslyism as the keystone of a plot to prevent "Americanization" of the Church and to Germanize the United States. Cahensly's apologists considered it nothing more than a pious, philanthropic movement to better the material condition and improve the spiritual welfare of Catholic immigrants to the United States. They thought that the charges of their opponents were deliberately malicious perversions of the truth designed to draw the attention of American Catholics away from the pernicious aspects of "Americanization" by turning attention upon Cahensly as a convenient scapegoat. Words of the harshest sort were used by both camps. Some members of the hierarchy who had opposed Cahenslyism when it was a clear and uncomplicated issue before 1891, found themselves allied with its supporters because of the larger questions involved after that date.[41]

The Cahenslyites joined forces with the conservatives in the school fight; hence, they were quite naturally committed to opposition to the university which was so closely identified by

[39] ACUA, "Chronicles," p. 54.

[40] John J. Meng, "Cahenslyism: The First Stage, 1883-1891," *CHR*, XXXI (January, 1946), 390.

[41] John J. Meng, "Cahenslyism: The Second Chapter, 1891-1910," *CHR*, XXXII (October, 1946), 315.

135

many with the liberals. The conservatives, on the other hand, gave strength and support to the Cahenslyite claims and aims.

Early in the summer of 1891, O'Connell told Gibbons:

It is likely that the German movement that the Amer. papers are now exploding will shake the foundations of the new departure that the Holy See was likely to adopt towards America. It was represented here that all were liberals except the Germans.[42]

A few days later O'Connell wrote: "The explosion of the Cahensly movement shatters the foundations of one of the supports of the new departure that some here contemplated making towards America."[43] It is not possible to state definitely what the effects of Cahenslyism were in Rome, but it certainly did cause additional problems for the university. O'Gorman was the first of the university professors to make a statement against Peter Paul Cahensly. The Washington *Post* reported:

Prof. O'Gorman, of Washington University, has had audiences with the Pope. His Holiness made many inquiries about the university and its courses of study, and about Archbishop Ireland and Bishop Keane, rector of the University.

Prof. O'Gorman has had interviews with many ecclesiastics high in rank. He found them all opposed to any such scheme as that proposed by Herr Cahensly, and hopeful that the Pope's prompt decision would keep the matter out of politics in America.[44]

Interviews such as this against the work of Cahensly heightened German-American ire against the university professor and caused a Buffalo German language paper to refer to him as the "fanatical Savonarola."[45]

Other university professors, however, were active in their support of the Cahensly cause. Schroeder and Pohle attended the general meeting of the German Catholics at Mayence in August, 1892, and Schroeder gave an address there before the general assembly of the St. Raphael Society in which he lauded the work of their general secretary, Cahensly.[46] The next month the univer-

[42] SMSA, D. J. O'Connell to A. Magnien, S.S., Rome, June 11, 1891.

[43] SMSA, D. J. O'Connell to A. Magnien, S.S., Rome, June 15, 1891.

[44] Washington *Post*, August 7, 1891.

[45] Buffalo *Christliche Woche*, February 3, 1892, cited in George Zurcher, "Foreign Ideas in the Catholic Church in America," *Roycroft Quarterly* (November, 1896), 46-47. This work will hereafter be referred to as Zurcher.

[46] NYAA, C-41, Peter Paul Cahensly to M. A. Corrigan, Limburg am Lahn, September 6, 1892.

136

sity professor attended the sixth *Katholikentag* held in Newark and he "spoke interestingly on his acquaintance with Cahensly, and defended the latter's endeavors."[47] This continued support of a position which was deemed untenable by the liberals was an additional cause for disagreement among the university faculty members. Keane reported:

Among us it [Cahenslyism] acted as a wedge to increase & intensify the spirit of disunion already manifesting itself. Dr. Schroeder having, during vacation, gloried in Cahenslyism, when I did what I considered my duty by expressing to him my disapproval of his having publicly advocated a policy condemned by the Holy See & the body of our Bishops, he received my words with contempt.[48]

As one might expect, Archbishop Ireland was also opposed to the activities of Schroeder and Pohle. Cahensly told Corrigan:

I know also from very good authority, that Msgr. Ireland, during his stay in Rome, passed unfair remarks about Msgr. Dr. Schroeder and Dr. Pohle, professors at the Catholic University in Washington, saying, that they must quit their chairs. He now will surely use all his endeavors with his friend Mgr. Keane, in order to get these men removed as soon as possible. Have the other Most Rev. Membres [*sic*] of the University-board then no influence in the appointment of Professors? In the interest of the Catholic Church of America would I be sorry, were these learned men to get lost for the University.[49]

In the same letter Cahensly indicated the type of accusations that were being made against the liberals, and, perhaps, even then were finding their way to Rome against the party and the university:

I am led to believe that the question at stake is: whether in the United States of N. America the principles of our holy Roman Catholic Church (as represented by Cahenslyism) will gain the victory or whether the Liberalism—as defended by Msgr. Ireland and colleagues— will conquer?[50]

After Schroeder and Pohle had made themselves the allies of the conservatives, the party of the opposition, being in the majority at the university, made their life extremely unpleasant in an

[47] New York *Katholisches Volksblatt*, September 29, 1892, cited in Zurcher, *op. cit.*, p. 37.

[48] ACUA, "Chronicles," p. 56.

[49] NYAA, C-41, Peter Paul Cahensly to M. A. Corrigan, Limburg am Lahn, October 31, 1892.

[50] *Ibid.*

effort to force them to resign their positions. Schroeder told Corrigan:

Meanwhile the day which will decide my fate and that of Dr. Pohle draws near. I have many reasons to believe that my silence in the controversies of the day was not enough for Mgr. Keane or his friends and that they are still determined to have their victim. I can assure you, Monsignor, that since October I have spent the most painful part of my life. Nevertheless, those gentlemen of the University are badly mistaken if they think that I am going to resign without being forced to do so. If they want to go to the extreme in this business of taking sides and forming parties, they will have to do it openly. They will not succeed in making me the scapegoat of the precarious situation of a University which, all during the past semester, has continually made itself the instrument, the active and avowed instrument, in public as well as inside, of the veritable conspiracy which is being plotted among the Catholics and against some Catholic prelates.[51]

Schroeder's suspicions about the designs against him were well-founded, for Keane told O'Connell a little later: "Schroeder holds on, & there is no way to oust him as yet, but he sees he has to be quiet."[52]

Pohle was the first to yield to the pressure brought against them. He accepted the chair of dogmatic theology at the University of Münster in Westphalia. When he tendered his letter of resignation to the Board of Trustees, he included many accusations about the partisan spirit in the university on the questions of the day, which he deplored as calculated to harm the institution, and he defended his own position and the position of Dr. Schroeder on those same questions. Concerning Schroeder he said:

But what has touched me most profoundly is the fact which I have observed the last two years, that Mgr. Schroeder, who as a man and a professor is, to say the least, equal to any of his colleagues, has become in consequence of his fearless attitude, at times the subject of treatment which is contrary not only to the courtesy due to such a distinguished man, but also to the most elementary principles of

---

[51] NYAA, CUA file, Joseph Schroeder to M. A. Corrigan, Reading, Pennsylvania, April 4, 1893.

[52] RDA, John J. Keane to D. J. O'Connell, Atlantic City, October 10, 1893.

138

Christian charity. I myself have witnessed attacks whose evident purpose was to render his position at the University unbearable.[53]

The rector later said that the contents of this letter had to be "honestly denounced as downright misrepresentation of the spirit & conduct of the great body of the Professors."[54] Nevertheless, there must have been some truth to it, for Ignatius F. Horstmann wrote to Corrigan:

I feel that if he [Schroeder] considered that he can retire with honor, he will not remain at the University. The atmosphere is too chilly for him. There are two professors who have not spoken to him for two years in spite of his having humbled himself to make them do so.[55]

Keane was elated when Pohle left Washingron but he was even more anxious that Schroeder should leave. He told O'Connell: "Would that Schroeder would do the same. He stands his ground, & the Board won't take action. But it won't last long so."[56] Notwithstanding their efforts to oust Schroeder during Keane's administration, the rector and his supporters failed.[57]

For a thorough understanding of the rector's antipathy to Schroeder, it is necessary to add that the professor was completely unsympathetic and unalterably opposed to Keane's views on total abstinence. It may even have been one of the major reasons for the attempt to get rid of him. The two liberal bishops, Ireland and Keane, were very active temperance workers, both attending Catholic Total Abstinence Union meetings and publicly appealing for the strict enforcement of Sunday laws. Schroeder, on the other hand, along with many German-Americans, was just as active in opposing the aims of the total abstainers. Typical of the

[53] BCA, 93-D-9, "Letter of Resignation to the Board of Directors of the Catholic University of America, sent to His Grace the Archbishop of Philadelphia, Chairman of the Committee for the appointment of Professors, March, 1894." Printed. This letter was signed by Pohle.

[54] ACUA, "Chronicles," p. 57.

[55] NYAA, CUA file, Ignatius F. Horstmann to M. A. Corrigan, Cleveland, March 9, 1894.

[56] RDA, John J. Keane to D. J. O'Connell, Washington, January 5, 1894. Shahan voiced similar sentiments to O'Connell: "You know of course that Pohle is leaving us. . . . He was a good professor, would it were the other German [Schroeder]" (RDA, O'Connell Papers, T. Shahan to D. J. O'Connell, Washington, December 13, 1893).

[57] For a sequel to this episode, cf. Peter E. Hogan, "Americanism and the Catholic University of America," *CHR*, XXXIII (July, 1947), 158-190.

statements that appeared in some German language papers at the time relative to the temperance question, was the one carried by the Baltimore *Katholicshe Volkszeitung*: "The Irish may need total abstinence; they know best. The Germans, as a rule, do not need it."[58] The Buffalo Catholic Total Abstinence Union protested to Keane, their ardent supporter, about some of the statements which Schroeder made about total abstinence in 1894, but the rector had to inform them that he had no right to interfere with the personal opinions expressed by professors outside the classroom.[59]

The rector's views on total abstinence, among other things, were responsible for aligning a powerful German language paper, the Illinois *Staats Zeitung*, against the university. When Keane wrote to Mr. A. C. Hesing, the president of the Illinois Staats Zeitung Company, to call his attention to the promise of a donation to the university, he recieved this reply:

As you are probably not acquainted with the circumstances and conditions under which my promise of aid was obtained, I take the liberty to trouble you with the following explanations.

When the members of the committee soliciting subscriptions for the University came to Chicago, I was invited to attend one of their meetings. At that meeting it was explicitly stated that the institution to be erected in Washington was intended to be—not a school for nursing and fostering certain narrow puritanical ideas apt to inculcate in the minds of the students dislike and prejudices against other nationalities, not a training school for riding a hobby horse of those of our bishops and prelates who can only see safety and salvation for our Church in this country by thoroughly "americanizing" as soon as possible everything that is called Catholic,—but an institution of learning on the broadest basis after the model of German or European Universities, one of the purposes being to elevate the standard of education of our clergy by establishing chairs of German literature, for the German and other languages, so as to enable them to administer to the spiritual wants of the many congregations in this country, composed of people of different nationalities. Moreover it was distinctly stated that the University should not be only a theological high school

---

[58] Baltimore *Katholische Volkszeitung*, March 26, 1892, cited in Zurcher, *op. cit.*, p. 15. The Buffalo *Christliche Woche* of October 9, 1891 cited in *ibid.*, p. 40, made an amusing statement during the school controversy: "If the devil and his grandmother can enjoy themselves at all, they must have danced a real Irish jig when the parochial school of Faribault was given over to the State."

[59] Zurcher, *op. cit.*, pp. 15-16.

or seminary. To every young man, wishing to apply himself to other faculties, the best opportunities should be given to accomplish his aims and ends.

In this respect I myself made a few remarks before the Committee. When I had finished Rt. Rev. Bishop Spalding of Peoria arose and said that he fully agreed with my views, that the new University would be everything I had stated. Relying on this assurance I readily signed the sum you have found standing against my name, and I also did my best to induce other Catholic citizens to lend their aid to such a worthy undertaking.

However, the assurance then given and my expectations, I am sorry to say, have not been realized. For one reason or another Bishop Spalding, who always had my highest esteem and fullest confidence has withdrawn from the management of the University and the control of the institution is now altogether in the hands of prelates who have made themselves conspicuous by their bitter opposition to everything that has a German name, going in their aversion against the Germans, their language, customs, and habits even so far, as to denounce, traduce, accuse and malign the German Catholics, priests, and bishops of this country before the Propaganda and the Apostolic See at Rome.

Under existing circumstances I was not much surprised when I found it stated in the papers the other day that the managers of the University were anxious and had resolved to establish above all other things a chair for temperance and prohibition doctrines. This may lie in their eyes more important and more appropriate for an American Catholic University than German literature and German language, but it certainly cannot be brought in accordance with the prospectus given out at the time when the subscriptions were solicited.

My friends do me the honor to call me a representative German Catholic. This is no doubt to a large extent a flattery I do not deserve. It is however true that my influence is great as Pres. of the Ills. Staats Zeitung, probably the best known and most influential paper printed in the German language, with a large number of German Catholic readers. When the "German Question" turned up, when the doings and machinations of our accusers came to light, I considered it a paramount duty for the Staats Zeitung to enter the lists for the defense of the rights of the German Catholics, and I am proud to say that I have done everything in my power to let the accusations officially brought against us, appear in the true light. You will no doubt readily understand now, that my actions would badly suit my words indeed, if I should pay my subscription for the Catholic University of America,—a subscription obtained and made under the gravest misapprehensions.[60]

It cannot be doubted that the influence of this paper was far-reaching, nor can it be doubted that the editors of other German

[60] ACUA, A. C. Hesing to John J. Keane, Chicago, May 21, 1890.

language papers entertained the same views and exerted a powerful influence on their readers to the detriment of the university.

There was still another question that divided the bishops of iber al and conservative views during the same period, namely, whether or not Catholics should participate in the World's Parliament of Religions in 1893. Keane's participation in that gathering was seized upon as another manifestation of the liberalism that was taking hold in the university. It is fairly safe to say that Rome was made aware of his part in it through denunciatory letters, but the rector foresaw that such would be the case. He wrote Denis O'Connell:

I think he [Satolli] looks askance at our part in the Parliament of Religions, as do, no doubt, all the ultra conservatives. I got into it, first at the urgent solicitation of Abp. Ireland—then at the request of the Abps. at their meeting in N. Y.—and I am confident that the result is an enormous advantage to the Church. But I take it for granted that I shall be denounced for it. So be it.[61]

He was not disappointed. The *Western Watchman* was loud in its condemnation of all the Catholics who participated in the parliament and it was especially vociferous in its denunciation of the university's rector.[62] Father Henry Tappert of Covington, Kentucky, the delegate of the Commissary of the *Katholikentag* in America to the *Katholikentag* in Cologne, in 1894, in a speech there condemned the liberalistic tendencies among some Catholics in the United States and cited the participation in "the Chicago religious Parliament of unholy memory" as an outstanding example.[63] Finally the Holy Father condemned the participation in such gatherings in a letter to the apostolic delegate on September 18, 1895:

We have known that meetings are held, from time to time, in the United States, at which Catholics and dissenters from the Catholic Church assemble to discuss together religion and right morals. We, indeed, recognize in this a zeal for religion, by which that nation is daily more ardently moved. Now, although those general meetings have

---

[61] RDA, John J. Keane to D. J. O'Connell, Washington, October 10, 1893.

[62] *Western Watchman* (St. Louis), October 28, 1893.

[63] Zurcher, *op. cit.*, pp. 52-53.

142

been tolerated by a prudent silence to this day, it would seem, nevertheless, more advisable for Catholics to hold their assemblies apart.[64]

There were many recriminations lodged against the university during the years 1892-1893. The rector answered some of them at a special session of the Board of Trustees on April 14, 1893. He recognized that they could not forbid the professors from talking and writing and he was particularly vehement in denying that the university was guilty of partisanship and that it was guilty of instilling insubordination against episcopal authority.[65] The same year the chancellor, in his annual letter to the bishops of the country on the university, attempted to remove any misapprehensions about the university that the bishops may have acquired as a result of the controversies:

In answer to the question which solicitude for the welfare of the University may have raised in some minds, I deem it opportune to state my firm conviction that the controversies on Catholic questions, which have so largely occupied the press and the public of late, have in no degreee penetrated into the work of the University nor hindered its inmates from steadily and harmoniously pressing on in their own legitimate lines. And so, we trust, it shall ever be. The Board of Directors are fully aware of their responsibility to the Holy See and to the Episcopate of the country, and there is no ground for any apprehension that the work or the spirit of the University will deviate in the least from their due purpose and direction.[66]

When conditions seemed dark and foreboding for the rector during the summer of 1893, he received encouraging news through Cardinal Gibbons, when O'Connell reported to the chancellor about an audience with the Pope:

Then we went fully into the situation in America. His Holiness said he would write you "to display a little more authority." He will also write to the opposition to desist. He said the opposition which I

---

[64] *Leonis XIII Acta*, XV, 323 ff, cited in Zwierlein, *op. cit.*, III, 238. A poor translation of the document appeared in the Buffalo *Catholic Union and Times*, October 24, 1895, cited in Zurcher, *op. cit.*, p. 50.

[65] ACUA, "Sessio. Extr. on April 14, 1893." This was a small card with notes. When writing to O'Connell about the meeting of the Board of Trustees in 1893, Gibbons said: "Of course many things occurred at the meeting which are not recorded in the minutes" (RDA, J. Card. Gibbons to D. J. O'Connell, Baltimore, October 16, 1893).

[66] ACUA, J. Card. Gibbons to Our Venerable Brethren, The Archbishops and Bishops of the United States, Baltimore, May 24, 1893. Printed. The same document may be found in NYAA, G-4.

named was always writing him most submissive letters, but I said they were insincere. He and Rampolla will both undertake now the support of the University, and they are resolute.[67]

This heartening information was corroborated in a letter that the rector received from Bouquillon. Keane told Gibbons:

I have had a splendid letter from Dr. Bouquillon. The Pope & Rampolla, & the Vannutellis also, are heartily with the University and against the Jesuits. The Pope promises a strong letter to that effect.[68]

Despite the resolve of Leo XIII and his Secretary of State to support the university, so many adverse reports about the institution had reached Rome as a result of the controversies, that the Pope requested an investigation be made and a report on the findings sent to him. Keane told O'Connell:

Attacks on the University in Rome have culminated in a request from the Pope for a report by Satolli. I am very glad of it. We have nothing to fear in the facts of the case, & Satolli says it will redound to the good of the Univ'y.[69]

The apostolic delegate made a careful inquiry into the past work and the condition of the university and then made a detailed report to the Sovereign Pontiff. Keane told the Board of Trustees the next year that Satolli had received from the Holy Father "an assurance of his entire satisfaction." He also asked the members of the board: "Is it not greatly to be desired that the guardians and friends of the University were as vigilant and active as its enemies?"[70]

The enemies of the university had continued their attacks against it even after the Holy Father had ordered the opposition to desist. In the fall of 1893 Ireland asked O'Connell:

Have you seen the late despatch to the N. Y. Herald—an interview with a prominent Jesuit, saying that Satolli is, of course, accepted, but that no peace can be made with Ireland or the Catholic University. I presume this is their program. Bp. Keane answered their attack on the University. He fears with reason that the war will continue.[71]

[67] BCA, 91-R-5, D. J. O'Connell to J. Card. Gibbons, Rome, August 4, 1893.

[68] BCA, 91-T-4, John J. Keane to J. Card. Gibbons, August 25, 1893.

[69] RDA, John J. Keane to D. J. O'Connell, Atlantic City, October 10, 1893.

[70] *Fifth Annual Report of the Rector*, p. 5.

[71] RDA, John Ireland to D. J. O'Connell, New York, October 23, 1893. In the interview with the prominent Jesuit it was stated: "It is not exact to say that we [Jesuits] are making war on the University of Washington, but it must

The rector suspected that the prominent Jesuit was the same S. M. Brandi who had written against the University in *Civiltà Cattolica* during the school controversy. Keane told O'Connell about the whole affair:

Fr. Brandi tried a trick on me lately. I rec'd a letter a few days ago from Card. Rampolla, saying that the Holy Father had learned that I had accused Fr. Brandi of being the author of an attack on the Univ. in the N. Y. Herald—that Fr. B. denied it, and that the Holy Father w'd be pleased if I would correct it. I answered by a statement showing that the charge ag'st Fr. B. was made by the Herald, an issue of veracity in which I could not interfere, & showing that as Fr. B. must have clearly understood this, his charge ag'st me was dishonest. The Cardinal forwards my letter with one of his own. I trust all will pass thro' your hands. Then comes a letter from Fr. B. to me, saying that he "repudiates & condemns" the attack on the Univ., and complaining that *the Herald* should have attributed it to him. I have answered, expressing my satisfaction at receiving his repudiation & condemnation, suggesting that he make it public, & expressing my amazement that, knowing the charge to have come from the Herald, he should have accused me of it to the Pope. They too seem on the defensive, but their "art is long." [72]

Keane informed Ireland shortly thereafter that Brandi actually was the author of the attack and the St. Paul prelate minced no words when he informed O'Connell about it: "Brandi is a devil. He now writes to Keane that he never spoke against the Univer-

---

not be forgotton that for a century past the Jesuits have had a flourishing university.

"When there was a question of establishing a Catholic University the Jesuits pointed out that it would be better to locate the projected university in some other city, as there was already such an institution in Washington" (New York *Herald*, October 13, 1893).

[72] RDA, John J. Keane to D. J. O'Connell, Washington, November 16, 1893. After Brandi had protested to the Holy Father about Keane accusing him of being the author of the attack on the university, Rampolla wrote to the rector for an explanation (M. Card. Rampolla to John J. Keane, Rome, October 30, 1893 (Italian)). When Keane answered he sent clippings of the newspaper items in question which absolved him of any accusation against Brandi (ACUA, John J. Keane to M. Card. Rampolla, Washington, November 12, 1893 (French), copy). O'Connell presented Keane's letter to Rampolla and in his report to the rector, he said: "The Pope would support the University. We agreed that Father Brandi was provoking too many complaints" (ACUA, D. J. O'Connell to John J. Keane, Rome, December 4, 1893).

sity, but the Herald told Keane that Brandi was its informant."[73] When Cardinal Gibbons transmitted the rector's reply to Rampolla's letter, he told the Cardinal Secretary of State: "I cannot forbear showing you the deep sorrow I feel at the continuation of attacks against the University in spite of the well-known intentions of His Holiness."[74]

There had been so many trials during the early days of the infant institution that it is a wonder that many bishops did not despair entirely of its survival. O'Connell told Gibbons: "I see a great deal of Bp. Spalding. He will do no harm tho' he does not hesitate to proclaim everywhere that the University is a failure."[75] Yet there were other bishops who were more optimistic, such as Thomas S. Byrne of Nashville, who "spoke strongly in favor of the University" on the day of his consecration (July 24, 1894), and Jeremiah O'Sullivan, Bishop of Mobile, who told O'Connell in 1894: "I hope the Holy Father will continue to uphold it. The failure of the University would be a calamity to the Church in the U. S."[76]

The university, its rector, and its professors continued to be a source of annoyance to Bishop McQuaid of Rochester, who wrote to Corrigan:

The Boston Pilot had a very mean letter from Dr. Garrigan of the U. anent the reported refusal of a New York court to permit the mort-

---

[73] RDA, John Ireland to D. J. O'Connell, St. Paul, November 24, 1893. It is difficult to determine whether Keane actually received explicit information on the authorship of the attack on the university. In a letter from the Washington Bureau of the New York *Herald* it was stated: "By reference to the original manuscript I find that Father Brandi is given as authority for the statement to which you replied just as it appears in the clipping I mailed you last night.

"It seems quite evident, therefore, that the error was made by the gentleman in this office who wrote the introduction to the interview with you — a mistake probably caused by a hasty reading of the statement upon which the interview was based" (ACUA, George W. Rouzer to John J. Keane, Washington, November 13, 1893). After Keane had been dismissed from the university the same Jesuit told Corrigan: "If the 'Canon' is hardly worked, nobody knows it in Rome. So far, he has not been consulted by any congregation" (NYAA, G-24, S. M. Brandi, S. J., to M. A. Corrigan, Rome, May 1, 1897).

[74] BCA, 92-R-2, J. Card. Gibbons to M. Card. Rampolla, Baltimore, November 14, 1893 (French), copy.

[75] BCA, 93-B-3, D. J. O'Connell to J. Card. Gibbons, Rome, January 17, 1894.

[76] RDA, Jeremiah O'Sullivan to D. J. O'Connell, Mobile, August 8, 1894.

146

gaging of its property, insinuating that the story originated in N. Y. from some enemy of the U.

It is about time for a fresh cable from Rome summoning you to trial or something else equally ridiculous.[77]

The Rochester prelate had another occasion to write his friend about the university early in 1894 when he was defeated for the nomination as a regent of the University of the State of New York at the hands of Father Sylvester Malone of Brooklyn. McQuaid rightly suspected that persons outside of New York had been instrumental in causing his defeat and he was determined to find out who those persons were. He told Corrigan:

It is all important to find out all about the outside clerical meddlers in the affairs of this state. Archbp. Ireland is one, but there are others. I shall not be surprised to learn that among them are some University professors. It is just what O'Gorman would do.[78]

By that same fall he had become certain of the identity of the "meddlers" and his patience with them had reached the breaking point. He preached a sermon from the pulpit of the cathedral in November, 1894, in which he assailed John Ireland by name for taking part in Republican politics in the State of New York. Besides his accusations against the St. Paul prelate, he claimed:

He was helped, in this political and behind-the-door crusade against the Bishops of the State of New York by high dignitaries on the Pacific Coast. There was sojourning in San Francisco, at the time, a high dignitary from the East [Bishop Keane, Rector of the Catholic University of Washington],—the same who afterwards was the panegyrist of the Rev. Mr. Malone on the occasion of his jubilee.[79]

When Rochester's bishop explained his attack on Ireland at the request of Rome, he seized the opportunity to unburden himself of all his grievances against the liberals and the university. He told Cardinal Ledochowski:

These priests of New York [Ducey, Nilan, Burtsell, Malone, Corrigan of Hoboken], with the help of two or three professors at the Washing-

---

[77] NYAA, G-9, Bernard J. McQuaid to M. A. Corrigan, Rochester, February 16, 1894.

[78] NYAA, Bishops &c., Bernard J. McQuaid to M. A. Corrigan, Rochester, March 31, 1894, cited in Zwierlein, op. cit., III, 204.

[79] Rochester Democrat and Chronicle, November 26, 1894, cited in Zwierlein, op. cit., III, 209. The brackets are Zwierlein's.

ton University, poisoned the mind of the Apostolic Delegate against Mgr. Corrigan, making him believe that the latter was opposed to the delegation. . . .

Of late years, a spirit of liberalism is springing up in our body under such leaders as Mgr. Ireland and Mgr. Keane, that, if not checked in time, will bring disaster on the church. Many a time Catholic laymen have remarked that the Catholic Church they once knew seems to be passing away, so greatly shocked are they at what they see passing around them.[80]

Such accusations against the university's rector had no immediate effect in Rome, but they may have had a cumulative effect and contributed to bringing about his dismissal a few years later.

The year 1894 was another trying one for the university and its rector. The Board of Trustees, at their meeting on April 4, received a report from the committee on studies and discipline in which it was recommended that an investigation be made into the cause of the lack of interest in the university on the part of many of the hierarchy and clergy which was the chief drawback to its success.[81] Ignatius Horstmann told Corrigan that when this report was read "Keane immediately demanded whether that was intended as a reflection on him and the faculty." The chairman of the committee, Placide L. Chapelle, assured the rector that such was not their intention, but "*fact* confronted us and that it was necessary to find out the causes of that fact."[82] As a result of the committee's recommendation, the archbishops of the board were appointed to confer with the other metropolitans of the country to find out as far as was possible why there was such lack of interest among the bishops and clergy.[83] They were to make a report at the next meeting of the board, but, if they did so, the writer could find no record of it.

As far as the rector was concerned the meeting of the board was "very satisfactory," for he was anxious about matters that seemed to be more important in his mind, namely, Rome's atti-

[80] Bernard J. McQuaid to M. Card. Ledochowski, 1895, original draft in the possession of F. Zwierlein, cited in Zwierlein, *op. cit.*, III, 223-224.

[81] ACUA, MMBT, Washington, April 4, 1894, p. 46.

[82] NYAA, CUA file, Ign. F. H. Horstmann to M. A. Corrigan, Cleveland, April 21, 1894.

[83] ACUA, MMBT, Washington, April 4, 1894, p. 46.

tude towards the university. After the meeting he told Denis O'Connell:

Our Faculty has been very anxious, as also Mgr. Satolli, that the Cardinal should go to Rome at the earliest possible day, in order to dispel these clouds of whisper & suspicion which so assiduously are gathered around the Holy Father, in regard to Mgr. Satolli, in regard to the University, in regard to the general tendency of so-called "liberalism" among us. . . .

The faculty urged very strongly that I, as rector, ought to go to Rome along with the Cardinal. They think the University ought to show itself boldly & speak out strongly,—that we greatly need another clear and strong word from the Holy Father, in view of recent attacks on the University, and because of our opening the next Faculty, for the laity, in October '95, which calls for endless activity & generosity for the raising of funds & securing of students & for general encouragement and cooperation.[84]

The rector took the advice of his faculty, probably seconded by O'Connell without whose approval no move was made in Rome. Keane and O'Gorman set out for Rome in the summer of 1894. O'Gorman arrived in Rome ahead of the rector. He had a long talk with Rampolla who "pumped him thoroughly, & arranged that he should see the Pope, who for over an hour eagerly probed the condition, as to the delegation, as to the University, as to the condition of things in general."[85] O'Connell later told Gibbons that "the Pope took a great fancy to O'Gorman and attaches much weight to his opinions."[86] Thus the ground was prepared for Keane when he arrived at the Vatican. He was given an hour and a half audience with Leo XIII and he informed Cardinal Gibbons later in a lengthy letter about what had transpired:

. . . . we got at the University. First I explained our success and presented an album of photographic views. Then we came to our difficulties, and discussed fully the opposition 1° of the Germans, 2° of the Jesuits, 3° of N. Y.—4° of all opposed to Mgr. Satolli and his policy, with which they identify the University. The last point launched us into the discussion of the delegation and Mgr. S. Here is where the Pope is most determined, because the delegation is simply an element in his "policy", which is, the breaking down of the influence

---

[84] RDA, John J. Keane to D. J. O'Connell, Washington, April 13, 1894.

[85] BCA, 93-J-7, John J. Keane to J. Card. Gibbons, Pegli, July 31, 1894.

[86] BCA, 93-K-7, D. J. O'Connell to J. Card. Gibbons, Grottaferrata, September 9, 1894.

of the Triple Alliance,—which means monarchism, militarism, and the oppression of the Papacy,—by enhancing the influence of democratic France and democratic America—an influence which presages democratic Italy, or Federated Italy, with the Pope in a position suitable to him. On this policy he is inflexibly bent, and the welcome given to the representative of the Pope in America was a most hopeful sign of the rallying of all democracy around the Pope. In this there may be an exaggeration, but there is also a great truth,—the Church and the Democracy are fast drawing nearer. Hence opposition to Satolli and the delegation was the worst hostility to the Pope, and he is ready to discipline the opposition and to enhance the authority of the delegation. This is going to be the central feature and motive of what he will say and do,—and he told me plainly that he was going to speak and act. He did not give me details, and of course I did not venture to ask for them. But it seems most likely that he will make the delegation the *final and obligatory* court of appeal from the Metropolitan courts of the country, and enhance Mgr. S's personal dignity as much as possible.

He regards the University as bound up with the same "policy", as an integral part of it, and it too shall be absolutely sustained against all opposition. He intends to speak strongly of it in the Encyclical which he is preparing to send to America in the near future,—*how* near we could not ascertain.[87]

The rector was entirely satisfied with the outcome of his visit to Rome. After leaving he wrote to O'Connell: "I leave Rome with a more contented and hopeful mind than ever before. A wonderful transformation is being operated there."[88] He thus returned to his post with renewed strength and with high hopes for a more peaceful year.

On January 6, 1895, the promised encyclical—in the preparation of which O'Gorman had a hand[89]—and which the liberals awaited so expectantly, was finished and dispatched to America. Keane had accurately foretold the contents of the encyclical letter *Longinqua oceani* in his letter to Gibbons. The apostolic delegation was the central theme; it was to be accepted by all parties because the delegate was the representative of the Sovereign

[87] BCA, 93-J-7, John J. Keane to J. Card. Gibbons, Pegli, July 31, 1894.

[88] RDA, John J. Keane to D. J. O'Connell, Pegli, August 3, 1894.

[89] BCA, 93-K-7, D. J. O'Connell to J. Card. Gibbons, Grottaferrata, September 9, 1894. The Pope told O'Connell: "O'Gorman helped me a great deal: He gave me many notes but now I must go over them myself and make them my own, I shall give them another coloring, but the substance will be there."

Pontiff. He was the symbol of unity and his presence in America should be conducive to unity. In his excellent commentary on the encyclical in the *American Catholic Quarterly Review*, Schroeder said:

Unity is an essential quality of the Church; it is at the same time the strength of the hierarchy, the clergy, and the people; it must be the characteristic mark of every Catholic institution; it will insure the success of every work of faith or of charity. Hence the Holy Father insists on unity in several parts of the encyclical.[90]

Discord, the result of the lack of unity, had been the lot of the American Church for some years previous, just as it had been the curse of the university faculty. With regard to the university, the Holy Father first cited the "prosperity and glory" of the Belgian nation that was ascribed to the influence of the University of Louvain and then he added:

Equally abundant will be the benefits proceeding from the Washington University if the professors and students (as we doubt not they will) be mindful of Our injuctions, and, party spirit and strife being removed, conciliate the good opinion of the people and clergy.[91]

Yet "party spirit and strife" continued. Neither in the university nor in the American Church at large was the goal of unity reached. Neither could it have been expected after so many issues, based on party adherence, had precluded rational consideration of the harm that was being done to the Church and to the university. Neither liberals nor conservatives could be immediately purged of their mutually obnoxious tenets by a single letter from the See of Peter.

Faculty discord continued at the university. A few months after the encyclical had been published Dumont told his friend, Rex, in his usual shaky English:

Fr. Orban was yesterday in Balto. & really there is there much talk about the University & against it; what good does this talk do us? & it is carried on in the presence of University students, were all the sayings brought back to the Professors? Will all this help much the 2 Sulpicians now at the University? Will not or at least may it not be

---

[90] Joseph Schroeder, "Leo XIII and the Encyclical 'Longinqua'," *A CQR*, XX (April, 1895), 379.

[91] "Encyclical Letter," *C UB*, I (April, 1895), 236. The Latin text and an English translation of the encyclical may also be found in *A CQR*, XX (April, 1895), 346-368.

said that all these reports originate with them; practically we are made victims, indeed a very unenviable position.[92]

Just before the close of the scholastic year in 1895, Dumont again wrote his friend:

Dissentions [sic] between Professors are far from healing. Last Sunday they had a very stormy meeting, 2 left the room, one was threatened with polite intervention & with expulsion, Dean followed 2 through the hall ways, angry discussions, students hearing all, a P. one insulted in the room being qualified as the meanest fellow ever known leaves the meeting, students know who used the language & against whom used. Enough of it, such a state of things is sickening.

Fr. Orban is well, greatly enjoys the comedy, as one of the Professors told me: what is worse is: so petty are the causes of such dissentions [sic]; Fr. Hogan would immensely enjoy all this.[93]

This letter probably referred to the difficulties that had arisen over the *Catholic University Bulletin*, the first issue of which was published in January, 1895. Keane reported the difficulties thus:

These alienations [that existed between Peries and some members of the faculty] were intensified by an event which ought to have had a different effect. This was the establishment of the University Bulletin. Dr. Peries was on the committee which discussed the matter with me. Dr. Shahan was chosen as editor. The bulk of the Professors rallied to the work, as requested in general invitation. The first number was a great success. It had no article from Drs. Schroeder, Peries, & Hyvernat. The cry was raised that they had been excluded, "boycotted." The committee met & repudiated any exclusion of any Professor, & declared the Bulletin was open to all. The Senate endorsed this. But it did not satisfy Drs. S. & P. Dr. Hyvernat yielded and contributed. The others demanded public apology! and, this being very properly refused, as no offence had been given, or intended, they maintained their injured attitude. It was sent forth to the press, and the German papers of the country were full of "the boycott," & of denunciations of the Bulletin, of the University & its officials.[94]

The rector evidently began to look for some legal means to rid the faculty of one of the causes of discord, for in the late summer of 1895 he requested the opinion of George E. Hamilton, the same

[92] SMSA, L. F. Dumont, S.S., to Charles B. Rex, S.S., Washington, March 20, 1895.

[93] SMSA, L. F. Dumont, S.S., to Charles B. Rex, S.S., Washington, June 6, 1895.

[94] ACUA, "Chronicles," pp. 58-59.

152

lawyer who had refused Satolli's invitation to aggregate the faculty of law at Georgetown University with the Catholic University of America in 1894.[95] Keane interrogated Hamilton on the rights of a professor in a sample case which he presented.[96] He received an answer that assured him that he would be able to proceed with his plans without any fear of legal complications, for the sample case was in reality the case of Peries who, according to the rector, had been engaged for three years in 1893. Before coming to the university the canon law professor had known Shahan and Bouquillon but after his arrival he "associated almost exclusively with Dr. Schroeder." The rector claimed "it was a taking of sides, & of course resulted accordingly. Moreover, he from the first acted as one victimized by the Faculty & the officials. Outbursts of the saddest character ensued."[97] Peries probably was informed that he would not be retained beyond that scholastic year (1895-1896), so he wrote to Corrigan in February:

I am sending you by the same mail a copy of my letter of resignation to my chair of C. L. in the Catholic University, in which I protest in moderate, but forcible words against the bad treatment inflicted on me and the violation of the Constitutions.

I spent my vacation with my dear mother, trying to obtain from her the leave of coming back to the United States, for I like to live there and feel there is for me a large and useful field to work in. I told her how good your Grace had been to promise me an official situation in New York. I hope she would give me her consent if you had a definite position to propose to me and I could thus persuade her to cross and live with me at least a few months every year. The Card. Richard, when I saw him, told me he wanted my services and would give me a nice place in Paris.[98]

He must have changed his mind about resigning, for the board decided to engage him for another year when they met on April 15, 1896.[99] This decision was reconsidered three days later at another meeting of the board. During these three days a confidential report was made to the chancellor by Bouquillon, Shahan, and Grannan in which they rejected the board's decision

[95] *Supra*, p. 102.

[96] ACUA, G. E. Hamilton to John J. Keane, Washington, September 3, 1895.

[97] ACUA, "Chronicles," pp. 57-58.

[98] NYAA, G-20, G. Peries to M. A. Corrigan, St. Mande, February 14, 1896.

[99] ACUA, MMBT, Washington, April 15, 1896, p. 56.

to retain the professor of canon law for another year. Among other things they claimed:

1. To compromise further would only destroy the prestige & dignity of the University. . . .

2. It is to the interest of the University & of this gentleman that he should not be reengaged for another year. If he remains, we are exposed to the danger of intrigues & calumnies both among our students & in the city. If he remains, he will place himself in an equivocal position,—in a position of inferiority & not enjoying the confidence of his colleagues, nor of the Rector, nor of the Board of Directors.

3. His presence for even one year longer would diminish the devotion & self-sacrifice of those professors who have borne the brunt & the burden of the hard work for years past, & who are still willing to bear it for the future; but to bear it they need peace. No man can be in his normal condition nor do effective work, while living in a turmoil. . . .

4. We desire to protest against the disloyal manner in which the Rt. Rev. Rector was treated, so long as it was supposed that there was no written documentary evidence for the three year contract.[100]

At the meeting of the board on April 18, the rector made a statement to the members in which he affirmed that he had contracted with Peries for only three years and he read a letter that had been written to Bouquillon at the time the contract was made to corroborate his statement. It was recorded in the minutes of the meeting:

The rector declared that Dr. Peries was incompetent to teach Canon Law for this country; that his students were dissatisfied with him; that his language concerning him as Rector had been most contemptuous, and that he had spoken publicly in Washington against the Rector and the University.

Archbishop Ireland confirmed this last charge declaring that he had abundant evidence of the fact.[101]

Peries had anticipated such action and he gained some advocates, chief among whom was Bishop Ignatius Horstmann of Cleveland. The rector reported:

A document was read for himself denying that his contract was for 3 years. He presented letters from the Sulpitians above named [Dissez and Many]; but written before the contract was presented to him at all, and coming from parties who had no part in the contract.[102]

[100] BCA, 94-Y-1, Th. Bouquillon, Chas. P. Grannan, Thos. J. Shahan, Confidential Report to Cardinal Gibbons, n.d.

[101] ACUA, MMBT, April 18, 1896, p. 58.

[102] ACUA, "Chronicles," p. 59.

After all the evidence had been presented, the board decided not to engage the professor for another year. Archbishop Ryan did not vote on the issue and "Bishop Horstmann and Father Lee demanded that their vote in the negative [for retention] be entered in the minutes."[103]

Peries then carried his case to the apostolic delegate in spite of the fact that the delegate tried to persuade him not to present his brief.[104] The brief was submitted to the rector for reply. Bouquillon prepared the reply which "was so clear & crushing that the Delegate declared that Dr. Peries had no case."[105] Peries then withdrew his appeal and wrote Cardinal Gibbons that he had come to the university with the conviction that he had been appointed to a "perpetual chair as my colleagues have been." He proposed that the cardinal and the delegate ask the board to allow him to retain his chair for two more years and that he would present his resignation the "next year or sooner" if he could find an honorable position.[106] In response to this plea an extension of one year was granted "at the end of which time his connection with the Univ'y would expire, *ipso facto*."[107] Peries did not avail himself of the extension. Keane recorded: "At the end of vacation he writes that he will not return to the Univ'y, and sends

[103] ACUA, MMBT, April 18, 1896, p. 59.

[104] BCA, 94-L-12, Francesco Satolli to J. Card. Gibbons, Washington, April 26, 1896. Cf. ACUA, G. Peries to Ign. F. Horstmann, Washington, April 20, 1896.

[105] ACUA, "Chronicles," p. 60. Peries' brief consisted of six typewritten pages, in French (ACUA, Francesco Satolli to John J. Keane, Washington, April 16, 1896). The reply, composed by Bouquillon, consisted of nine typewritten pages, in French, accompanied by pertinent documents, the most important of which was a letter written to Bouquillon by Keane at the time that Peries was engaged, in which the rector stated: "Immediately on receiving your letter, I laid the case of M. Peries before the Directors. Their vote is in the affirmative; and by the same mail I send him our invitation, and proposal for a contract for three years, renewable at the pleasure of both parties. I have also written to Cardinal Richard" (ACUA, John J. Keane to Th. Bouquillon, Washington, August 11, 1893). Peries claimed to have lost the letter written by Keane so when this letter was produced his case was practically closed. All these documents are in ACUA under the covering letter of John J. Keane to Francesco Satolli, Washington, May 4, 1896.

[106] ACUA, G. Peries to J. Card. Gibbons, Washington, May 9, 1896 (French); G. Peries to Francesco Satolli, Washington, May 10, 1896 (French), copy.

[107] ACUA, "Chronicles," p. 60; J. Card. Gibbons to G. Peries, Baltimore, May 21, 1896. On this letter Peries signed his name under the sentence: "I subscribe to the above."

his 'resignation' to Abp. Ryan to be presented to the Board."[108] The documents show that in the same month of May, 1896, Gibbons wrote a letter to Peries' superior, Cardinal Richard, in which he recommended the professor as a talented and zealous priest who had worked diligently for three years and who had attracted a great number of students to his class. The chancellor expressed the hope that the Cardinal Archbishop of Paris would give the professor a position in keeping with his zeal and with his capacities.[109] Also during the same month of May, Keane wrote to Gibbons:

I am glad indeed that the matter with Dr. Peries has been finally settled. But I shall daily pray that he may be kept in Paris,—for his mercurial temperament would keep us in constant uncertainty all next year.[110]

All these facts in the case of George Peries were important in view of his activities in France a few years later during the controversy over Father Hecker's doctrine when he wrote scathing articles against the American Catholic liberals in *La Vérité* under the name of "Saint-Clement."[111] Keane told Walter Elliott of the Paulists during the trying days of the Americanism quarrel that Peries was "trying to take the revenge which he threatened" when he was removed from the chair of canon law at the university.[112]

Towards the close of the scholastic year 1896, the university faculty's relations approached the ideal of unity that had been so strongly desired and urged by the Holy Father in his encyclical. Keane said:

[108] ACUA, "Chronicles," p. 60; G. Peries to J. Card. Gibbons, St. Mande, September 8, 1896; G. Peries to P. J. Ryan, St. Mande, September 11, 1896; "Letter of Resignation to the Board of Directors of the Catholic University of America sent to his Grace the Archbishop of Philadelphia chairman of the Committee for the appointment of Professors," St. Mande, September 8, 1896, printed.

[109] BCA, 94-M-11, J. Card. Gibbons to François Card. Richard, Baltimore, May 21, 1896 (French), copy.

[110] BCA, 94-M-13, John J. Keane to J. Card. Gibbons, Washington, May 23, 1896. At the meeting of the Board of Trustees on October 26, 1896, "The letter of resignation of Rev. Dr. Peries as Professor of Canon Law was ordered to be preserved in the archives" (ACUA, MMBT, Washington, October 26, 1896, p. 63).

[111] Peter E. Hogan, "Americanism and the Catholic University of America," *CHR*, XXXIII (July, 1947), 158-190.

[112] PFA, John J. Keane to Walter Elliott, Rome, April 19, 1898.

All elements of discord seemed to have burned themselves out. Dr. Schroeder, after a conversation with Abp. Ireland, expressed his good will for peace, & promised to write for the Bulletin[113] & work for the establishment of a Chair of German, which I had public [*sic*] recommended & strongly urged. He was met more than half way by myself and all. And so harmony and union seemed to have prevailed at last.[114]

Within a brief time the temporary peace was violently disturbed once more, but when that occurred Bishop Keane was no longer there to help in its restoration.[115]

While the rector was working for what he believed was the elimination of the causes of discord in the university faculty, the institution and some of its professors were still being attacked on the grounds of liberalism. O'Gorman and Pace had been invited to lecture before the Columbian Catholic Summer School in Madison, Wisconsin, by John Zahm, C.S.C., chairman of the school's committee on study and lectures. After the arrangements had been agreed upon by the professors and the chairman, both O'Gorman and Pace received a letter from Sebastian Messmer, a former professor at the university, who was then Bishop of Green Bay and President of the Columbian Catholic Summer School, informing them that he regretted that they had been engaged.[116] To O'Gorman he wrote:

We had laid it down as a rule last year not to engage, or invite any professor from the University for our platform. Again, having been

---

[113] Gibbons wrote Schroeder on April 23, 1896: "I earnestly hope that in the next and future numbers of the Bulletin your name will appear" (BCA, 94-L-10, copy). Schroeder answered on April 26: "I shall cheerfully comply with your request as well as that of the Apostolic Delegate" (BCA, 94-L-13).

[114] ACUA, "Chronicles," p. 61.

[115] Peter E. Hogan, "Thomas J. Conaty, Second Rector of the Catholic University of America, 1896-1903" (Unpublished master's thesis, Department of History, Catholic University of America, 1947), pp. 106-112; 155-161. Maurice Francis Egan, professor of English Literature at the university during these years, made this observation in his *Recollections of a Happy Life*: "The discord of opinions or convictions among the ecclesiastics themselves was a constant source of embarrassment and difficulty. Cardinal Gibbons, making no reference whatever to the laity, often declared that it was harder to govern the University than the whole of his diocese; and I always thought that the war march of the priests from *Attila*, which the organist played for the opening procession at the beginning of the year, was singularly appropriate" (Egan, *op. cit.*, p. 189).

[116] ACUA, S. G. Messmer to Edward A. Pace, Green Bay, January 20, 1896.

157

exposed to a great deal of incrimination last year on account of Dr. Zahm's expression on the evolution of man, we have to be much more careful this year to have no theories or opinions put forth from our boards which would not find acceptance with all. For this reason myself and others objected at once to arrangement made by Dr. Zahm. But to relieve him of his delicate position we compromised by instructing him to inform you of the sentiments of the Board and to ask you— in case you still desire to lecture to us—to choose a subject where there will be no danger of advancing theories or opinions which would or might involve the school into difficulties or controversies.[117]

Messmer did not know at the time he wrote his letter that O'Gorman was the Bishop-Elect of Sioux Falls. Ireland had written Gibbons the week before to tell him that he had been informed in the strictest confidence that O'Gorman had been chosen for Sioux Falls and that, "ferocious attacks had been made on the whole list submitted to Rome, as liberals, semi-heretical, etc., especially was O'Gorman torn to pieces." In spite of these attacks Ireland's recommendation was sustained.[118]

To Pace the Green Bay prelate wrote substantially the same as he had written to O'Gorman, substituting the name of Faben for that of Zahm, as chairman of the committee on studies and lecturers and adding:

Whatever each one's private opinion may be, the fact cannot be denied that the Catholic University and its Professors and Rector are not looked upon with favor by many of our Catholics. Together with others I therefore objected at once to the arrangement made by Rev. Faben.[119]

Messmer then told Pace that a compromise had been made whereby they would consent to his lecturing *only in the clear understanding* that you will not treat or give rise to dispute and unpleasant objections." Messmer went on to tell him that since the meeting he had regretted the compromise, and now "I most respectfully ask you to kindly cancel your engagement." He assured Pace that it was not personal antipathy that forced him to make such an unseemly request and he felt sure that the university professor would understand.[120]

[117] ACUA, S. G. Messmer to Thomas O'Gorman, Green Bay, January 20, 1896.

[118] BCA, 94-G-8, John Ireland to J. Card. Gibbons, St. Paul, January 13, 1896.

[119] ACUA, S. G. Messmer to Edward A. Pace, Green Bay, January 20, 1896.
[120] *Ibid*.

158

If Pace had not understood he was enlightened by Zahm, whom Messmer had informed about his request that Pace cancel the promised lectures. The chairman wrote to Washington immediately:

I trust you will do nothing of the kind. The board was unanimous in asking you to lecture, & is still unanimous in desiring to hear you give the promised course. Only two persons opposed your appointment, & neither of these belong to the board of Studies. One of these was Bishop Messmer himself, & the other a layman, a follower of Fr. Hughes. The only reason assigned by either of these gentlemen was that you were not sound in philosophy, that you were dangerously liberal, etc. The board knows what all this means, & hope that you will favor us with your presence as agreed between us. There is a principle and a cause at stake & I trust that you will not see them sacrificed to satisfy two self-constituted inquisitors. . . . The interests of the Catholic University are at stake, & you being forced out by one or two who do not express the wishes of the majority will eventually have a bad effect on our institution—the Catholic University—whose success we so much desire.[121]

The two professors did not disappoint the chairman, for they shared his desire for the success of the university,[122] and, presumably, the vindication of their own views.

In an attempt to explain this attitude on the part of Messmer, Keane recorded in the "Chronicles" that when Messmer was chosen for the See of Green Bay, he had co-operated with him in his attempt "to escape the mitre."[123] The rector said:

Since then I have learned to my dismay & disgust that I have been represented as having worked to "get him out of the University !" When I wrote to him about it, he disclaimed responsibility for the rumor, but went on, while writing very kindly of myself personally, to write of all those associated with me, that is the Professors, in the most condemnatory terms.[124]

Therefore, Bishop Keane considered this portrayal of Messmer's animus towards the institution and its professors as "unpardonable." In reality it was probably just another expression of the conservative tendencies of the party to which Messmer belonged,

---

[121] ACUA, John Zahm to Edward A. Pace, Notre Dame, January 27, 1896.
[122] ACUA, "Chronicles," p. 56.
[123] *Supra*, pp. 50-51.
[124] ACUA, "Chronicles," pp. 55-56.

the party that could see nothing good in the institution which Keane directed.

Discord also continued in the press, in spite of Leo XIII's admonitions in *Longinqua oceani*. In the enclyclical he had advised:

Those who desire to be of real service to the Church, and with their pens heartily to defend the Catholic cause, should carry on the conflict with perfect unanimity, and, as it were, with serried ranks; for they rather inflict than repel war if they waste their strength by discord. In like manner their work, instead of being profitable and fruitful, becomes injurious and disastrous when they presume to call before their tribunal decisions and acts of Bishops, and casting off due reverence, cavil and find fault, not perceiving how great a disturbance of order and how many evils are thereby produced. Let them then, be mindful of their duties and not overstep the proper limits of moderation.[125]

Still editors of Catholic papers failed to heed the desires of the Sovereign Pontiff which were so clearly stated. Keane wrote George Zurcher, a priest of the Diocese of Buffalo and an ardent temperance advocate:

Permit me to ask of you a great favor. You have doubtless noticed the persistency with which many of the German Catholic papers have kept up an attack of insults and misrepresentations against the institution. Every approval of the Holy Father here only serves to intensify their malignity. You have yourself suffered enough from similar attacks to be able to appreciate the animus of them. We have thus far let these insults and calumnies pass unnoticed, but now it seems plainly our duty to ask the attention of the board of directors to the matter. . . . . Could you, dear friend, from such of these papers as you are acquainted with, make a small collection of such pieces, with name of paper and date, and send them to me? [126]

The continued agitation over the university in the press was probably a reflection of the opposition that must have been carried on in Rome by those hostile to the institution and its rector.

In 1896 the liberals received their greatest surprise when one of their constant and most influential supporters deserted them. Keane had been at first the close friend of Francesco Satolli, the apostolic delegate, and their friendship continued for a number of years. He was one of the rector's chief advisers during the search

[125] "Encyclical Letter," *CUB*, I (April, 1895), 244-245.
[126] Cited in the Buffalo *Express*, October 6, 1896.

for the first faculty. When he came to America as ablegate in 1892, he was cordially received by the liberals and carefully "shielded" from the influence of the conservatives. He took up residence at the university and remained there until his own home was provided after he had been appointed the first apostolic delegate. He supported the liberal wing of the hierarchy in the school controversy and in its stand against Cahenslyism. He further deprecated the attacks against the university and castigated the perpetrators of such charges. But just when the so-called liberals felt themselves in final possession of the results of the campaign they had so carefully waged, Satolli deserted them. With his former support now changed to active participation in the conservative campaign against the liberal causes, there was no dam to stem and to divert the flood of complaints and accusations that made their way to Rome against the university and its rector. Rome finally made a decision that changed the fortunes of the liberals for a time and caused the problems of the Church in America to be once more aired before the general public. The Holy See dismissed John J. Keane from his position as rector of the Catholic University of America.[127]

[127] Pope Leo XIII to John J. Keane, Rome, September 15, 1896, cited in "Right Rev. John Jospeh Keane, D.D.," *CUB*, II (October, 1896), 583.

CHAPTER V

KEANE'S DISMISSAL AND VINDICATION

Bishop Keane spent the summer of 1896 resting at St. Gildas de Rhuys in Brittany, and in the Channel Islands. When he returned to America for the re-opening of the university, he looked forward to a peaceful year, since the differences among the faculty members had been settled in the main the previous spring. Then on September 28 Cardinal Gibbons telegraphed for him to come to Baltimore and there he handed him the following letter from Pope Leo XIII:[1]

To our Venerable Brother, John Joseph Keane, Bishop of Ajasso:

Venerable Brother Health and Apostolic Benediction: It is customary that they who are appointed to preside over Catholic universities should not hold the office in perpetuity. This custom has grown up through wise reasons, and the Roman pontiffs have ever been careful that it should be adhered to. Since, therefore, Venerable Brother, You have now presided for several years over the University at Washington, in the first establishment and subsequent development of which you have shown laudable zeal and diligence, it has seemed best that the above-mentioned custom should not be departed from, and that another, whose name is to be proposed to us by the Bishops, should be appointed to succeeed you in this honorable position. In order, however, that in your resigning this office, due regard may be had to your person and your dignity, we have determined to elevate you to the rank of Archbishop.

Being solicitous for your future welfare we leave it to your own free choice either to remain in your own country, or, if you prefer it, to come to Rome. If you choose the former, we will destine for you some archiepiscopal see, by vote of the Bishops of the United States. If you prefer the latter we shall welcome you most lovingly, and will place you among the Consultors of the Congregation of Studies and the Congregation of the Propaganda, in both of which you could do much for the interest of religion in the United States. In this case we would also assign you a suitable revenue for your honorable maintenance.

Confidently trusting, Venerable Brother, that you will accept this, our administrative act, with hearty good will, we most lovingly bes-

---

[1] ACUA, "Chronicles," pp. 60-61.

162

tow upon you the apostolic benediction, as a pledge of our paternal affection.

Given at Rome, from St. Peter's, this 15th day of September, 1896, in the nineteenth year of our pontificate.

Leo XIII, Pope.[2]

Under the circumstances such a letter would have caused thoughts of resentment and rebellion to crowd the mind of the ordinary man. The rector's reactions were conveyed to Rampolla in a letter from Cardinal Gibbons:

Bishop Keane received the letter by which the Holy Father discharged him from his functions with the greatest calm and, without a moment's hesitation, received that decision not only with the respect due to the will of the Pope, but also, I am able to say, with a sensible joy, seeing in it more the manifestation of the will of God in his regard.[3]

Yet cannot the reader detect a little more closely the more intimate feelings of the rector as portrayed in the last paragraph of the letter which he immediately sent to the Holy Father?

Most Holy Father:

His Eminence, Cardinal Gibbons, yesterday handed me the letter in which your Holiness has made known to me that my administration of this University now comes to an end, and that another rector is to be appointed.

Without a moment of hesitation I accept the will of your Holiness in the matter as a manifestation of the providence of God, and from this instant I resign into the hands of His Eminence, the Chancellor, the office of Rector, with all the rights thereto attaching.

Thanking your Holiness for the freedom of choice granted me, I choose to remain in my own country, and, moreover, without any official position whatsoever, in tranquillity and peace. Your Holiness' most humble son in Christ.

JOHN J. KEANE
Bishop of Ajasso.[4]

[2] Pope Leo XIII to John J. Keane, Rome, September 15, 1896, cited in "Right Rev. John Jospeh Keane, D.D.," *CUB*, II (October, 1896), 583.

[3] BCA, 94-T-7, J. Card. Gibbons to Mariano Card. Rampolla, Baltimore, November 24, 1896 (French), copy.

[4] John J. Keane to Pope Leo XIII, Washington, September 29, 1896, cited in "Right Rev. John Joseph Keane, D.D.," *CUB*, II (October, 1896), 584. An editorialist in the Hartford *Times* (October 5, 1896) pointed out the note of displeasure in Keane's reply to the Holy Father: "That the change is not pleasing to Bishop Keane is shown by his declination of an influential position as a member of the propaganda in Rome, and a renunciation of all aspirations for preferment in the Church."

163

Neither the rector nor the cardinal had any intention of making this correspondence public, but, as often happened during those years, the newspapers obtained it in some way. The rector was approached for a statement, which he courteously gave, and on October 4 the country was informed of what had transpired. The news was truly astonishing to everybody and it was received with mixed emotion. The day before the general public was informed, McQuaid wrote to Corrigan:

The news from Rome is astounding. The failure of the University is known in Rome at last, and the blame is thrown on Keane. Much of it is due to him, but other causes are there. These causes are irremediable now. The failure implicated the Holy Father, who was made to father the undertaking from the beginning.

What collapses on every side! Gibbons, Ireland, and Keane! ! ! They were cock of the walk for a while and dictated to the country and thought to run our dioceses for us. They may change their policy and repent. They can never repair the harm done in the past.[5]

On the following day John Farley wrote to Corrigan: "I see the Pope's letter to Bp. Keane is out. I am somewhat afraid that the tone of the Bp's reply will get him into trouble. I don't like it, I must say."[6] Corrigan wrote the deposed rector to express his condolence, and Keane answered: "I welcome the release as a great blessing, but am none the less thankful for your kind sympathy."[7]

Among many people there was profound sorrow and indignation that the man who had given himself so unsparingly to the cause of the university should be thus humiliated before the world. Emotions were deeply affected at the opening exercises of the new year in the chapel in Caldwell Hall on October 4, when the rector read the Holy Father's letter and his own in reply and then addressed the assembly, telling them: "I had a secret to tell you this morning. It is a secret no longer." He then spoke in the

[5] NYAA, Dignitaries, 1896, Bernard J. McQuaid to M. A. Corrigan, Rochester, October 3, 1896, cited in Zwierlein, *op. cit.*, III, 241.

[6] NYAA, G-23, Jno. M. Farley to M. A. Corrigan, New York, October 5, 1896.

[7] NYAA, G-23, John J. Keane to M. A. Corrigan, Washington, October 23, 1896. To Archbishop Chapelle's letter of sympathy, Keane replied: "From the first I have found in my removal only the greatest relief, for which I am profoundly grateful to our Divine Master. And I welcome the act of the Pope without the slightest desire to ask why it has been taken, or how it was brought about" (NOAA, John J. Keane to P. L. Chapelle, San José, October 26, 1896).

same terms as the published statement that appeared in some of the papers that day, in which he had told the public:

I welcome my release from the office of Rector of the University with profound gratitude, both to Divine Providence and to the Pope. While I always regarded its duties as a labor of love, they had grown to be far beyond my strength and abilities, and the deliverance from the burden is a response to my prayers. I am too loyal a soldier to ask to be relieved from my post, no matter what its difficulties; but feeling that my nine years of strain and solicitude in the work had brought me close to the end of my brain and nerve powers, I was fully ready to welcome what has been done. . . . Of course no one needs to be assured that the action of the Holy Father is prompted not only by personal kindness toward myself, but also by earnest solicitude for the best interests of the University.[8]

The rector concluded his remarks by telling his audience: "I asked no reasons why. I request you, my friends and students, to do likewise. Do not question why the Holy Father has done this. It is sufficient that he has done it, therefore it is wisely and well done."[9]

The *Irish World* reported with, perhaps, some exaggeration:

Many of the students and visitors sobbed audibly; but the one who seemed the most deeply affected was Cardinal Gibbons. When he rose to speak he was trembling so violently that for a moment it seemed that he would faint. When he began to speak his voice trembled and broke, and he made no effort to hide the tears that rushed to his eyes. The Cardinal's face was as white as the marble statue of St. Thomas Aquinas, the patron of the university, near which he was standing, and the drawn look about his deep-set eyes and his mouth marked the emotion under which he was laboring.

"I am a hard man to move," he half sobbed, "but to-day I am moved with the most profound sorrow I have ever felt in a long life full of sorrow."

"I trust," he concluded, "that the Catholic University is destined to have a long line of distinguished and able rectors, but I know that none will be more courtly, more able, more thoroughly a man of God than the one we lose to-day." [10]

Immediately after the ceremonies in the chapel, the vice rector and the members of the faculties retired to one of the parlors to

[8] "Right Rev. John Jospeh Keane, D.D.," *C UB*, II (October, 1896), 584.

[9] *Irish World* (New York), October 10, 1896.

[10] *Ibid.* For a more complete account of Cardinal Gibbons' address cf. "Right Rev. John Joseph Keane, D.D.," *C UB*, II (October, 1896), 585.

draw up resolutions which were formally presented to the former rector by a committee consisting of the deans of the three faculties. They expressed their "deep and sincere regret" at parting with him and they assured him of their "unalterable affection, of their prayers, and of their determination to work unitedly and perseveringly for the great object to which he has consecrated so large a portion of his life."[11] Twenty-nine students signed resolutions in which they expressed their appreciation for his work and their sorrow at the loss of their father. They told him that "his manner of departure was worthy of those heroes and saints, whose example, his words and work have taught them to follow."[12] After lunch the bishop received some of the students[13] and then left for California.[14] On his way he stopped in Chicago to see Archbishop Riordan of San Francisco who was visiting there. From there he wrote to Gibbons telling him that both Riordan and Ireland would see the Cardinal the following week and confer on the situation, "concerning which they feel very gloomy."[15]

The citizens of Washington did not let the deposed rector depart without sending after him an expression of their admiration and regret. A public mass-meeting was held on the evening of October 8 in the hall of Carroll Institute which, according to the Washington *Post*, was attended by "a crowd which filled the hall and galleries and overflowed into the corridors and reception rooms."[16] Judge Martin F. Morris, an intimate friend of the former rector and a frequent lecturer at the university, presided at the meeting which was attended by the heads of all the universities of Washington, by representatives of the local and national governments, by generals of the army, and by men prominent in society and business.[17] The professors of the university took no part in the meeting either as a body or as individuals according to the express wish of Bishop Keane that "they would make no public demonstration whatever of their feelings at his removal."[18]

[11] "Right Rev. John Joseph Keane, D.D.," *C UB*, II (October, 1896), 586-587.

[12] ACUA, "Resolutions." These are signed by twenty-nine students.

[13] PFA, "Student's Book. St. Thomas College, 1890-1906."

[14] "Right Rev. John Joseph Keane, D.D.," *C UB*, II (October, 1896), 587.

[15] BCA, 94-R-6, John J. Keane to J. Card. Gibbons, Chicago, October 7, 1896.

[16] Washington *Post*, October 7, 1896.

[17] "Right Rev. John Joseph Keane, D.D.," *C UB*, II (October, 1896), 587.

[18] Washington *Post*, October 7, 1896.

The meeting was addressed by J. Havens Richards, S.J., president of Georgetown University, J. E. Rankin, president of Howard University, B. L. Whitman, president of Columbian University, General A. A. Greely, District Commissioner Truesdell, and Denis J. Stafford, pastor of St. Patrick's Church. Resolutions, embodying expressions of the esteem of all for their fellow citizen, were reported and read by Father Joseph F. McGee of St. Patrick's Church and adopted by the meeting.[19]

William L. Starr, pastor of Corpus Christi Church in Baltimore, was disappointed when his fellow-townsmen did not follow the example of the Washingtonians, as he expressed himself in a letter to Cardinal Gibbons:

In the absence of any concerted action upon the part of Baltimore Catholics to express their admiration of the Rt. Rev. Bishop Keane & their regret at his withdrawal from the high offfice which he has so aptly & acceptably filled, I cannot refrain from the impulse to convey to your Eminence the assurance of my burning indignation at the manner of his removal & of the indignity thereby put upon your Eminence. As a devoted and loyal son of the Holy Father, I have no word of condemnation for him. I know that his position is always a trying one & that he is liable to be betrayed into false positions by the acts of his trusted agents. He has no means of knowing what goes on in remote parts of the world excepting the reports of his agents. It has happened in the history of the Papacy with lamentable frequency that the Sovereign Pontiffs have been sold, like their Divine Master, by those of their own household. I am sure that I voice the feelings of your own clergy when I say that we feel keenly the scandalous manner in which this whole business concerning Bishop Keane has been conducted, without the slightest reference to your Eminence.[20]

Such manifestations of esteem and appreciation for the work that he had endeavored to accomplish must have come as a balm to Keane's spirit.

Naturally Ireland was among the first to be approached by the newspaper correspondents when the news of the dismissal was published. The Archbishop of St. Paul stated that the Pope's letter simply established for the university the rule which generally obtained for other Catholic universities:

The reasons for a rule of this kind are obvious. A University is too important an institution to be, at any time, constrained, under a plea

---

[19] *Ibid.*, October 9, 1896.

[20] BCA, 94-R-9, William L. Starr to J. Card. Gibbons, Baltimore, October 9, 1896.

of personal rights or personal equity, to retain as its rector a man who would no longer be the best to be found. The present constitution of the Washington University specified no limit of time to the holding of the office of rector. The defect will be remedied at the next meeting of the directory, October 21st.

At the same meeting, Bishop Keane may possibly be chosen to be his own successor. His election would, beyond all doubt, be ratified by the Roman authorities.[21]

A number of papers on October 5 printed Ireland's statement without comment, along with the letter of Leo XIII and Keane's answer.[22] Other papers gave an indication of the spectacular and fanciful stories that were printed during the succeeding months. On October 5 the Buffalo *Enquirer* printed a long editorial in which it stated:

> The removal of Bishop Keane from the rectorship of the Catholic University, at Washington, no matter in what honeyed phrases it may be disguised, is a victory for the conservative party in the Catholic Church in America. . . . It has been the aim of the liberal Catholic party, led by a few able prelates, to put church government on a better basis, but the majority of the bishops have stood strongly for the interests of their own order. . . . The establishing of the Catholic University at Washington and the appointment of Bishop Keane as rector looked like another liberal victory . . . . The men who sustained the University were the leaders of the liberal party and the Rector represented them. There can be little doubt, therefore, that the conservative bishops, constituting a great majority of the Catholic Prelates, have made up their minds that they will control the University of Washington, and mar its career or shape it, as seems best. . . . The Catholic Church in the United States ought to have a new system of government; the missionary fiction worked well during the period of growth and formation, but it is now a source of weakness and danger.[23]

The Springfield *Republican* for the same day found the deposition of Keane highly significant:

> The inevitable inference in American minds is not that this is a case of a church principle of "rotation in office," but that Bishop Keane has been a trifle too American—somewhat too willing to affiliate in a

---

[21] St. Paul *Pioneer Press*, October 5, 1896.

[22] *Ibid.*; Hartford *Times*, October 5, 1896; Milwaukee *Herald*, October 5, 1896; New York *Morning Advertiser*, October 5, 1896; New York *Times*, October 5, 1896; Worcester *Telegram*, October 5, 1896.

[23] Buffalo *Enquirer*, October 5, 1896.

168

degree with other Christians, somewhat too Catholic to be Roman Catholic. . . . How long will it be before James Gibbons, the Baltimore Cardinal Archbishop, is warned as to his public utterances, or has he already been warned, and accepted the admonition? This deposition of Bishop Keane is significant.[24]

On the same day the Buffalo *Commercial* inferred from the removal that the "American wing" was losing favor in Rome and that its enemies had scored a notable triumph. The paper did not accept Keane's statement: "They [the duties as rector] had grown to be beyond my strength and abilities," at its face value, but speculated that "probably the affiliations and views of his successor will go farther towards explaining the deposition of Bishop Keane than the documentary evidence given to the public."[25]

After the first day an increasing number of papers, with the exception of such Catholic journals as the *Catholic Telegraph*, the *Catholic Standard and Times*, and the Boston *Pilot* which contained such mild terms as "resigns" and "retires" with simple statements of praise for his work,[26] began the publication of sensational stories in which the controversies of the past few years were aired once more and in which, too, much space was given to the two parties in the hierarchy and the varying fortunes of each one. The Buffalo *Express* for October 6 stated that "the removal of Bishop Keane from the American University at Washington looks very much like a triumph for the anti-American party in the Catholic Church."[27] The New York *Herald* for the same day found that the belief had grown that the removal of Bishop Keane "is an outward sign of an inward movement which is to shake the entire American hierarchy."[28]

As the days went on the stories became more fantastic. Schroeder was forced to deny the report that it was he who urged the Pope to remove the rector when he had an audience with him that summer. The Washington *Post* published an interview with

[24] Springfield *Republican*, October 5, 1896.

[25] Buffalo *Commercial*, October 5, 1896.

[26] *Catholic Telegraph* (Cincinnati), October 8, 1896; Boston *Pilot*, October 10, 1896. *Catholic Standard and Times* (Philadelphia), October 10, 1896.

[27] Buffalo *Express*, October 6, 1896.

[28] New York *Herald*, October 6, 1896.

the university professor which also appeared in the *Catholic Universe* two days later:

Mgr. Schroeder laughed at the report that he was the head of the opposition among the professors at the university to the rector. "I am the only German here," said he, "and if I head the party, I am also the whole of it."

He denied that the Germans had refused to endow the chair while Bishop Keane remained the rector. . . . He concluded by saying that whatever differences of opinion might have existed between himself and the Archbishop as to the policy of the university, their personal relations were of a very friendly character.[29]

The *Evening Star* for the same day had a front page story on "Bishop Keane's case" in which Schroeder's interview was questioned by an unnamed person:

Monsignor Schroeder, who spent the summer in Rome, and who, with Cardinal Satolli, is the head of the reactionists, has been quick to rush into print to deny rumors which have never taken tangible shape, that he was the agent which brought about the demand for Bishop Keane's resignation. It is singular, to say the least, that he would be so ardent and vigorous in his self-defense in the face of an indictment so impalpable. As soon as Monsignor Schroeder returned to this country from Rome the German papers began to announce that Bishop Keane was to retire from the university. This was a peculiar coincidence, to say the least. Cardinal Satolli knew, without question, that the deposition of the bishop was decided upon, but he thought that the actual fact would occur after his departure for Europe. I do not think that the action they have taken should have the effect of retarding the liberal spirit of the American Church, but that it will have such an effect is beyond question.[30]

The same paper reprinted an interview which had appeared in the Philadelphia *Public Ledger* the day before in which Major John M. Carson stated:

Among the Catholic clergy and laity in this city the deposition of Bishop Keane is quite generally taken as an overwhelming defeat for Archbishop Ireland and the so-called American school in the Catholic Church, of which Bishop Keane has been one of the strongest advocates.[31]

[29] Washington *Post*, October 7, 1896; *Catholic Universe* (Cleveland), October 9, 1896.

[30] *Evening Star* (Washington), October 7, 1896.

[31] *Ibid.*

170

The Protestant papers joined with the secular press in giving their views on the causes for Keane's dismissal. The *Congregationalist* of Boston for October 8 stated:

The public must be pardoned if they wonder whether, if Bishop Keane had been less liberal, less charitable, less fraternal in his dealings with Protestant Christians, he would not have been permitted to remain at the head of the institution to which he had given so much of his energy and devotion. . . . Fathers McGlynn and Burtsell, Archbishop Ireland and now Bishop Keane have all had to submit to the inevitable. Will Cardinal Gibbons, the leader of the liberal wing, be the next one to be humiliated and chastised? [32]

On the same day the *Christian Advocate* of Nashville surmised that the real ground for the dismissal of Bishop Keane was his "sympathy with Archbishop Ireland's views on education."[33]

The few Catholic papers that joined with the secular newspapers of the country in expressing their opinions as to the cause of Keane's removal were a little less daring, with the exception of the *Western Watchman*. Father David S. Phelan, the *Western Watchman's* editor, presented his usual unflattering opinions about Bishop Keane. He claimed that the rector was removed "for persistently maintaining a wrong position in regard to public schools and other public institutions. . . . The German Catholics had nothing to do with it."[34] The Louisville *Catholic Advocate* for October 8 merely stated that the action of the Holy Father had occurred "in such a strange combination of circumstances."[35] A few days later the *Catholic Citizen* of Milwaukee claimed to be only giving information when it stated:

When an office is resigned by suggestion, it is only honest to say that there has been a "removal." When a removal is made despite an able and faithful administration of the office, it is fair to presume that the exigencies of party controversy have determined it so. . . . We note this as another blow at the Home Rule heretofore enjoyed by the American Catholic Church. . . . Every issue upon which there is an acute divergence of opinion among the Archbishops seems to be adjusted not as heretofore by conference among themselves, but by appeal, anticipatory or otherwise, to Rome.[36]

[32] *Congregationalist* (Boston), October 8, 1896.

[33] *Christian Advocate* (Nashville), October 8, 1896.

[34] *Western Watchman*, October 9, 1896, cited in Washington *Times*, October 10, 1896.

[35] *Catholic Advocate* (Louisville), October 8, 1896.

[36] *Catholic Citizen* (Milwaukee), October 10, 1896.

Day after day secular newspapers printed sensational stories about the parties in the Catholic Church, their differences, and the causes for the dismissal of the rector. The Washington *Post* and the New York *Herald*—the two papers always carried substantially the same stories—gave a positive answer to the question: Who is responsible for Keane's dismissal?

It can be stated on the positive declaration of those who know that Cardinal Satolli caused the removal of Bishop Keane from the rectorship of the Catholic University. This statement is not only from the friends but from the opponents of Bishop Keane. It comes in a way which makes it authentic.[37]

On the same day the New York *World* quoted a statement by an unnamed priest:

The Jesuits are the ones wholly responsible. . . . probably he might be found in Rome in the College of Cardinals, and in the person of the German Jesuit, Andreas Steinhuber. Events will prove whether American Catholics will tamely allow Jesuitism to rule them.[38]

A few days later the *Monitor* of San Francisco, probably reflecting in this case the views of Archbishop Riordan, welcomed the former rector in their midst and told its readers:

Every student of the University and every man who believes in the higher learning and every Catholic who hopes to see the broad and liberal sentiment of the Church triumph in the world of thought will regret the resignation of Bishop Keane.[39]

On October 10 the Washington *Star* announced, probably with the hope that it was true:

The impression is gaining ground that the controversy which will result from the action of the pope will be bitter and prolonged . . . . An observant Catholic said today that it was a significant fact that the demand for Bishop Keane's resignation came from the Catholic University, and it was the belief of friends of the late rector that the intention on the part of those who gave out the information was to humiliate Bishop Keane by making it necessary for him to explain publicly the causes that led to the severance of his relations with the university. . . . It is known that Cardinal Satolli was astounded at the announcement and was indignant that it had been made before he left this country,

---

[37] Washington *Post*, October 8, 1896.

[38] New York *World*, October 8, 1896.

[39] San Francisco *Monitor*, October 10, 1896.

because he wished to go away leaving kindly feeling behind him, whereas now there is no covering up the fact that he is pursued by the maledictions of many.[40]

On the same day the Baltimore *Sun* was presumptious enough to give the so-called party alignment of each member of the university's Board of Trustees.[41] This was too much for Cardinal Gibbons. He publicly denied "any disagreement or antagonism or want of harmony among the members of the Board of Directors of the University of Washington."[42]

The statement of the cardinal was not enough to stop the press from making use of what they considered to be good copy. On October 14 the *Staats Zeitung*, a German language paper of New York, published a long story in which Keane's stand on the school question was emphasized as a cause of his dismissal.[43] The next day the New York *World* printed a front page story about "The German Crusade—Bishop Keane's removal only an incident in the movement— New College in Rome the object—How the Conspiracy was carried out by Mgr. Schroeder at the Vatican— Mgr. Jessing the Prime Mover of it."[44] The *Congregationalist* of Boston continued its guessing by stating that "it looks as if Pope Leo had played with liberalism as a cat plays with a mouse as long as it served his own interests, but with the fixed purpose that it should be swallowed up at last."[45] The *Churchman* of New York took the occasion to abuse Romanism and to indicate its Apaism:

There is a party in the papal Church in this country who call themselves "liberal, or American School" of Romanism. This "school of thought" is American before everything else. The American system of public school education is dear to it. A liberal charitableness toward other Christians who are not Romanists also distinguishes it. Italian narrowness, Italian intrigue, Italian interference it abhors. Ultramontanism it detests with more than Gallic intensity. Two conspicuous leaders of this "American School" are Archbishop Ireland and Bishop

---

[40] Washington *Star*, October 10, 1896.

[41] Baltimore *Sun*, October 10, 1896.

[42] Rochester *Union and Advertiser*, October 12, 1896.

[43] New York *Staats Zeitung*, October 14, 1896. On October 7, 1896, the *Herold des Glaubens* merely printed the texts of the letters without comment.

[44] New York *World*, October 15, 1896.

[45] *Congregationalist* (Boston), October 15, 1896. The same day the *Christian Register* (Boston), made a statement without any inferences.

173

Keane. Ireland is great as an educationalist, and, like many Americans, does not favor parochial schools. It was to the talent and ability of Keane, a former lecturer at Harvard, that the Roman Catholic University at Washington owes its great success. From the headship of the university, however, Dr. Keane has been suddenly removed by mandate from Rome. . . . . Perhaps the most remarkable evidence that could be given to the Pope's power in America is furnished by this incident. A large institution founded with American money, ostensibly directed by American trustees, and engaged in the education of American citizens, is suddenly dealt a death blow, not by those who have charge of it in America, not because Americans are dissatisfied with its teaching and administration, but by an Italian Pope, and that on the ground that Bishop Keane is too little of an Italian and too much of an American to please the Italian authorities in Rome. This sort of high-handed interference in American affairs seems to be mildly resented by American Romanists, and even by the submissive rector of the university himself.[46]

The *Irish World* published a summary of the stories that had appeared in the sensation-loving New York *World* and attributed them to "anti-Catholic animus." It claimed that "The public is regaled with accounts of plots and counterplots which have no existence outside the fertile brains of the sensation-loving journalists."[47]

The news about Keane's removal from the Catholic University of America was not confined to the United States. In France *Le Peuple Français* and *Le Bien Public* published the letters that had appeared in the American papers[48] and the *Courrier de Bruxelles* printed a story about "Liberalism in the Church" in which it was stated that the removal of Keane was "just another proof of the Holy Father's solicitude always to maintain integrity of doctrine."[49]

While the newspapers continued to print their rumors and sensational stories the Board of Trustees met on October 21-22 to decide upon the *terna* to be sent to Rome from which the Holy

[46] *The Churchman* (New York), October 17, 1896.

[47] *Irish World* (New York), October 17, 1896. Cf. New York *Freeman's Journal*, October 17, 1896.

[48] *Le Peuple Français*, October 21, 1896; *Le Bien Public*, October 21, 1896.

[49] *Courrier de Bruxelles*, October 25, 1896.

See would select a successor to the deposed rector. The secretary
of the board first read Keane's letter of resignation:

To the Most Rev. and Rt. Reverend, The Directors of the Catholic
University of America.

The letter of our Holy Father the Pope, relieving me from the office
of rector of the University is in your hands. My reply of unhesitating
acquiescence was sent at once. My connexion with the University is
therefore at an end. In the welfare of the institution I shall ever feel
the profoundest interest, and for its Directors shall ever cherish the most
respectful affection.

Most respectfully,
John J. Keane [50]

The board could do nothing else but accept his resignation as
rector, but they retained Keane as a member of the Board of
Trustees.[51] The members of the board then chose by secret ballot
the three names that were to be sent to Rome after the chancellor
had read all the names that had been proposed for the position by
the various members of the board. Thomas J. Conaty, a prominent priest of the Diocese of Springfield, was the first choice of
the trustees[52] and subsequently he was appointed to take up the
reins reluctantly released by Keane. The board then adopted the
motion that the term of office for the rector would be fixed at six
years with eligibility for re-election at the end of each term.[53] A
committee of two, the Archbishop of St. Paul and the Bishop of
Covington, were appointed by the chancellor to draft a letter
expressing the sentiments of the members of the board "for the
exalted services rendered to the University by the late rector."[54]
The letter was drafted later and sent to Keane in California:

It is the unanimous desire of the Board of Directors of the Catholic
University that I write to express to you their profound sorrow at your
departure from the University, with which your name has been, and I
trust, ever will be irrevocably associated.

They feel your departure the more keenly in that they were not able
to personally manifest their appreciation and bid you farewell. But

---

[50] ACUA, MMBT, Washington, October 21, 1896, pp. 60-61.

[51] *Ibid.*, p. 61.

[52] *Ibid.*, p. 60. On the *terna* submitted to Rome, Daniel Riordan, a priest of
the Archdiocese of Chicago, was *dignior*, and Monsignor Joseph Moody of the
Archdiocese of New York was *dignus*.

[53] *Ibid.*, p. 61.

[54] *Ibid.*, p. 63.

Bishop Keane was never known to hesitate or ask explanations when the command was given.

For nine years untiring labor in building the Halls of Divinity and Philosophy, your indefatigable zeal in collecting the funds necessary to defray the expenses of the rapidly growing institution, your numberless sermons and addresses, always interesting, in every part of the land, in the presence of Catholic and Protestant audiences, young and old, in churches, seminaries and halls, eliciting by your magnetic enthusiasm for higher education, the sympathy of your hearers, attracting the attention and interest of those already well-known in the world of theology, philosophy, science and letters, and inspiring with a noble ambition young men who were capable of appreciating your high ideals, and above all, your apostolic disinterestedness (for we know you leave the university as poor as when you began it), have merited the well-earned admiration, and drawn to you the unfeigned affection of your fellow-citizens, Protestants as well as Catholics, throughout the land.

Your departure will be deeply felt by professors and students, to whom you have endeared yourself by fatherly interest and whole-souled affection. The University, extensive as were its labors and exacting in its demands, did not absorb your efforts for good. While the professors feel that they have lost a leader whose place will not be easily filled, while students are grieved for the departure of their Rector who was ever a kind friend, there are a great many others, whose sad hearts and tear-dimmed eyes speak of the absence of one who was father of the poor.

We desire to assure you of our sincere appreciation of your labors, and to offer you our deep affection and sympathy, with earnest hopes for your future peace and happiness. The public demonstration in Washington, participated in by Protestants and Catholics alike, finds an echo in our hearts.

Your noble soul has grown from your noble undertaking. You have proven the efficiency of the University to train young men to generous self-forgetfulness for the welfare of others in your sublime resignation to the will of the Holy Father. You are the masterpiece of your own training.

When in future we shall have occasion to point to an exemplar for the imitation of young men who will reap the fruit of your labors, we shall feel an honest pride in setting before them the first rector of the University, the generous, high-minded, much beloved Bishop Keane.[55]

[55] ACUA, J. Card. Gibbons to John J. Keane, Baltimore, October 31, 1896. On the same day Gibbons sent a letter to Philip J. Garrigan, the forgotten man during all the excitement over Keane's dismissal. He thanked the vice rector for his valuble services and he hoped that nothing would happen to "disturb

The rector's reply was characteristic of him:

I most gratefully return thanks to your Eminence and the Board of Directors of the University for the exceedingly kind sentiments conveys to me by your Eminence's letter of Oct. 31.

I am very far from flattering myself that I deserve a tithe of the praise prompted by the goodness and the sympathy of your own generous hearts. While I did my best for the interests of the great work to which obedience had consecrated my energies, yet I was always conscious that my best was far from being up to the requirements of the case. Hence I have not for a moment questioned the wisdom of the Holy Father in desiring a change of administration.

May the best blessings of Providence and the loyal co-operation of our Catholic people prosper the University in all its future.[56]

The members of the Board of Trustees also decided that a letter should be written to the Holy Father in which these sentiments would be incorporated:

1° that the Board accepts with filial submission His decision concerning the late Rector. 2° its regret, that because of the great commotion caused in this country, such action had not been communicated through the Board; 3° its hope that our Holy Father, knowing the high esteem with which Bishop Keane is held by this Board and his great services to the University would extend to him marks of his esteem and care for his welfare.[57]

A letter was drafted by Bishops Maes and Farley and read at the meeting on October 22 but all the members would not subscribe to its contents. It was then decided that a committee, appointed by the chancellor, would prepare another letter within a month or two to be sent to each member of the board for his approval.[58] The cardinal later called a meeting of Patrick J. Ryan of Philadelphia and Michael A. Corrigan of New York for November 17

---

your official relations with the Institution in the near future." Gibbons seemed concerned about impressing him with the desirability of the vice rector serving under several successive rectors: "The interests of the University also demand that the Vice-Rector remain after the incoming rector arrives because he is so closely connected with discipline and internal management" (ACUA, Garrigan Papers, J. Card. Gibbons to P. J. Garrigan, Baltimore, October 31, 1896; BCA, 94-S-6, copy).

[56] ACUA, John J. Keane to J. Card. Gibbons, San José, California, November 5, 1896.

[57] ACUA, MMBT, Washington, October 21, 1896, p. 63.

[58] ACUA, MMBT, Washington, October 22, 1896, p. 63.

to draft such a letter. When Ryan received the notice from the chancellor he told Corrigan:

I wrote to the Cardinal that it would be difficult to write such a letter as will please both Pope & Board. Indeed I believe it impossible & the gold of silence better than the silver of speech in such circumstances as the present.[59]

Ryan's views must have prevailed, for the drafting of a satisfactory letter was delayed so long that no communication, in the sense indicated by the minutes of the trustees' meeting, was forwarded to Rome.

The board also took cognizance of the rumors and stories that appeared in the daily journals, and it issued a statement with a view to putting a stop to them. The New York *Tribune* reported:

The Board wishes it to be understood by the public that there are absolutely no factions nor sectional differences among the members. The election of the candidates for the rectorship was practically unanimous. To speak of the triumph of this or that party as conservatism or liberalism, Nationalism or Americanism, is to misrepresent the whole situation. All the members of the Board are equally American in spirit. They have but one thought, and that is the welfare of the University and its steady progress to the highest Catholic education.[60]

Actually the meeting of the trustees neither brought peace to the university nor did its pronouncement cause the press to cease printing its quota of rumors. Patrick A. Ludden, Bishop of Syracuse, wrote to Archbishop Corrigan:

It appears that peace does not yet reign in ecclesiastical circles at Washington. I hope religious wars will be confined to that neighborhood. There is a rumor here that Monsignor Mooney has declined to be a candidate for President of the University; if so I rejoice at his good sense in steering clear just now of that unfortunate institution.[61]

On October 24 the *Literary Digest* presented a summary of the various opinions that had appeared in the religious papers on

[59] NYAA, G-23, P. J. Ryan to M. A. Corrigan, Philadelphia, November 1, 1897. On this subject Ryan told Chapelle: "Plain blunt men like you & I prove bad diplomats & I intend to leave the work to the tact of my colleagues" (NOAA, P. J. Ryan to P. L. Chapelle, Philadelphia, November 10, 1896).

[60] New York *Tribune*, October 23, 1896.

[61] NYAA, G-23, P. A. Ludden to M. A. Corrigan, Syracuse, October 30, 1896.

Keane's dismissal.[62] A few days later the *Morning Star* of Boston reported:

The *Independent* of Oct. 22 says that the *Western Watchman* declares that Bishop Keane was removed from the presidency of the Catholic University of Washington on the advice of Card. Satolli, because "Rome did not want the young priests of America to be taught Pelagianism. Bishop Keane's Pelagianism is his having said that any form of Protestantism is better than no religion at all. He has said that several times." [63]

The *Catholic Times* of London also kept its readers informed about the latest developments on the American Church scene by printing:

The strong feeling against what is called "the German Party" excited amongst the Catholics of the United States by the removal of Bishop Keane from the rectorship of the Catholic University has by no means subsided, and the American papers are still full of protests against what are described as intrigues having for their object to un-Americanise the Church in the States, and unduly restrict the freedom of its members.[64]

The *Review of Reviews* for November repeated the viewpoints of some Protestants papers, notably the *Congregationalist*, when it reported:

The Pope's action had an arbitrary appearance that goes somewhat against the American grain. The University at Washington was established solely upon American initiative, without any aid from Rome, Dr. Keane beings its most active promoter, and Dr. Keane's personal influence securing practically all of the money. It seems to be the prevailing opinion that the University rector has suffered from the fact that his leaning was toward the so-called liberal or American wing of the Catholic Church in the United States.[65]

During the first weeks in November the press carried reports that Cardinal Gibbons and Archbishop Ireland would be called to Rome for the purpose of removing them from their high posts.[66]

[62] *Literary Digest*, XIII (October 24, 1896), 821.
[63] *Morning Star* (Boston), October 29, 1896.
[64] *Catholic Times* (London), October 30, 1896.
[65] *Review of Reviews*, XIV (November, 1896), 531.
[66] New York *Tribune*, November 13, 14, 20, 1896.

There was also a widely circulated rumor that three of the professors in the university would be removed from their positions:

The published statement that Cardinal Satolli was to report that Rev. Dr. Bouquillon, Rev. Dr. Shahan, and Rev. Dr. Pace, three leading professors at the Catholic University, should be removed has caused inquiries to pour into the city from all quarters asking if the report were true.[67]

The rumors were so persistent that the new apostolic delegate, Sebastian Martinelli, wrote to Rome to find out if there was any truth in them. He received a reassuring reply which he communicated to Cardinal Gibbons to set his mind at rest:

I beg to inform your Eminence that I have just now received a Cablegram from the Secretary of State in answer to my letter in which I informed him about the rumor spread in the Newspapers about the deposition of some American Prelates, and removal of some professors from the Catholic University.

His Eminence says that the Holy Father was very sorry on hearing the agitation caused by these false news; and meantime he authorizes me to contradict the assertion as a lie.[68]

Ireland wrote Gibbons a very gloomy view of the whole situation just before the cardinal had received the delegate's letter assuring him that no Roman action against him or others was contempalted:

But, really, what is to become of religion—if things continue as they have come. There is, no doubt, a well-organized conspiracy. A villainous letter from Paris? appears in the N.Y. Sun of Nov. 29—and an article in the same strain in the Germania, of Berlin.

Many Americans are beginning to believe that there is some truth in all those reports of papal disfavor. Something is to be done to stop this dreadful and diabolical conspiracy. . . . Nothing but stern courage on our part will avert disaster from us. We are timid children, & we are treated as children. Our enemies are not timid.

The university is dead: nothing can revive it. The Jesuits have triumphed there for good.[69]

The university was far from being dead. Its life continued with the installation of the new rector, Thomas J. Conaty, on January

[67] Baltimore *Sun*, October 18, 1896.

[68] BCA, 94-U-2, Sebastian Martinelli to J. Card. Gibbons, Washington, December 3, 1896.

[69] BCA, 94-U-1, John Ireland to J. Card. Gibbons, St. Paul, December 2, 1896.

180

19, 1897.[70] The former rector was not ignored on this occasion, for the papers published a cablegram from Keane in which he sent his successor "cordial greetings; crosit [*sic*] prosperity,"[71] and at the ceremony the chancellor praised the university's "second founder," John J. Keane:

The University may claim two founders. The first and chief of these is the Pontiff happily reigning. From the day of its inauguration to the present moment the Holy Father has taken an active personal and fatherly interest in its welfare and progress.

After the Holy Father, what name can I more fittingly mention than that of Bishop Keane? He is justly entitled to be called its second founder. When the Bishop was appointed Rector the land for the institution had not been bought. He traversed the length and breadth of the land, everywhere delivering sermons and lectures in the interest of higher education. These discourses were rewarded by munificent contributions. He did not neglect the higher interests, and it is due to him that the university contains today professors who are the peer of any in the land.[72]

After Keane had left the university he spent some time with his intimate friend, Myles P. O'Connor, at San José, California.[73] Judge O'Connor had been a generous donor to the university. The former rector must have given much time to pondering over his future. The Holy Father had offered him two alternatives: either he could accept an archbishopric in the United States; or he could go to Rome and receive an appointment to honorable positions there. His first decision, made in haste, was a flat refusal of both alternatives and a request to remain in the United States "without any official position whatsoever, in tranquillity and peace."[74] Yet all knew that he would not be granted that request. The Metropolitan of New York and his suffragans feared that the former rector would be appointed to the See of Buffalo that had been vacant since the death of Stephen V. Ryan on

[70] Hogan, "Thomas J. Conaty," pp. 31-32.

[71] New York *World*, January 20, 1897.

[72] *Ibid.*

[73] Washington *Post*, October 8, 1896. The sanitarium founded by Judge O'Connor at San José was Keane's home during these days (NOAA, John J. Keane to P. L. Chapelle, San José, California, October 26, 1896).

[74] *Supra*, p. 177.

April 16, 1896.[75] Winant M. Wigger, Bishop of Newark, wrote to Corrigan shortly after Keane's dismissal:

You will probably be pleased to learn that Cardinal Satolli does not at all believe that Mgr. Keane will be nominated for Buffalo. I hope he is right in his positive declaration that he will *not* be appointed to that important See.[76]

McQuaid of Rochester also had feared that Keane would be appointed to the neighboring diocese, for he wrote to Corrigan later:

It seems that nothing kept Keane out of Buffalo but his own folly in publishing, as he did, the Pope's letter asking for his resignation. Divine Providence often intervenes to upset man's plans. The first news kept me awake two nights in succession. An unusual occurrence.[77]

While Keane was in California contemplating his future the Washington *Post* informed its readers that their former fellow-citizen was happy in his exile:

We are glad to hear that he is happy, content and hopeful in his new abiding place in San José, in California; full of affection for those he has left behind; zealous with fresh plans for work; instinct with the same noble aims and purposes that have made him beloved and honored everywhere; free from the smallest taint of anger or reproach toward any living thing. He is there what he was here—a pure and gentle heart, a lofty soul, an exalted and commanding mind. He puts his hand to the plow, looks not behind him with repining or complaint, and runs the furrow true. The love of those who knew him here will mingle with the loves that spring up in his pathway there, and so anoint and bless him.[78]

Yet the bishop could not live on plans for work. He had left the university without any source of revenue from salary or pension

[75] Maynard, *op. cit.*, p. 620.

[76] NYAA, G-23, Winant M. Wigger to M. A. Corrigan, South Orange, New Jersey, October 9, 1896.

[77] NYAA, C-40, Bernard J. McQuaid to M. A. Corrigan, Rochester, January 20, 1897. In the same letter McQuaid said: "Evidently over in Rome they can't bear me much ill-will for the lecture I gave Ireland, or they would not enlarge the diocese of Rochester in my lifetime." This was a reference to the sermon delivered in the pulpit of his cathedral in November, 1895, in which he assailed Ireland and concerning which Rome demanded an explanation.

[78] Washington *Post*, cited in New York *Democrat*, November 8, 1896. This item may have been given to the papers by Garrigan for he had received a letter from Keane written November 1, in which the former rector said: "I

and he had not saved for such an eventuality. Two days after he departed from Washington he wrote to Gibbons:

May I beg a parting favor of your Eminence? Among the charity pensioners whom I now must cease to provide for, is poor old Mrs. C——, mother of Sister St. ———. For many months I have been sending the destitute old lady $30 per month. If abandoned, her case is desperate. Could your Eminence assume this burden of charity? [79]

The chancellor must have indicated Keane's financial difficulties to the members of the Board of Trustees, for a month later William Henry Elder, Archbishop of Cincinnati, questioned the cardinal:

At our meeting in Washington, I understood you to say that some provision would be made on behalf of Rt. Rev. Bishop Keane. Has it been accomplished or decided on? [80]

Unfortunately, it was not possible to discover the answer to the question, but there was evidence that the cardinal was generous in sending sums of money at a later date so the former rector could meet his many obligations. [81]

After Keane had spent a month considering his plans for the future he decided to acquiesce in the repeated offers from Leo XIII of positions mentioned in the letter that announced his dismissal from the university. [82] Gibbons so informed Rampolla as soon as the decision had been reached:

I am happy with the decision that Bishop Keane has made. I have well-founded confidence that by his piety, his intelligence and his zeal,

---

cannot lose sight of the fact that I am in exile; yet no place of exile was ever sweeter, and no exile was ever more peacefully content that I" (ACUA, Garrigan Papers, John J. Keane to P. J. Garrigan, San José, California, November 1, 1896).

[79] BAC, 94-R-6, John J. Keane to J. Card. Gibbons, Chicago, October 7, 1896.

[80] BCA, 94-T-3, William Henry Elder to J. Card. Gibbons, Cincinnati, November 20, 1896.

[81] BCA, 95-C-4, John J. Keane to J. Card. Gibbons, Rome, January 18, 1897.

[82] NOAA, John J. Keane to P. L. Chapelle, San José, California, November 18, 1896; ACUA, Garrigan Papers, John J. Keane to Philip J. Garrigan, San José, California, November 19, 1896. The former rector told both these correspondents that it was Archbishop Riordan who had convinced him "to sacrifice the sweet retirement in which I am so content." The San Francisco prelate also advised Keane to "demand an investigation of the charges of heterodoxy made against me by Card. Satolli." For this purpose he asked for

he will usefully serve the general interests of the Church and in particular the interests of the Church in the United States in Rome.[83]

Shortly before he left for Rome he indicated his continued interest in the institution that had so completely filled a portion of his life:

I had a long and very satisfactory talk with Dr. Garrigan this evening. He rejoices at the opening prospect of better things. And the dawn of hope makes him desire all the more earnestly *one thing,* which he, and many others, think would secure the future of the Univ'y, now so seriously imperiled.

He insists that not to have a Bishop for Rector will hopelessly lower the Univ'y to the level of a mere college or seminary, deprive it of all its prestige, and ensure its utter failure. This I have heard declared by Abp. Riordan & others with an emphasis that Dr. G. would be incapable of.—As I wrote your Eminence, the word "sacerdos" in the Constitution *absolutely does not* exclude a Bishop, but only a layman.

Now Dr. G. says he is *sure* that Bp. Maes would accept the position, & that he would fill it most satisfactorily & save the situation. Dr. Conaty's appointment, if made, has not been officially promulgated. I ask you, as a favor to the imperilled cause, to cable immediately a request that *if not* promulgated, they sh'd delay till I arrive there shortly. I could then discuss the matter with them. Satolli will likely not resist, & good will be done.[84]

Gibbons did not grant this favor to his friend because he did not consider it important enough that a bishop should be appointed and, probably a more weighty reason, he felt that if the appoint-

---

pertinent documents from his correspondents.   When Archbishop Ireland received the news he wrote to Magnien: "Bp. Keane has recovered himself: and he is willing to be the soldier rather than the hermit. He has realized that he is disgraced, that he must fight for his honor, & for the cause which he represented" (ACUA, Bouquillon Papers, John Ireland to A. Magnien, S.S., St. Paul, November 19, 1896). Cf. Zwierlein, *op. cit.,* III, 245. Also cf. NYAA, G-19, Thomas F. Gambon to M. A. Corrigan, Rome, December 10, 1896.

[83] BCA, 94-T-11, J. Card. Gibbons to M. Card. Rampolla, Baltimore, November 30, 1896 (French), copy.

[84] BCA, 94-Y-2, John J. Keane to J. Card. Gibbons, Washington, n.d. Soon after his dismissal Keane had placed his hopes in George Montgomery, the Coadjutor Bishop of Monterey and Los Angeles, as a suitable successor. Archbishop Riordan, however, considered him "utterly unfit" for the rectorship (ACUA, Garrigan Papers, John J. Keane to P. J. Garrigan, San Francisco, October 11, 1896).

184

ment was delayed beyond a reasonable time the papers would begin their round of rumors, surmises, and suspicions.[85]

Before the former rector left for Rome on December 5 he took a parting shot at the rumor-mongers in an interview that appeared in many papers:

I very much regret that there has been a bureau of mischief at work in this country and in Europe, founded for the manufacture and dissemination of pernicious rumors of all sorts against Christians and distinguished Catholic prelates in this country. I am delighted to see the crushing blow inflicted upon them by the telegram from Cardinal Rampolla to the Apostolic Delegate. I hope the telegram will convince the American public that they ought never again to pay heed to the fabrications of the mischief bureau.[86]

On the day after Keane sailed from New York, accompanied by John Gloyd, a priest of the Archdiocese of Baltimore, John Lancaster Spalding wrote to his friend, Daniel Hudson, the editor of the *Ave Maria*:

The impression in Rome is that the Pope, in slapping Bp. Keane in the face, has given a death blow to the University. With Bp. Keane himself I have lost patience. If the Pope had him down on all fours kicking him, each time he lifted his foot, the enthusiastic Bishop would shout;— See how the Holy Father honors me. A more disgusting state of things than our ecclesiastical situation is hardly conceivable. The only important question, it seems, is whether Abp. Ireland is falling or rising in favor with Rome. If we could only hear nothing more of him, it matters little whether he rise or fall. I am sick of it all and only wish I were away from it all. I have suffered much with rheumatism since my return and doubt whether I can get rid of it in this climate.[87]

---

[85] Hogan, "Thomas J. Conaty," p. 27.

[86] Rochester *Union and Advertiser*, December 5, 1896, cited in Zwierlein, *op. cit.*, III, 245.

[87] AUND, photostat, John Lancaster Spalding to Daniel Hudson, Peoria, December 6, 1896. The Peoria prelate wrote the same friend later: "Abp. Ireland, I think, is a hoodo — whatever he touches seems to go wrong" (AUND, photostat, John Lancaster Spalding to Daniel Hudson, Peoria, February 7, 1897). In his correspondence with Hudson, Spalding frequently mentioned that he was suffering from rheumatism (AUND, photostat, John L. Spalding to Daniel Hudson, Peoria, April 16, 1897). Besides mentioning his rheumatism, he said: "I had an interview with Abp. Ireland ... Though I have a certain sympathy with some of his views, we are, I believe, radically unlike."

On the same day Thomas Gambon, a priest of the Diocese of Louisville, wrote Corrigan one of his interesting letters:

The newspapers are trying for their own interest to make mischief and though their reports are without foundation they set somebody, will mention on my return, trembling in their boots in fear and expectation of what [is] supposed to [be] coming on. . . . Keane I have been told will visit the Eternal City very soon and the storm will have subsided by the time I will have reached New York, the Capitol of the Catholic and Commercial world. . . . His Eminence [Satolli] is enjoying good health and amuses himself and entertains me at times by pulling sweet music out of his American Aeolian instrument. . . . We smoke cigars together the same as two old Mountaineers and I am glad to know that he will always be the friend of Americans.[88]

Keane arrived in Rome on December 18 and made an application for an audience with the Holy Father immediately. Father Gloyd informed his superior as to what then transpired:

It is evident that the Pope was anxious to see him, for he at once named the following Sunday at 12 [December 20] for the audience which lasted I would say about ½ hour. Bishop Keane stated that His Holiness gave him a most hearty welcome, and listened to what he had to say with the greatest interest. When he finished the Holy Father said "It is God who is directing you; you did well in taking the advice of Archbishop Riordan and Ireland: you did well in coming here, etc."

Having stated to the Pope, said the Bishop, what an excitement his removal from the University caused in America, that some had even gone so far as to declare that the Holy Father had changed his policy, etc. To this last assertion the Pope replied "I assure you I have not changed my policy in the least." The Holy Father appointed him Canon of St. John Lateran, but I do not think the Bishop has yet accepted, at least his friends have advised him not to do so until his position is more clearly defined.

The Bishop has strong backing here in persons of Bro. [sic] David who is regarded as the most learned man in his order; and is reported as having great influence here, Mgr. Mourey, Dr. O'Connell and others. When this difficulty will be settled I am unable to say. He insists upon our remaining until his position is definitely known.[89]

---

[88] NYAA, G-19, Thomas F. Gambon to M. A. Corrigan, Rome, December 6, 1896.

[89] BCA, 94-W-4, John Gloyd to J. Card. Gibbons, Rome, December 29, 1896. Bishop Carl Mourey was an official in the Holy Roman Rota. Father David Fleming, O.F.M., was a consultor in the Congregation of the Inquisition. Cf. *La Gerarchia Cattolica* (Rome, 1897), pp. 675, 708.

After Keane had arrived in Rome McQuaid wrote to Corrigan: "Did you notice the letter of the Roman Correspondent of the London Tablet of Jan. 9? They are trying to puzzle over Keane's coming to Rome ... and what he is going to do."[90] It was not long before the former rector informed the cardinal concerning the matter that was a "puzzle" to others. On January 15 he wrote:

Final action has been taken at last, and I am made Abp. of Damascus, Assistant at the Pontifical Throne, Canon of St. John Lateran, and Consultor to the Propaganda. The latter is the only position that I really value, it means *practical* utility, work for the Ch. in the U. S., while the others are simply tinsel honors. Strong effort was made by all the hostile influences, especially American, to hinder my being admitted to the Propaganda; and even Rampolla, while talking fair, was at least passively holding the appointment back. But Card. Vincenzo Vannutelli, at O'C's [Denis O'Connell] suggestion, spoke plainly and strongly to the Pope about it, day before yesterday; the H. F. agreed with him, & asked him to go himself to Ledochowski (who was of course opposed to it) and order the appointment to be made out at once. He did so; and yesterday Ledoch. told me that he had directed biglietto to be drawn up; this to be signed by Rampolla, & then all the docs. will be given me together. All is now certain; but still I make no move, and publish nothing, til the docs. are in my hands. Then I must at once secure my apartments. Preliminary inquiries have already been made to that end. A heavy expense will thus rest on me, and my total Roman salary will not be over $850, the canoncy bringing $60 a month, I am told, and the Consultorship $80 a year! I have to enter on my new career, with all its difficulties & financial responsibilities, trusting to the Providence of God and the kindness of my friends in America, and must pray: "non confundar in aeternum."

O'C. has done nobly. His advice has been invaluable, & his influence with the Vannutellis has been the main element in our success. Their friendliness as members of the Propaganda will be my chief dependence for making my Consultorship of practical utility, for the others would, I am sure, gladly ignore me if they could. This appointment, & that of Fr. David in the Holy Office, are considered facts of extreme importance, inaugurating a new method & new life in the Roman Congregations.[91]

Archbishop Keane must have cabled the news the same day that he sent the letter giving the information in full, for Cardinal Gibbons wrote a letter that day to Cardinal Rampolla in which he

[90] NYAA, C-40, Bernard J. McQuaid to M. A. Corrigan, Rochester, January 23, 1897.

[91] BCA, 95-B-9, John J. Keane to J. Card. Gibbons, Rome, January 15, 1897.

informed the papal Secretary of State that the honors given to the former rector had been "a great consolation to his numerous friends." He said that Keane had waited a long time uncertain of his position even after the letter of the Holy Father promising dignities had been published, yet he had been humble in accepting the will of the Supreme Pontiff. Gibbons went on to say that many saw in the delay a change of view on the part of the Pope and Rampolla but he himself did not believe they had changed. He also told Rampolla that he wanted him to see to it that Keane was appointed to consultorships in the Congregations of the Propagation of the Faith and in the Congregation of Studies as the Holy Father had promised in his letter. "It is important not to revive the public sentiment which has calmed. A long delay would make them angry and respect for pontifical authority would suffer."[92] On January 18 Keane wrote that he actually had been appointed to all the offices mentioned in his previous letter and that he valued only the appointments to the consultorships.[93] On January 28 John Gloyd informed his cardinal archbishop that "the Bishop is now *active* Consultor at the Propaganda and already busily engaged in some cases affecting American interests, and that he had made arrangements for the time being to take rooms at the Canadian College."[94]

After Keane's position was clearly defined he took another shot at the "mischief bureau" in the United States by issuing a statement to the press which appeared in the New York *Journal*:

The Pope said to me: "I am greatly shocked and grieved by these mischief makers who are so busy in the American press. I protest against this malice and falsehood. The idea that anyone would try to put me in the position of disapproving the splendid service of Cardinal Satolli or of publicly disgracing you never occurred to me. The change in the rectorship at the Washington University was submitted to me as a purely pedagogical routine matter. I was astonished and indignant when I learned that mischief makers had misrepresented the meaning of my act. I desire to denounce their statements and to give evidence of my love and esteem for you. My answer to your enemies will be a substantial one. The policy of the Holy See in America is unchanged!"

It is remarkable that when the so-called liberals are dominant in

---

[92] BCA, 95-B-10, J. Card. Gibbons to M. Card. Rampolla, Baltimore, January 15, 1897 (French), copy.

[93] BCA, 95-C-4, John J. Keane to J. Card. Gibbons, Rome, January 18, 1897.

[94] BCA, 95-E-6, John Gloyd to J. Card. Gibbons, Rome, January 28, 1897.

America no one is attacked by them, but when the so-called conservatives appear to have gained a victory the mischief bureau in New York suddenly starts into activity, and the whole press of the country teems with scandal, falsehood and venomous abuse.

All these stories originating in New York are pure inventions of malignant minds. I would be sorry to hold Archbishop Corrigan responsible for all that has been said or written by those who appear to be his friends, and cannot be brought to believe that he would consent to or authorize all of this mischievous work.[95]

After this statement had appeared Thomas F. Gambon wrote to Corrigan:

You will learn from the enclosed clippings that there is a financial blizzard in the North West and a loud mouthed Canon by the Tiber.

From the tone of the Canon's utterances one can easily fancy that Keane feels that he is in tight traces but this roar across the waters will make the Archpriest of St. John's [Satolli] keep his eye on some of his Canons and he is the man that will do so.[96]

A few weeks later the same correspondent told Corrigan: "You are perfectly correct. Keane is making a mistake in keeping up these sensational reports and if this means he wants to get even with Satolli he is very much mistaken."[97]

After Keane had taken his Roman offices his friends still looked for some means to vindicate him by bringing him back to an honorable position in the United States. It appeared to them that they could accomplish their purpose when the Archdiocese of New Orleans was left vacant by the death of Francis Janssens on June 9, 1897.[98] The former rector's name appeared first on the

[95] New York *Journal*, February 12, 1897.

[96] NYAA, G-25, Thomas F. Gambon to M. A. Corrigan, Louisville, February 20, 1897. Father Gambon displayed a dislike for Keane in an earlier letter: "He [Keane] will be made Canon of St. John Lateran where he can say his office piously according to the Roman Ritual, and will have an opportunity to study sound Catholic Philosophy if he feels so inclined" (NYAA, G-19, Thomas F. Gambon to M. A. Corrigan, Rome, December 10, 1896). The same priest took great pride in his friendship with Satolli: "In writing to Satolli I said that the loyalty and generous devotion to Leo XIII and the Holy See was the predominating atmosphere of the N. York diocese. As he is an intimate friend of mine I wrote freely to him and any points of information you may wish to give will be judiciously used by your devoted servant" (NYAA, G-25, Thomas F. Gambon to M. A. Corrigan, Louisville, March 5, 1897).

[97] NYAA, 95-G-25, Thomas F. Gambon to M. A. Corrigan, Louisville, March 5, 1897.

[98] Maynard, *op. cit.*, p. 634.

terna selected by the bishops of the province.[99]   Camillus P. Maes, whose name was second on the same list, wrote Gibbons shortly after the *terna* had been submitted to Rome:

I would be the first one to welcome the Most Rev. Archbishop Keane to the vacant Archbishopric, more especially so because his exaltation would be looked upon as a vindication of our self-sacrificing friend whose treatment by passing powers has aroused the best feelings of the whole Catholic world. During my recent trip through Europe, I have been able to guage the Catholic opinion of many lands: all agree that the vindication of this good man by the Holy Father was called for and was not made too emphatic. I had occasion to tell His Holiness so during my private audience, and I have reason to think that the Supreme Pontiff and Cardinal Rampolla were impressed by what I had to say. But I have also witnessed the work which Archbishop Keane is doing in Rome. There we have a man occupying the position, enjoying and asserting the influence over American interests, which had been denied for years to the entreaties of Your Eminence and of the whole American hierarchy; he is doing an untold amount of good. Besides, the Archbishop himself asserts that he has never been so happy; he realises that he is doing a good work; he is enthusiastic about his many and great opportunities in Rome to serve the Church in America. I therefore agree with your Eminence, that it is better for the good of religion to allow Archbp. Keane to have his wish and have him remain in the Eternal City to watch and further the Catholic interests of the United States.[100]

Keane was very emphatic when he told Denis O'Connell that he did not want New Orleans: "What a hornet's nest I would be in if sent there. I have done all I could to hinder it & hope there is no danger."[101] He also so informed the press of the United States when he arrived in September to attend the yearly meeting of the Board of Trustees of the university:

The Bishops of the province, notwithstanding my protest, have put my name on the list of candidates for that office. I take it as a high compliment but I have no desire to be appointed. How I feel on the matter is well known in Rome and here, so I may say I do not think that there is any danger or probability that I will be appointed Archbishop of New Orleans.[102]

[99] NYAA, C-40, F. Heslin to M. A. Corrigan, New Orleans, July 5, 1897.

[100] BCA, 95-R-5, Camillus P. Maes to J. Card. Gibbons, Covington, July 19, 1897.

[101] RDA, John J. Keane to D. J. O'Connell, Saratoga, New York, September 20, 1897.

[102] ACUA, clipping.

190

If the former rector had known the powerful influences at work against his appointment he need not have feared that he would be appointed. O'Connell told Gibbons: "Nothing has been done at the Prop. about N.O. and I hear again the Pope would not approve the nomination of Mgr. Keane. Satolli's opposition is like a passion."[103]

Keane's return for the board meeting was utilized by his many friends to indicate their affectionate regard for him by paying him public honor. Alphonse Magnien told O'Connell:

Abp. Keane's friends are happy to have him in their midst: a banquet is going to be given to him next month in Washington. It will be a grand affair owing to the quality of many of the guests: not even the rapporteurs of the french "La Vérité" will be able to deny that the elite were there & that Abp. Keane occupies a prominent place in the esteem of the American Church.

But, inter nos, please to watch his tongue: I always fear that he will commit himself to some extraordinary & very suspicious statement.[104]

The press tried to stir up rumors and indulged itself in conjectures about the purpose of his visit to America which the archbishop attempted to spike immediately by giving an interview to a representative of the Boston *Herald*:

I did not slight Archbishop Corrigan in New York by not calling on him. My feelings for him are nothing but friendly. I did not have any secret conference with Archbishop Ireland, nor discuss any Church quarrels, as some papers have reported. We met in a friendly chat, and that was all there was to it. When I left the United States I made public announcement that I would return in time to attend the meeting of the directors of the Catholic University. . . . There are no controversies in the Church, and my mission is one of peace. The reports that there is trouble in the Catholic University are mean and false, and that contributions to the University from wealthy friends of mine have not been paid because I resigned are ridiculous, and are hardly worth denying. The management of the University will continue as it is without friction, and I do not fear but there will be sufficient funds to run it in the future as in the past.[105]

After the university meeting the archbishop returned to his work in Rome. During the next two years he took a very active

[103] BCA, 95-U-5, D. J. O'Connell to J. Card. Gibbons, Genazzano, October 21, 1897.

[104] RDA, A. Magnien, S.S., to D. J. O'Connell, Baltimore, September 27, 1897.

[105] ACUA, clipping.

part in the controversy over Americanism that had been touched off by the publication of the French translation of the life of Father Isaac T. Hecker, founder of the Paulists, early in 1897.[106] Again in the fall of 1898 Keane returned to the United States to be present at the meeting of the university's Board of Trustees. At this meeting it was decided that a letter requesting permission for the former rector to return to America to collect for the university, which was at the time in a precarious financial condition, should be sent to the Holy Father.[107] The chancellor dispatched the request to Rome[108] and he received a reply immediately, informing him that the Holy Father did not regard it as opportune then to grant the request.[109] As for Keane, he was very willing to enter on this work and Spalding, who had revived his interest and renewed his faith in the university, wrote to Hudson of the Keane offer: "This is generous and I think he may meet with success. The future of the University is more promising."[110]

While Archbishop Keane was taking care of the interests of the American Church in Europe during the Americanism troubles and awaiting permission to return to begin the work of collecting for the university, the Archdiocese of Oregon City was left vacant by the death of William H. Gross on November 14, 1898.[111] Gibbons wrote Cardinal Ledochowski, the Prefect of the Congregation of the Propaganda, that the bishops of the Province of

---

[106] The PFA contain many letters that indicate that Archbishop Keane's interest in the controversy was of great help to the Paulists. The definitive history of this controversy remains to be told, but there is, fortunately, an abundance of material which will enable the historian of Americanism to give a full account of the unfortunate affair. For some phases of the controversy, cf. Peter E. Hogan, "Americanism and the Catholic University of America," *CHR*, XXXIII (July, 1947), 158-190; Thomas T. McAvoy, "Americanism, Fact and Fiction," *CHR*, XXXI (July, 1945), 133-153; Vincent F. Holden, "A Myth in *L'Americanisme*," *CHR*, XXXI (July, 1945), 154-170.

[107] ACUA, MMBT, Washington, October 11, 1898. For further information on Keane's activities as a collector of funds for the university, cf. Peter E. Hogan, "Thomas J. Conaty," pp. 43-48.

[108] BCA, 96-S-1, J. Card. Gibbons to M. Card. Rampolla, Baltimore, November 1, 1898 (French), copy.

[109] BCA, 96-T-3, M. Card. Rampolla to J. Card. Gibbons, Rome, November 17, 1898 (Italian). Americanism was a flaming issue in French clerical circles at that time.

[110] AUND, photostat, John Lancaster Spalding to Daniel Hudson, Peoria, October 28, 1898.

[111] Maynard, *op. cit.*, p. 638.

192

Oregon City had informed him that they would be happy to have Archbishop Keane as their metropolitan and the cardinal was simply adding his voice to theirs. He told the cardinal prefect that the former rector was eminently qualified for the office "because of his great reputation in the country, the respect that Americans without distinction have for his character and his person, his great virtue and his eloquence will give him weighty authority and his influence will help all the province."[112] The authorities in Rome indicated that they were unfavorable to the cardinal's petition by transferring Alexander Christie to the vacant see from Vancouver Island on February 12, 1899.[113]

Finally Rome saw fit to grant the repeated requests of the chancellor of the university that the former rector be left free to collect for the institution.[114] The archbishop returned to America to assume his new duties a few days before the meeting of the Board of Trustees in the fall of 1899.[115] He began his work almost immediately[116] and during the ensuing months he met with moderate success.[117] Keane told Denis O'Connell how pleased he was with his work: "I meet nothing but friendliness so warm & sincere that it makes my heart young again—and it had grown right old."[118]

While the former rector was engaged in collecting the Archdiocese of Dubuque became vacant by the death of John Hennessy on March 4, 1900.[119] Keane's name appeared in first place on the *terna* submitted by the bishops of the province and in second place on the list submitted by the consultors and irre-

[112] BCA, 97-B-9, J. Card. Gibbons to M. Card. Ledochowski, Baltimore, January 24, 1899 (French), copy.

[113] Maynard, *op. cit.*, p. 638.

[114] NYAA, G-36, J. Card. Gibbons to M. A. Corrigan, Baltimore, November 20, 1899.

[115] "University Chronicle," *C UB*, V (October, 1899), 523.

[116] RDA, John J. Keane to D. J. O'Connell, Baltimore, November 3, 1899. The archbishop told O'Connell: "Ireland, who used to be so hopeless about the Univ'y, acknowledged that the prospects were never as bright as at present."

[117] RDA, John J. Keane to D. J. O'Connell, Washington, December 25, 1899; ACUA, John J. Keane to Thomas J. Conaty, Philadelphia, December 20, 1899; NYAA, G-36, John J. Keane to M. A. Corrigan, Washington, January 2, 1900.

[118] RDA, John J. Keane to D. J. O'Connell, Washington, December 25, 1899.

[119] Maynard, *op. cit.*, p. 624.

movable rectors of the archdiocese.[120]   Immediately all the friends of the archbishop rallied to the cause and began to work for his appointment.   His ever-faithful and influential friend, Cardinal Gibbons, wrote a letter to Cardinal Ledochowski urging the appointment of the archbishop since he appeared on both lists, stressing particularly the fact that the Holy Father had promised Keane an archbishopric in the United States when he dismissed him from the university and insisting "now is the best opportunity to follow the counsel of the Holy Father."[121]   On the same day Gibbons wrote the papal Secretary of State, Cardinal Rampolla, telling him substantially the same thing and urging him to recommend Keane to the Holy Father in a special way. He informed the cardinal that the See of Dubuque was suitable to the archbishop's dignity and he reminded him of the "emotion produced in the United States by his dismissal from the university." He also told Rampolla that the position Keane occupied at the time was "regarded as humiliating."[122]   Rampolla, in a reply shortly thereafter, informed Gibbons that Leo XIII had seconded the desires of the Baltimore prelate.[123]

Patrick W. Riordan, Archbishop of San Francisco, told O'Connell:

His appointment would be most acceptable to all the educated Catholics of America, who still feel bitterly the removal from the University. He has the ability, the zeal and piety needed for such a place as Dubuque, and his appointment would be a great blessing to the entire Province. There is no one on the list that can be compared to him. Now do your best and if our friend of Peoria [Spalding] be still in Rome get him to see some of the Cardinals and even the Pope in favor of Damascus.[124]

A short time later the same correspondent wrote that he had seen

120 BCA, 98-C-4, Henry Cosgrove to J. Card. Gibbons, Davenport, March 28, 1900. The same information may be found in NYAA, G-36, Henry Cosgrove to M. A. Corrigan, Davenport, March 28, 1900.

121 BCA, 98-D-6, J. Card. Gibbons to M. Card. Ledochowski, Baltimore, April 15, 1900 (Latin), copy.

122 BCA, 98-D, J. Card. Gibbons to M. Card. Rampolla, Baltimore, April 15, 1900 (French), copy.

123 BCA, 98-D-12, M. Card. Rampolla to J. Card. Gibbons, Rome, April 30, 1900 (Italian).

124 RDA, P. W. Riordon to D. J. O'Connell, Paris, April 18, (1900).

194

in the papers that Archbishop John J. Kain of St. Louis had left New York for Europe:

You will not fail to get him to speak in favor of our friend of Damascus for Dubuque. Abp. Kain has shown himself a true friend of Damascus and I am sure will do what is in his power to aid him. I thought of writing to Satolli a frank letter on this subject. If the Archbp. is not sent to Dubuque it will be solely because Satolli opposes him. What do you advise? I will do nothing until I receive an answer from you.[125]

Archbishop Kain later wrote to Gibbons that in an audience with the Holy Father he had been told that Keane's appointment had been confirmed and Cardinal Ledochowski had assured him that Keane would be selected:

Whilst Mgr. Keane was not a *persona grata* to Cardinal Satolli yet seeing that all wanted Mgr. K. in Dubuque, he [Ledochowski] would not oppose the appointment. . . . Rampolla was strongly of the opinion that Mgr. Keane would be the next Abp. of Dubuque. . . . Cardinal Parocchi was loud in his eulogies of Mgr. Keane's learning & eloquence & piety and expressed his confidence that, if he would accept, he would certainly go to Dubuque.[126]

Bishop Spalding told O'Connell: "If you think a letter to Card. Serafino or anyone else might help Abp. Keane please let me know."[127]

Finally the archbishop's friends received the news that they had worked and prayed for. O'Connell cabled Gibbons: "Keane indubitanter nominabitur."[128] Denis O'Connell could entertain no doubt that this news pleased the mutual friends of Archbishop Keane from the letters he received. J. R. Slattery wrote:

Liberty Hall [American College in Rome] never sent forth a more joyous message than yesterday's; that Damascus will be swallowed up in Dubuque. It was told me sub secreto secretissimo but I feel it no breach to express my joy to yourself. . . . It will as much as any other step, tend to rehabilitate the Delegation Apostolic, which as you know, suffered from Keane's dismissal at Washington. . . . We know how glad J. J. K. will be to find himself once more anchored and beyond the call of the chapter of San Giovanni in Laterano.[129]

[125] RDA, P. W. Riordan to D. J. O'Connell, Paris, April 29, (1900).

[126] BCA, 98-F-12, John J. Kain to J. Card. Gibbons, Lucerne, June 27, 1900.

[127] RDA, John Lancaster Spalding to D. J. O'Connell, Paris, May 3, 1900.

[128] BCA, 98-E-2, "Marathon" (D. J. O'Connell) to J. Card. Gibbons, Rome, May 21, 1900 (cablegram).

[129] RDA, J. R. Slattery to D. J. O'Connell, Baltimore, May 22, 1900.

Jospeh E. Hayden, American consul at Castellammare di Stabia, joined in the chorus of exultation:

Thanks be to God for the freedom of Bishop Keane; I formed a resolution while in America to watch and wait for an opportunity to read the riot act to his keepers in Rome. I saw my time for action had arrived when I was about to write my reply to Maigen [sic]; and without mentioning Bishop Keane's name, I sent a shot into that old ark called the Vatican that shook it from stem to stern—and now poor Bishop Keane is free; all glory to God and no thanks to them. Is it not strange that they continue to say the Lord's Prayer; for surely with the "coming of His Kingdom" there would be an end to theirs. You see I can't help being critical—but this is all right as long as I remain just.[130]

When O'Connell had sent absolutely certain news of the appointment to the former rector, who was vacationing at Bad Nauheim, Germany, Keane wrote: "I must and do say Deo Gratias from the depths of my heart for this solution to my life problem." The archbishop especially thanked Cardinal Serafino for his influence in bringing about the appointment, and he indicated the sentiments that he had buried deep in his heart since his dismissal from the university:

The action of the Holy Father in sending, virtually, his instructions to the meeting of the Propaganda in my favor, seems to me very unusual and significant. It is a very nice and welcome settling of the score, which, after all, really stood between us.[131]

The archbishop received the official notification of his appointment on his sixty-first birthday, September 12, 1900, while he was still in Germany. He sailed two days later and on his arrival in New York on September 22, he set out for Washington where he received the papal brief of July 24, 1900, "together with a personal letter from the Holy Father." The archbishop reached Dubuque on the afternoon of Thursday, September 27, and he was then installed in St. Raphael's Cathedral according to the ceremonial prescribed in the *Pontificale Romanum*.[132]

Indeed, the former rector's "life problem" had been solved.

130 RDA, Joseph E. Hayden to D. J. O'Connell, Castellammare di Stabia, July 19, 1900.

131 RDA, John J. Keane to D. J. O'Connell, Bad Nauheim, Germany, July 27, [1900].

132 DAA, "Record of the Administration of John J. Keane, Archbishop of Dubuque," p. 1. This is a one hundred and fifty-two page diocesan diary in Keane's hand.

While retaining the affection of thousands of Catholics through-out the United States and Europe, the bishop of deep faith won the esteem and love of most of his spiritual children during his administration of eleven years at Dubuque. During those years the institution at Washington that he had fathered and solicitously watched over during its first years claimed a portion of his time and affection as it grew and prospered. A few months before he resigned as Archbishop of Dubuque because of failing health, he recorded in his diary in a hand that was no longer firm and sure:

Have just written to Mgr. Shahan, Rector of the Univ'y at Washington, congratulating him that our Univ., while splendidly fostering the Light of Faith and Science, is also nourishing the fire of practical charity by superintending the work of a great national Charity organization. So may it ever be in our Univ'y and so may it likewise be in the life of our Archdiocese, Faith and Charity, each fostering the other, both inseparable.[133]

Seven years after his resignation of Dubuque in 1911, the good Lord on June 22, 1918, granted John J. Keane's oft-repeated plea: "O how I long for our Eternal Home. May the sweet Lord soon take me there."[134]

[133] *Ibid.*, p. 145.
[134] *Ibid.*

BIBLIOGRAPHY

Manuscript Sources

Archives of the Catholic University of America. "Chronicles of the Catholic University of America from 1885." "Report of Ireland and Keane to Trustees of the University on Their Mission to Rome." "Minutes of the Meetings of the Board of Trustees." Miscellaneous Correspondence. Collected newspaper clippings on the university and the school controversy.

Archives of the University of Notre Dame. Photostats of the Hudson Papers pertaining to the Catholic University of America.

Baltimore Cathedral Archives. Gibbons Papers.

Dubuque Archdiocesan Archives. "Record of the Administration of John J. Keane, Archbishop of Dubuque, 1900-1911."

New Orleans Archdiocesan Archives. Chapelle Papers.

New York Archdiocesan Archives. Corrigan and Farley Papers.

Paulist Fathers Archives, New York. General File and Americanism File.

Richmond Diocesan Archives. O'Connell Papers.

St. Mary's Seminary Archives, Roland Park, Baltimore. Magnien and Rex Papers.

Printed Sources

Acta et Decreta Concilii Plenarii Baltimorensis Tertii. Baltimore, 1886.

Barrows, John Henry, *The World's Parliament of Religions.* 2 vols. Chicago, 1893.

By-Laws of the Board of Trustees of the Catholic University of America. Washington, 1900.

Constitutiones Catholicae Universitatis Americae a Sancta Sede approbatae cum documentis annexis. Romae, 1889.

"Encyclical Letter," *Catholic University Bulletin,* I (April, 1895), 231-247.

Fifth Annual Report of the Rector of the Catholic University of America, March, 1894. Washington, 1894.

Fourth Annual Report of the Rector of the Catholic University of America, March, 1893. Washington, 1893.

Inauguration of the Schools of Philosophy and the Social Sciences and Dedication of McMahon Hall, Catholic University of America, October 1, 1895 — Official Report. Washington, 1895.

"Leo P.P. XIII de Magno Lycaeo Washingtonensi," *American Ecclesiastical Review,* I (June, 1889), 223-226.

National Educational Association. Journal of Proceedings and Addresses. Session of the Year 1889, held at Nashville, Tennessee. Topeka, Kansas, 1889.

Official Announcements of the Catholic University of America, September, 1889. Baltimore, 1889.

Official Announcements for the Scholastic Year 1891-'92. Washington, 1891.

Second Annual Report of the Rector of the Catholic University of America, April, 1891. Washington, 1891.

Seventh Annual Report of the Rector of the Catholic University of America, March, 1896. Washington, 1896.

Sixth Annual Report of the Rector of the Catholic University of America, September, 1895. Washington, 1895.

Solemnities of the Dedication and Opening of the Catholic University of America, November 13th, 1889. Official Report. Baltimore, 1889.

Statement of the Financial Condition of the Catholic University of America from its Beginning to November 1, 1903. Washington, 1903. Personal and Private.

Third Annual Report of the Rector of the Catholic University of America, April, 1892. Washington, 1892.

"University Chronicle," *Catholic University Bulletin,* I (January, 1895), 90-98; I (April, 1895), 263-276; I (July, 1895), 402-409; I (October, 1895), 565-566; II (January, 1896), 97-116; II (April, 1896), 214-234; II (July, 1896), 421-436; II (October, 1896), 567-573.

Year Book of the Catholic University of America, 1893-'94. Washington, 1893.

Year Book of the Catholic University of America, 1894-'95. Washington, 1894.

Year Book of the Catholic University of America, 1895-'96. Washington, 1895.

Year Book of the Catholic University of America, 1896-'97. Washington, 1896.

Year Book of the Catholic University of America, 1897-'98. Washington, 1897.

Secondary Works

Egan, Maurice Francis, *Recollections of a Happy Life.* New York, 1924.

Ellis, John Tracy, *The Formative Years of the Catholic University of America.* Washington, 1946.

Gade, John A., *The Life of Cardinal Mercier.* New York, 1935.

La Gerarchia Cattolica. Rome, 1897.

Maynard, Theodore, *The Story of American Catholicism.* New York, 1946.

Rappenhöner, Joseph, *Allgemeine Moraltheologie.* Munich, 1893.

Reilly, Daniel F., O.P., *The School Controversy (1891-1893).* Washington, 1943.

Rommel, H., *Thomas Bouquillon.* Bruges, 1903.

Zwierlein, Frederick J., *The Life and Letters of Bishop McQuaid.* 3 vols. Rochester, 1925-1927.

Brochures and Pamphlets

Bouquillon, Thomas, *Education: To Whom Does It Belong?* Baltimore, 1891.

——————, *Education: To Whom Does It Belong? A Rejoinder to Critics.* Baltimore, 1892.

——————, *Education: To Whom Does It Belong? A Rejoinder to Civiltà Cattolica.* Baltimore, 1892.

Keane, J. J., *The Catholic Church and the American Sunday.* Buffalo, 1895.

[Purcell, Richard J.], *The Catholic University of America—A Half Century of Progress.* Washington, 1941.

199

Periodical Literature

Ahern, M. J., "Innsbruck University," *Catholic Encyclopedia*, VIII, 24-25.

Bengini, U., "University of Pisa," *Catholic Encyclopedia*, XII, 112.

Bouquillon, Thomas, "The Catholic Controversy about Education. A Reply," *Educational Review*, III (April, 1892), 365-373.

——————, "The University of Paris—I," *Catholic University Bulletin*, I (July, 1895), 349-369.

Bouquillon, Thomas, *et al.*, "Catholicism vs. Science, Liberty, Truthfulness," *Catholic University Bulletin*, II (July, 1896), 356-387.

Dengel, I. Ph., "Ludwig von Pastor," *Lexikon für Theologie und Kirche*, VIII, 1018-1020.

Dürr, L., "Fulcran Vigouroux," *Lexikon für Theologie und Kirche*, X, 611-612.

Freundorfer, J., "Louis Claude Fillion," *Lexikon für Theologie und Kirche*, IV, 1.

[Garrigan, Philip J.], "The First Lustrum of the Catholic University," *American Ecclesiastical Review*, I (September, 1889), 338-347.

——————, "Present Aspect of the Catholic University," *American Ecclesiastical Review*, I (August, 1889), 281-298.

"Graduating Exercises," *Catholic University Bulletin*, II (July, 1896), 444-454.

Guilday, Peter, "John Gilmary Shea," *Historical Records and Studies*, XVII (July, 1926), 5-171.

Herbermann, Charles G., "The Faculty of the Catholic University," *American Catholic Quarterly Review*, XIV (October, 1889), 701-714.

Hilgenreiner, K., "August Lehmkuhl," *Lexikon für Theologie und Kirche*, VI, 454.

Hogan, Peter E., "Americanism and the Catholic University of America," *Catholic Historical Review*, XXXIII (July, 1947), 158-190.

Holden, Vincent F., "A Myth in 'L'Americanism'," *Catholic Historical Review*, XXXI (July, 1945), 154-170.

"Inauguration of McMahon Hall," *Catholic University Bulletin*, I (October, 1895), 541-564.

Keane, John J., "A Chat about the Catholic University," *Catholic World*, XLVIII (November, 1888), 216-226.

——————, "Inauguration of McMahon Hall," *Catholic University Bulletin*, I (October, 1895), 535-541.

——————, "International Arbitration," *Catholic University Bulletin*, II (July, 1896), 305-309.

——————, "Leo XIII and the Catholic University," *Catholic World*, XLVI (November, 1887), 145-153.

——————, "The Catholic Universities of France," *Catholic World*, XLVII (June, 1888), 289-297.

——————, "The Catholic University of Louvain," *Catholic World*, XLVI (January, 1888), 525-534.

——————, "The Financial Side of the University," *Catholic University Bulletin*, I (April, 1895), 149-164.

——————, "The University of Strassburg," *Catholic World*, XLVI (February, 1888), 643-652.

Kerby, William J., "Keane, John Joseph," *Dictionary of American Biography*, X, 267-268.

——————, "Thomas Bouquillon," *Catholic Encyclopedia*, II, 716.

Lauchert, L., "Bernard Jungmann," *Lexikon für Theologie und Kirche*, V, 722.

Lobingier, Charles Sumner, "Robinson, William Callyhan," *Dictionary of American Biography*, XVI, 56-57.

McAvoy, Thomas T., "Americanism, Fact and Fiction," *Catholic Historical Review*, XXXI (July, 1945), 133-153.

Meng, John J., "Cahenslyism: The First Stage, 1883-1891," *Catholic Historical Review*, XXXI (January, 1946), 389-413.

——————, "Cahenslyism: The Second Chapter, 1891-1910," *Catholic Historical Review*, XXXII (October, 1946), 302-340.

Merk, A., "Gustav Bickell," *Lexikon für Theologie und Kirche*, II, 342.

de Moreau, E., "Godefroid Kurth," *Lexikon für Thoelogie und Kirche*, VI, 316.

"Necrologies," *Catholic University Bulletin*, I (April, 1895), 334-339.

O'Gorman, Thomas, "Leo XIII and the Catholic University," *Catholic University Bulletin*, I (January, 1895), 19-23.

——————, "The Educational Policy of Archbishop Ireland," *Educational Review*, III (May, 1892), 462-471.

Pace, Edward A., "Francesco Satolli," *Catholic Encyclopedia*, XIII, 486.

——————, "The McMahon Hall of Philosophy," *Catholic University Bulletin*, I (January, 1895), 53-64.

——————, "Universities," *Catholic Encyclopedia*, XV, 188-198.

"Prospectus," *Catholic University Bulletin*, I (January, 1895), i-iii.

Purcell, Richard J., "Corrigan, Michael Augustine," *DAB*, IV, 450-452.

——————, "Garrigan, Philip Joseph," *DAB*, VII, 167.

——————, "Gmeiner, John," *DAB*, VII, 335-336.

——————, "Kelly, Eugene," *DAB*, X, 307-308.

——————, "McQuaid, Bernard John," *DAB*, XII, 163-164.

——————, "Malone, Sylvester," *DAB*, XII, 226-227.

——————, "Marty, Martin," *DAB*, XII, 352.

——————, "Messmer, Sebastian Gebhard," *DAB*, XII, 579-580.

——————, "O'Gorman, Thomas," *DAB*, XIV, 3.

——————, "Ryan, Patrick John," *DAB*, XVI, 263-264.

——————, "Shahan, Thomas Joseph," *DAB*, XVII, 16-17.

——————, "Spalding, John Lancaster," *DAB*, XVII, 422-423.

——————, "Wigger, Winant Michael," *DAB*, XX, 89.

——————, "Williams, John Joseph," *DAB*, XX, 276-277.

"Right Rev. John Joseph Keane, D.D.," *Catholic University Bulletin*, II (October, 1896), 583-592.

Shahan, Thomas J., "The Catholic Congress of Brussels," *Catholic University Bulletin*, I (January, 1895), 73-85.

Schroeder, Joseph, "American Catholics and European School Legislation," *American Ecclesiastical Review*, XI (May, 1892), 366-393.

——————, "Leo XIII and the Encyclical 'Longinqua'," *American Catholic Quarterly Review*, XX (April, 1895), 369-388.

Sendfelder, Leopold, "University of Vienna," *Catholic Encyclopedia*, XV, 421-423.

Seppelt, F. X., "Max Sdralek," *Lexikon für Theologie und Kirche*, IX, 389.

Söhngen, G., "Ernst Commer," *Lexikon für Theologie und Kirche*, III, 18.

Zurcher, George, "Foreign Ideas in the Catholic Church in America," *Roycroft Quarterly* (November, 1896), 1-55.

Unpublished Material

Hogan, Peter E., S.S.J., "Thomas J. Conaty, Second Rector of the Catholic University of America, 1896-1903." Unpublished Master's thesis, Catholic University of America, Department of History, 1947. [This study is now in the process of publication.]

Newspapers

Permanent files as well as clippings collected by Keane were used by the writer.

Baltimore *American*, July 29, 1890.

Baltimore *Catholic Mirror*, March 9, 1889; January 21, 1893.

Baltimore *Katholische Volkszeitung*, March 26, 1892.

Baltimore *Sun*, June 18, 1890; October 10, 18, 1896.

Boston *Christian Register*, October 15, 1896.

Boston *Congregationalist*, October 8, 15, 1896.

Boston *Herald*, May 11, 1891.

Boston *Morning Star*, October 29, 1896.

Boston *Pilot*, March 30, 1889; June 15, 1889; October 26, 1889; July 12, 1890; October 10, 1896.

Buffalo *Catholic Union and Times*, September 19, 1895; October 24, 1895.

Buffalo *Christliche Woche*, February 3, 1892; October 9, 1892.

Buffalo *Commercial*, October 5, 1896.

Buffalo *Enquirer*, October 5, 1896.

Buffalo *Express*, October 6, 1896.

Cincinnati *Catholic Telegraph*, October 8, 1896.

Cincinnati *Evening Post*, August 29, 1890.

[France], *Courrier de Bruxelles*, October 25, 1896.

        Le Bien Public, October 21, 1896.

        Le Peuple Français, October 21, 1896.

        L' Universe, November 29, 1890.

        Revue Catholique de Bordeaux, October 10, 1894.

Harper's Weekly, November 16, 1889.

Hartford *Times*, October 5, 1896.

Indianapolis *Journal*, June 7, 1890.

London *Catholic Times*, October 30, 1896.

Louisville *Catholic Advocate*, October 8, 1896.

Milwaukee *Catholic Citizen*, October 10, 1896.

Milwaukee *Herald*, October 5, 1896.

Milwaukee *Sentinel*, January 29, 1890.

Nashville *Christian Advocate*, October 8, 1896.

New York *Catholic American*, November 24, 1888.

New York *Catholic News*, June 8, 1896.

New York *Churchman*, October 17, 1896.

New York *Democrat*, November 8, 1896.

New York *Evening Telegram*, May 16, 1889; June 11, 1890.

New York *Freeman's Journal and Catholic Register*, September 7, 1889; June 9, 1890; October 17, 1896.

New York *Globe Democrat*, November 29, 1891.

New York *Herald*, January 20, 1890; May 12, 1890; June 1, 1890; May 17, 1892; October 6, 1896.

New York *Irish World*, October 10, 17, 1896.

New York *Journal*, February 12, 1897.

New York *Mail and Express*, December 29, 1892.

New York *Morning Advertiser*, October 5, 1896.

New York *News*, September 27, 1895.

New York *Observer*, March 6, 1890.

New York *Sun*, September 2, 1890; October 24, 1890; September 29, 1892; February 8, 1900.

New York *Tablet*, June 14, 1890.

New York *Times*, October 5, 1896.

New York *Tribune*, March 31, 1890; April 19, 1890; May 12, 1890; July 28, 29, 1890; December 30, 1892; February 24, 1893; October 23, 1896; November 13, 14, 20, 1896.

New York *World*, February 3, 1893; October 8, 15, 1896; January 20, 1897.

Philadelphia *Catholic Standard and Times*, October 10, 1896; February 17, 1900.

Rochester *Democrat and Chronicle*, November 26, 1894.

Rochester *Union and Advertiser*, October 12, 1896; December 5, 1896.

St. Louis *Herold des Glaubens*, October 7, 1896.

St. Louis *Western Watchman*, October 28, 1893; November 21, 1895.

St. Paul *Pioneer Press*, October 5, 1896.

San Francisco *Chronicle*, February 12, 13, 15, 19, 1894.

San Francisco *Monitor*, October 10, 1896.

Sioux City *North American Catholic*, May 9, 1896.

Springfield *Republican*, January 26, 1890.

Washington *Church News*, May 12, 19, 1889.

Washington *Evening Star*, March 2, 9, 1891; August 5, 1891; February 4, 1892; October 7, 1896.

Washington *Post*, January 30, 1890; March 3, 1890; January 4, 1891; August 3, 7, 1891; December 18, 1891; February 5, 6, 1892; November 16, 1893; August 7, 1895; October 7, 8, 1896.

Washington *Star*, February 7, 13, 20, 1890; October 10, 1896.

Washington *Times*, October 10, 1896.

Worcester *Spy*, January 24, 1890.

Worcester *Telegram*, October 5, 1896.

York *Age*, June 21, 1890.

INDEX

206

207

ENDOWMENTS, *see* Finances
ENROLLMENT, *see* Students
EUCHARISTIC LEAGUE, *see* Priests' Eucharistic League
FACULTY
  committee appointed, 99
  discord, 151-3
  first members, 51-28
  objections to Hogan as professor, 55
  requirements for new members, 104-5
  resolutions presented to Keane, 166
  selection of deans and administrative officers, 36
  suggested candidates, letter from Keane to Pace, 8
  unity achieved, 156-7
  see also Bazerque; Bouquillon; Egan; Garrigan; Graf; Grannan; Hewit;
    Hogan; Hyvernat; Keane; Kerby; Messmer; O'Gorman; Orban; Pace;
    Peries; Pohle; Quinn, Daniel; Robinson, William; Schroeder; Searle;
    Shahan; Shanahan; Shea; Stoddard
FARIBAULT-STILLWATER PLAN, *see* Ireland; School question
FARLEY, JOHN M.
  letter to Corrigan *re* Keane, 164
  resignation as secretary, 74
FARREN, BERNARD N., replaced on board, 73
FEEHAN, PATRICK A., Archbishop of Chicago, present at Parliament of
  Religions, 68
FEES, justification by Keane, 78
FELTEN, JOSEPH, offer by Keane, 20
FILLION, LOUIS CLAUDE, S.S., recommended by Felton, 20n
FINANCES
  appeal to clergy and laity, 76
  associations formed, 81-2
  diocesan campaign plans and attitude of board, 79-80
  endowment of chairs, 77, 81, 108, 113
  increase of burdens, 112-3
  indebtedness incurred, 78-80
  justification of fees, 78
  Keane appointed to collect funds, 193
  recommendations for general collection, 113
  tuition, 105
FITZGERALD, WILLIAM J., president of alumni association, 58
FLASCH, KILIAN C., Bishop of LaCrosse, appointed to board, 73
FLETCHER, WILLIAM A., vice-president of alumni association, 58
FOLEY, JOHN, Bishop of Detroit
  attitude toward canon law, 31
  letter to Gibbons *re* faculty selection, 25
FOLEY, J. T., comments on Bouquillon, 129
FORESTIER, B., S.M., purchase of house, 88
FRANCISCUS, P. J., C.S.C., director of students, 88
FULTON, ROBERT, S.J.
  attitude on Holaind in letter to Richards, 127
  letter to Corrigan *re* faculty, 3

208

211

MAES, CAMILLUS P., Bishop of Covington
appointed to board, 73
appointed to write to Keane, 175
help to Keane in obtaining faculty, 14
meeting with Keane in Rome, 10

MAGNIEN, A., S.S.,
letter to Ireland *re* controversy, 132
letters to O'Connell *re* Bouquillon, 129; *re* Keane, 191; *re* school controversy, 132

MAGRUDER, G. L., dean of Georgetown Medical School, letter to Satolli, 102-3
MALONE, SYLVESTER, defeat of McQuaid, 147
MARISTS
agreement signed, 88
house of studies, 53
negotiations, 88

MARTINELLI, SEBASTIAN, apostolic delegate, letter to Gibbons *re* Rome and the university, 180

MARTY, MARTIN, O.S.B., Bishop of St. Cloud
consecration of O'Gorman, 59
designated as collector of funds, 76

MATHEW, FATHER, memorial chair, 81
MEAD, EDWIN D., Keane's answer of attack, 61
MENG, JOHN J., Cahenslyism articles, 135
MERCIER, DÉSIRÉ
letters to Keane *re* possibilities in America, 13-4
meetings with Keane, 11-4
plan for Louvain, 11-2
requested by Leo XIII to remain at Louvain, 14

MESSMER, SEBASTIAN G.
acceptance, 24
appointed Bishop of Green Bay, 50-1
biography, 24
letters to Gibbons and Corrigan *re* fitness, 24
objections to Bouquillon, 130
objections to O'Gorman and Pace, 157-8
urged on Keane for professorship, 73

MIDDLETON MANSION, called St. Thomas College, 33
MIVART, ST. GEORGE
recommended by Ireland for faculty, 27
rejection of Catholic doctrine, 28

MOORE, JOHN, Bishop of St. Augustine
objections to parting with Pace, 6
present at Parliament of Religions, 69

MORRIS, MARTIN F., address at public mass meeting, 166-7

O'CONNELL, DENIS J., rector of the North American College, Rome
letter from Keane *re* university, 19
letter from Moore *re* Pace, 7
letter to Keane to come to Rome, 10

O'CONNOR, JAMES, Bishop of Omaha, interest in affiliation, 88-9

214

217

[This index was compiled by Miss Ruth Harvey]